LANGUAGE IN SOCIETY 21
Intercultural Communication

Language in Society

GENERAL EDITOR
Peter Trudgill, Professor in the
Department of Language and
Linguistics, University of Lausanne

ADVISORY EDITORS
Ralph Fasold, Professor of Linguistics, Georgetown University
William Labov, Professor of Linguistics, University of Pennsylvania

Intercultural Communication

A Discourse Approach

Ron Scollon
and
Suzanne Wong Scollon

BLACKWELL
Oxford UK & Cambridge USA

First published 1995

Blackwell Publishers, the publishing imprint of
Basil Blackwell Inc.
238 Main Street
Cambridge, Massachusetts 02142
USA

Basil Blackwell Ltd
108 Cowley Road
Oxford   OX4 1JF
UK

Library of Congress Cataloging-in-Publication Data

Scollon, Ronald, 1939–
    Intercultural communication: a discourse approach / Ron
Scollon and Suzanne Wong Scollon.
        p.   cm. – (Language in society; 21)
    Includes bibliographical references (p.) and index.
    ISBN 0–631–19488–6. — ISBN 0–631–19489–4 (pbk.)
        1.   Intercultural communication.   I. Scollon, Suzanne B.
    K.
    II. Title.   III. Series.
    P94.6.S36   1994 1995
    306.4'4 – dc20   94–19318
                                                                CIP

British Library Cataloguing in Publication Data

A CIP catalogue record for this book is available from the British Library.

Typeset in 10½ on 12pt Erhardt
by Graphicraft Typesetters Ltd, Hong Kong
Printed and bound in Great Britain by
Hartnolls Limited, Bodmin, Cornwall
This book is printed on acid-free paper

Contents

Figures

Series Editor's Preface

A number of books in the *Language and Society* series have dealt with topics in the ethnography of speaking. The present volume draws on theoretical advances that have been made in this field over the past two decades, but also makes a very valuable contribution based on important descriptive work, including the authors' own, in the field of cross-cultural communication. The book is perhaps most noticeable, however, for the extent to which it represents an essay in applied sociolinguistics. Although theoretically founded and descriptively rich, *Intercultural Communication* also examines what conclusions can be drawn from sociolinguistic research for the practice of professional communication. This emphasis on practice makes the book a pioneering work which will have an impact well beyond the fields of socio-linguistics and foreign-language teaching. The authors' final conclusions are sober and paradoxical, namely that expert professional communicators are those who have come to appreciate their lack of expertise. Readers of *Intercultural Communication* will nevertheless come to appreciate not only the amount of variation to be found between human discourse systems, but also the amount of progress that has been made by sociolinguistic research-ers such as the Scollons in describing and understanding such systems.

Peter Trudgill

Preface

This book is about professional communication between people who are members of different groups. When as westerners or Asians we do business together, when as men or women we work together in an office, or when as members of senior or junior generations we develop a product together we engage in what we call "interdiscourse communication." That is to say, the discourse of westerners or of Asians, the discourse of men or women, the corporate discourse or the discourse of our professional organizations enfolds us within an envelope of language which gives us an identity and which makes it easier to communicate with those who are like us. By the same token, however, the discourses of our cultural groups, our corporate cultures, our professional specializations, or our gender or generation groups make it more difficult for us to interpret those who are members of different groups. We call these enveloping discourses "discourse systems."

Interdiscourse communication is a term we use to include the entire range of communications across boundaries of groups or discourse systems from the most inclusive of those groups, cultural groups, to the communications which take place between men and women or between colleagues who have been born into different generations. In interdiscourse analysis we consider the ways in which discourses are created and interpreted when those discourses cross the boundaries of group membership. We also consider the ways in which we use communication to claim and to display our own complex and multiple identities as communicating professionals.

This is a book on intercultural professional communication in English between westerners and East Asians, especially Chinese; but it is more than that. This book is on organizational communication, especially where conflicts arise between identity in the corporate culture and in one's professional specialization; but it is more than that. This book is about communication across the so-called generations gap; but it is more than that. This book is about miscommunications which occur between men and women; but it is more than that. This book is an interactive sociolinguistic framework for analyzing discourse which crosses the boundaries between these discourse systems. Because each professional communicator is simultaneously a member of a corporate, a professional, a generational, a gender, a cultural, and even other discourse systems, the focus of this book is on how those multiple memberships provide a framework within which all professional communication takes place.

Discourse analysis in professional communication is a new and rapidly developing field which integrates aspects of intercultural communication studies, applied interactional sociolinguistics, and discourse analysis. We have written this book to meet the needs of students and teachers in courses in English for professional communication, English for special purposes, or other such courses where the central focus is on communication in professional or business contexts. The book is designed for either classroom use or self-study, since many of those who are involved in intercultural professional communication have already completed their courses of study and are actively engaged in their professional work.

We have two main audiences in mind: (1) professional communicators who are East Asian speakers of English, and their teachers in courses on professional communication, whether in Asia or elsewhere, and (2) professional communicators who are concerned with any communications which cross the lines of discourse systems. The book has been field-tested in Hong Kong and therefore tends to emphasize examples of most direct relevance to Chinese (Cantonese) speakers of English. Nevertheless, the research on which this book is based covers a much broader range of East Asian English communication including Taiwan, Korea, Japan, Singapore, Mainland China, North America, Great Britain, and Australia.

In over twenty years of research on intercultural intra-organizational communication in North America as well as in Taiwan and in Korea, we have seen that most miscommunication does not arise through mispronunciations or through poor uses of grammar, as important as those aspects of language learning are. The major sources of miscommunication in intercultural contexts lie in differences in patterns of discourse. In our consulting work with major business, governmental, and educational organizations in North America and in Asia we have found that frequently intergroup miscommunication and even hostility arise when each group has failed to interpret the intentions of the other group as a result of misinterpreting its discourse conventions. In teaching a range of courses, from "cultural differences in institutional settings" to courses on discourse, sociolinguistics, and first and second language acquisition, we have found that careful attention to communication at this higher level of discourse analysis leads to an ability to return to original statements and to do the repair work that is needed to improve cross-group communication. In this book we have for the first time organized course topics from a range of diverse fields into a unified presentation specifically designed for the professional communicator.

Our research in Taiwan was supported by Providence University (Ching Yi Ta Hsueh), Shalu, Taiwan, and in Korea by the Sogang Institute for English as an International Language, Sogang University, Seoul, Korea. It received continued funding from the Alaska Humanities Forum, Anchorage, Alaska (a program of the National Endowment for the Humanities), and Lynn Canal Conservation, Haines, Alaska. We wish to thank these two universities as well as the two funding agencies for their support of our work. Of course, the ideas expressed in this book are not the responsibility of any of these agencies.

The principle foundation upon which we write is the ongoing discourse about discourse among our colleagues. We owe much of our general approach to discussions of intergroup discourse with John Gumperz. We wish to thank Deborah Tannen for critical reading and lively discussion of not only this manuscript but the many other papers upon which this book is based. We also thank Tim Boswood, Coordinator of the English for Professional Communication program at City Polytechnic of Hong Kong, for the pleasure of many thoughtful conversations about this material.

This book has been used in manuscript form as the textbook for several courses which we have taught at City Polytechnic of Hong Kong and Hong Kong Baptist College. Our students in those courses have provided many useful comments, raised important questions, and suggested further examples which have materially improved the clarity of this text. We wish to thank them for their interest and for their astute observations. We are indebted to David Li Chor Shing for many suggestions which have clarified our statements regarding Chinese cultural matters as well as for improvements in style. We have benefited greatly too from discussions with him of the book's contents. Judy Ho Woon Yee and Vicki Yung Kit Yee have also given critical and helpful readings. As well, we thank Tom Scollon for his assistance in preparing the figures and Rachel Scollon for her editorial assistance. While we are deeply indebted to all of these people as well as to many others for their help in making our ideas clearer, we ourselves remain responsible for infelicities, eccentricities, and failures to get it right.

1

What is a Discourse Approach?

In a business meeting between Hong Kong Chinese and Anglo-North American businessmen, one of the Chinese businessmen might say the following:

> Because most of our production is done in China now, and uh, it's not really certain how the government will react in the run-up to 1997, and since I think a certain amount of caution in committing to TV advertisement is necessary because of the expense. So, I suggest that we delay making our decision until after Legco makes its decision.

This short excerpt is like many others which occur when Chinese or other Asians speak in English to native English speakers from other parts of the world. In most cases there is little difficulty in understanding at the level of the words and sentences. There is the normal amount of "uh's" and other disfluencies found in any section of authentic, real-life language use whether the speakers are native or non-native speakers of the language. Nevertheless, even though the words and sentences of the speaker are quite clear, there is a feeling that it is not quite clear what the speaker's main point is.

Research on discourse shows that this confusion in goals or in interpreting the main point of another's speech is caused by the fact that each side is using different principles of discourse to organize its presentations. In this case the Asian speaker uses a "topic–comment" order of presentation in which the main point (or comment) is deferred until sufficient backgrounding of the topic has been done. The most common form of this structure is this:

> *because* of
> Y (topic, background, or reasons)
> X (comment, main point, or action suggested)

On the other hand, a western speaker of English tends to expect a discourse strategy of opening the discussion with the introduction of the speaker's main point so that other speakers may react to it and so that he or she can develop arguments in support as they are needed. That form would be as follows:

X (comment, main point, or action suggested)
because of
Y (topic, background, or reasons)

In the case given above the westerner might expect something more like the following:

I suggest that we delay making our decision until after Legco makes its decision. That's because I think a certain amount of caution in committing to TV advertisement is necessary because of the expense. In addition to that, most of our production is done in China now, and it's not really certain how the government will react in the run-up to 1997.

This would put the suggestion to delay the decision right at the beginning and then follow this with the speaker's reasons for doing so. The Asian speaker feels uncomfortable putting his suggestion first before he has given his reasoning. This difference in discourse pattern leads the westerner to focus on the opening stages of the discourse as the most crucial while the Asian speaker will tend to look for the crucial points to occur somewhat later.

The result of these different discourse strategies is that there arise the unfair and prejudicial stereotypes of the "inscrutable" Asian or of the frank and rude westerner.

Our purpose is to introduce professional communicators to the basic principles of discourse as they apply to communication between members of different groups or, as we will put it, interdiscourse communication. In addition, we describe salient differences which can be expected between speakers of English who come from different cultural backgrounds. We focus particularly on communication between North American or European speakers of English and their East Asian counterparts in contexts of international professional communication.

The Topic

An interdiscourse framework for professional communication can be applied to any situation in which professional communicators are involved in communication between members of different groups. As we will argue, each of us is simultaneously a member of many different discourse systems. We are members of a particular corporate group, a particular professional or occupational group, a generation, a gender, a region, and an ethnicity. As a result, virtually all professional communication is communication across some lines which divide us into different discourse groups or systems of discourse. It is for this reason we are approaching discourse in professional communication from the point of view of an interdiscourse framework of analysis.

Professional communication

By "professional communicators" we mean anyone for whom communication is a major aspect of his or her work. This includes a very broad range of positions in business and in government, from executives or executive secretaries to translators and copywriters. A recent study in a major East Asian city of positions which could be considered to require professional communication included the following list:

Accountant	Merchandizer
Account executive	Officer
Assistant auditor	Receptionist
Assistant manager	Reporter
Copywriter	Sales executive
Designer	Senior administrative assistant
Editor	Senior clerk
Executive	Senior engineer
Executive secretary	Tour guide
Manager	Trainee manager
Marketing executive	Trainee programmer
Media executive	Translator

Such a list does not, of course, exhaust the positions in government and in business in which professional communicators work. It is only given to suggest the range of employments in which we believe interdiscourse professional communication is a significant aspect of day-to-day professional competence.

We would also like to add teachers (at all levels) to this list of professional communicators. That, of course, raises the question of the possible misinterpretation of the term "professional communication." For some this term might mean "the communication of professionals" (such as doctors, lawyers, or teachers). We see no need to exclude that use of the term since such professionals find that communication is at the heart of their professional activities as well. Our main concern is that we should not limit our definition of "professional communication" to just those positions which are usually called professional. We believe that intercultural professional communication is a central aspect of the work life of anyone whose work is based upon communication.

Interdiscourse communication

We do not just focus on professional communication but take as our main concern the interdiscourse aspects of such communication. This is because not only in contemporary Asian society, but worldwide as well, a very large segment of day-to-day professional communication takes place in the international language, English. In many cases this communication is between one non-native speaker of English and another. When Chinese from Hong Kong do business in Japan, many aspects of this communication take place in English. When Koreans open an industrial complex in Saudi Arabia, again, English is generally the language in which business is transacted. As a result, the use of English carries with it an almost inevitable load of interdiscourse or intercultural communication.

We do not take the extreme deterministic position that a language solely determines the thought patterns of its speakers. We believe that reality is far too complex to allow for such a simple statement. Nevertheless, we believe that many aspects of western culture, especially western patterns of discourse, which ultimately lead to confusion or to misinterpretation in intercultural discourse are carried within English as well as transmitted through the process of the teaching and learning of English. These distinctive patterns of discourse are the focus of this book.

We have chosen to present as our primary examples, especially in the opening chapters, communications which involve East Asian speakers of English and western native speakers of English. This is partly because this is a rapidly expanding area of research and of perceived need. At the same time, we believe that these examples will be found to also illustrate general principles of interdiscourse analysis which readers may use in situations very different from those presented in this book. Ultimately we will argue that the cultural differences between people in professional communication are likely to be rather less significant than other differences which arise from being members of different gender or generational discourse systems, or from the conflicts which arise between corporate discourse and professional discourse systems.

Discourse

Discourse as a field of study includes many different aspects of language use. Discourse analysts study everything from the topic–comment structures of sentences or paragraphs through the analysis of rambling conversations or jokes. In recent years the study of discourse has been extended to include literary discourse and whole fields of culture and symbolic systems. Our basic interest is in face-to-face conversation within speech events such as meetings, conversations, or interviews. From such forms of discourse we will derive the principles upon which we base our study.

The Limits of Language

Mr Wong and Mr Richardson have a conversation. Mr Richardson has enjoyed this conversation and when they are ready to part he says to Mr Wong that they really should get together to have lunch sometime. Mr Wong says that he would enjoy that. After a few weeks Mr Wong begins to feel that Mr Richardson has been rather insincere because he has not followed up his invitation to lunch with a specific time and place.

The difference in discourse patterns expected by many Asian speakers of English and by western speakers of English is the source of the problem between Mr Wong and Mr Richardson. The pattern which we have mentioned above of displacing important points until nearer the end of a conversation, which is often found in East Asian discourse, has led Mr Wong to think that this mention of lunch at the end of the conversation is of some importance to Mr Richardson. Whether it is important to Mr Wong or not, he believes that Mr Richardson is seriously making an invitation to lunch. Mr Richardson, on the other hand, has made this mention of having lunch together sometime at the end of his conversation because it is of little major significance. For him it does not signify any more than that he has enjoyed his conversation with Mr Wong. It is not a specific invitation, but just a conventional way of parting with good feelings toward the other.

This difference in discourse pattern results in a confusion between the two participants in this hypothetical conversation. The problem at root is that language is fundamentally ambiguous. While it is important for both speakers to distinguish between the main point and "small talk," there is nothing in the language used itself to say "This is the important point." That emphasis is supplied by the expectations each speaker has that the other speaker will use language in the same way that he or she does.

The field of conversational analysis has been an active area of research for well over two decades now. On the basis of this research Stephen Levinson (1990) has argued that it is possible to draw four quite general conclusions:

1   Language is ambiguous by nature.
2   We *must* draw inferences about meaning.
3   Our inferences tend to be fixed, not tentative.
4   Our inferences are drawn very quickly.

In the sections which follow we will take up each of these conclusions in more specific detail.

Language is ambiguous by nature

When we say that language is always ambiguous, what we mean is that we can never fully control the meanings of the things we say and write. The meanings we exchange by speaking and by writing are not given in the words and sentences alone but are also constructed partly out of what our listeners and our readers interpret them to mean. To put this quite another way, meaning in language is jointly constructed by the participants in communication. This is the first general conclusion reached in the research on communication.

I may say something is blue in color but it is another question altogether what the color blue means to you. There is never complete agreement among speakers of a language about the semantic ranges of such items as color terms. This is just one example.

Word-level ambiguity in language

Such words as the prepositions "in" or "at" are notoriously difficult to teach and to learn, and this is because their meanings reside only partly in the words themselves. Much of their meaning is given by the situations in which they are used.

For example, if we say:

There's a man *at* the front door

the preposition "at" tells us something about where the man is located, but it does not tell us very much. We know that he is outside the door. We even go further in assuming that he is standing within reach of the door where he has probably just knocked or rung the bell.

It is not clear just how much it is safe to read into such a sentence, and that is the whole point. This sentence is quite ambiguous in that we do not know very much about just how this man is "at" the door. If we use what is a very similar sentence:

There's a taxi *at* the door

we can see that there is a very different way of being "at" the door. In the case of a taxi we would expect the taxi to be at some distance from the door, in a roadway or a driveway, probably waiting with its motor running. Furthermore, the taxi includes a driver.

One could say that the difference in these two sentences lies not in the preposition "at" but in the two subject nouns "man" and "taxi." The difference lies in what we know about men and taxis and how they wait "at" doors. The point we want to make, based on Levinson's argument, is that what is different in meaning between these two sentences is how objects are "at" a location and that the preposition "at" does not give us enough information in itself. In order to understand these sentences we must call upon our knowledge about the world, which does not reside in the sentences or in any of the words of the sentences.

This is what we mean when we say that language is always ambiguous at the word level. The words themselves do not give us enough information to interpret their meaning unequivocally.

To give just one more example, if we say:

The coffee is *in* the cup

you may draw a number of inferences about just how the coffee is in the cup. You may assume that it is coffee in its brewed, liquid form. You will most likely not assume that we are talking about coffee beans or a jar of frozen coffee powder.

By the same token, if we say

The pencil is *in* the cup

it is likely that you could draw a picture of that cup and the pencil. The pencil would be sticking out of the cup but more of it would be inside rather than outside because otherwise the pencil would fall out of the cup. What you do not understand from that sentence is that we have ground the pencil into fine powder, poured boiling water over it, and made a brew of pencil to drink. But there is nothing in the differences between those two sentences or in the words "in" or "cup" which tell you that. These are assumptions you make on the basis of what you know about the world, and the words and sentences only serve to point you in the direction of what you already know.

Sentence-level ambiguity in language

You might think that if words such as the prepositions "at" or "in" or the names of colors are naturally ambiguous, the ambiguity could be cleared up at the level of sentences. Unfortunately, sentences are equally ambiguous.

Our colleague Ray McDermott (1979) has given the example of the simple sentence, "What time is it?," as an excellent example of the ambiguity of language at the sentence level.

If I am walking down the street and I stop you to ask:

What time is it?

your answer is likely to be something like, "It's two o'clock," or whatever time it is. I will then thank you and go on. Nothing out of the ordinary is understood. But let us change the context to the elementary school classroom. The teacher asks Frankie,

What time is it?

And Frankie answers, "It's two o'clock." In this case the teacher answers,

Very good, Frankie.

Notice the difference here. In the first case the sentence, "What time is it?," is part of the speech act of requesting the time and as such it forms a set with the other sentence, "Thank you." In the second case the same sentence, "What time is it?," is part of the speech act of testing a child for his or her ability to tell the time. As such this sentence forms a pair not with, "Thank you," but with, "Very good."

If you doubt that this is true, you can go along the street after reading this and ask somebody the time. When they tell you the time, you answer by saying, "Very good." We assure you that they will consider this to be very odd in the mildest cases or even hostile behavior in more extreme responses.

There are, of course, also many other meanings for this same sentence. If a husband and a wife are at dinner in the home of friends and she asks him, "What time is it?," this question almost certainly could be better translated as something like, "Don't you think it is time we were leaving?"

The point we are making is simply that the meaning of the sentence, "What time is it?," resides not in the sentence alone but in the situation in which it is used as well. Knowing how to interpret the meaning of this sentence requires knowledge of the world as well as knowledge of words and sentences.

Discourse-level ambiguity in language

As a last resort, it might be hoped that we could find unambiguous meaning in language at the level of discourse. Perhaps we could find some way of being specific about the contexts in which sentences are used, and if enough of that information could be made explicit then we could say that language was not ambiguous at least at the level of discourse. Unfortunately, this approach cannot work either. Language remains inherently ambiguous at the level of discourse as well.

Deborah Tannen's (1990a) book *You Just Don't Understand* shows how men and women from the same culture, even from the same families, often misunderstand each other because of different assumptions they make about the purposes or goals of their communication. A man may wish to make a woman happy by giving her a gift of something she really wants. He asks her what she would like to have for her birthday – she can ask for anything. Unfortunately, what she wants more than anything else is for him to know intuitively what she would like to have. According to Tannen, men and women, at least in North American society, tend to differ in their concern for explicitness or for indirection. A woman, according to Tannen, is likely to think it is important for someone to show how well he knows her by not having to ask explicitly what she wants. A man in that situation, however, feels best about the situation if he is told quite directly and explicitly how he can make her happy.

No amount of language used directly could ever clear up this sort of ambiguity. The more clearly they discussed the situation the happier one of the participants would become at the expense of the other. The situation is like that of two little children, a brother and a sister. He wanted to have a chocolate ice-cream cone, so his sister said she also wanted chocolate. The boy then changed his mind and said he wanted strawberry. That made the sister change her request to strawberry. The problem is that he wanted what she did not have and she wanted to have the same as he had.

This sort of difficulty is, unfortunately, in the nature of human interaction and makes it impossible for language to ever become clear and unambiguous.

In the example given earlier in this chapter, Mr Wong expects that the information which comes at the end of a conversation will be the most significant, and so he gives this information special attention. Mr Richardson assumes that what comes at the beginning is most significant, and so he plays down the value of what comes nearer the end. What becomes ambiguous is the emphasis placed on different topics in the discourse. While it might be fairly clear what the actual sentences mean, it is not at all clear how to evaluate them in light of the other sentences.

The ambiguity of language is not the result of poor learning

In this book, which emphasizes interdiscourse aspects of professional communication, it is important to emphasize now that the ambiguity of language is not the result of poor learning. In other words you should not think that if people just had better vocabularies, better grasp of English grammar, or better concepts of the nature of discourse these ambiguities would be cleared up. The point we are making is that ambiguity is inherent in all language use. There is no way to get around the ambiguity of language. What is most important is to recognize that this is the nature of language and to develop strategies for dealing with ambiguity, not to try to prevent it from developing.

We must *draw inferences about meaning*

We hope that by now our position is clear. Language is always, inherently, and necessarily ambiguous. That leads to the second point we want to make about communication. It means that in order to communicate we *must* always jump to conclusions about what other people mean. There is no way around this. A crossword puzzle is much like the way language works. The first few entries are somewhat difficult, but where we are not sure, a few guesses seem to fit. These then fill in a couple of squares and help us to make more guesses. If those guesses seem to work, we will consider our first guesses to be fairly reliable. We do not consider them to be right answers until the whole puzzle is done and there are no more squares to fill in. If all of the words we have guessed fit in then we draw the final conclusion that our earliest guesses were correct.

Language works in a comparable way. When someone says something, we must jump to some conclusion about what he or she means. We draw inferences based on two main sources: (1) the language they have used, and (2) our knowledge about the world. That knowledge includes expectations about what people would normally say in such circumstances.

Our inferences tend to be fixed, not tentative

A third conclusion of the past two decades of research on conversational inference and discourse analysis is that the inferences we make tend to become fixed conclusions; they do not remain tentative in our minds.

There is a good reason why it should work this way. Otherwise we would be always wandering around in uncertainty about what anything might mean. When someone says, "There's a man at the door," we draw the inference that this means that the man is standing at the door and waiting for someone to go to answer his call. We do not immediately begin to consider all the possibilities of what such a statement might mean. That would lead to complete communicative immobilization.

Many researchers in the field prefer to use the distinction between "marked" and "unmarked" to capture this aspect of communication. When we say that we make certain assumptions about the man at the door, those are the unmarked assumptions we are making. In other words, as long as nothing to the contrary leads us to expect differently, we assume that the world will operate the way we have come to expect it to operate. The unmarked expectation for men at doors is that described above. If the man at the door was dead or injured and lying at the door, we would expect the speaker to say, "There's a man lying at the door," or, perhaps, "There's somebody at the door, and he's in trouble." Something would be said to indicate that the unmarked expectation was not in effect in this case.

In other words, when there is no reason to expect otherwise, we assume the world will behave normally and that our unmarked expectations about it will continue to remain true. These fixed expectations are not tentative but are really the main substance of our concept of the normal, day-to-day world that we take for granted without questioning.

Our inferences are drawn very quickly

The fourth and final point we want to make based on the research of the past two decades is that the inferences we draw in ordinary conversation (as well as in reading written text) are drawn very quickly. Most researchers suggest that such inferences must be drawn every time it becomes possible for speakers to exchange turns, and that such occasions occur approximately once every second in normal conversation.

What is Successful Interdiscourse Professional Communication?

Language is ambiguous. This means that we can never be certain what the other person means – whether in speaking or writing. To put it another way, language can never fully express our meanings. Of course it is not surprising that research should confirm what philosophers in both the east and the west have told us for millennia. But what does this mean for inter-cultural professional communication?

In the first place it should be clear that communication works better the more the participants share assumptions and knowledge about the world. Where two people have very similar histories, backgrounds, and experiences, their communication works fairly easily because the inferences each makes about what the other means will be based on common experience and knowledge. Two people from the same village and the same family are likely to make fewer mistakes in drawing inferences about what the other means than two people from different cities on different sides of the earth.

The ambiguous nature of language is one major source of difficulties in interdiscourse communication. Where any two people differ in group membership because they are of different genders, different ages, different ethnic or cultural groups, different educations, different parts of the same country or even city, different income or occupational groups, or with very different personal histories, each will find it more difficult to draw inferences about what the other person means.

In the contemporary world of international and intercultural professional communication, the differences between people are considerable. People are in daily contact with members of cultures and other groups from all around the world. Successful communication is based on sharing as much as possible the assumptions we make about what others mean. When we are communicating with people who are very different from us, it is very difficult to know how to draw inferences about what they mean, and so it is impossible to depend on shared knowledge and background for confidence in our interpretations.

Expecting things to go wrong

Let us return to the example we gave above. Mr Wong feels that Mr Richardson has been insincere because he did not live up to his suggested invitation for lunch with Mr Wong. Mr Richardson probably feels that Mr Wong has been vaguely difficult to understand because he is not likely to have placed his main topics at the beginning of the conversation. Each has formed a somewhat negative opinion of the other on the basis of his wrong inferences about what the other meant. What do we do to fix this sort of miscommunication?

One solution might be to teach both Mr Wong and Mr Richardson what the other person's expectations are. Then Mr Richardson will know that Mr Wong will want to pay close attention to what comes at the end of their conversation, and Mr Wong will know that Mr Richardson will want to pay more attention to what comes at the beginning.

But have we fixed things? In this scenario they have just switched assumptions. The problem is that now neither of them knows which system the other is likely to use, since they now know both systems.

And yet to some extent we have fixed things. What both Mr Wong and Mr Richardson now know is that they cannot be certain how to interpret the speech of the other. That, in turn, means that they should hesitate to draw any negative conclusions about the actions of the other, since they cannot be sure whether they have correctly interpreted the other's intentions.

It also means something else. If both Mr Wong and Mr Richardson know that there are two possible systems for arranging topics and for giving emphasis to a topic in a discourse, they are both likely to pay closer attention to topics at both the beginnings and the endings of their conversations. In other words, they have both come to expect problems of interpretation. This leads them to question their own immediate interpretations and will also lead them to probe the other conversationalist further to see if their interpretations are correct.

Two Approaches to Interdiscourse Professional Communication

We have adopted two approaches to improving professional communication between members of different discourse systems. The first approach is based on knowing as much as possible about the people with whom one is communicating. This approach might be called the approach of increasing shared knowledge. The second approach is based on making the assumption that misunderstandings are the only thing certain about interdiscourse professional communication. This approach might be called dealing with miscommunication.

Increasing shared knowledge

We begin in chapter 2 from the point of view of increasing shared knowledge. We focus on the scenes and events in which our communicative actions and activities take place. Chapter 3 then turns to the question of how our identities as participants in speech events are both developed and maintained in interpersonal communication. The overall goal of these two chapters is to outline the two major areas in which shared knowledge works to reduce the ambiguity inherent in communication.

Dealing with miscommunication

Chapter 4 turns the focus toward dealing with miscommunication. It begins by introducing discourse analysis through the study of conversational inference. Through a study of cohesive devices such as conjunction, schemata or scripts, prosodic patterning of rhythm, intonation, and timing, we discuss the processes used by participants in speech events to interpret meanings.

Chapter 5 picks up the question of what causes the widely observed difference between westerners and Asians in their use of deductive and inductive strategies for introducing topics. We argue that it is not any inherent difference between westerners and Asians, but what makes the difference is that relationships of face politeness are treated differently. Both strategies may be used either by westerners or by Asians, but there is a tendency for Asians to be concerned with showing deference or respect in interactions with non-intimates, in contrast to westerners, who tend to emphasize egalitarian interpersonal relationships. These differences in face relationships lead to the use of different rhetorical strategies.

Because differences in rhetorical strategies can lead to the development of differences in interpersonal power, chapter 5 discusses the sources of power disparities in discourse. The chapter closes with a study of focused and non-focused interaction.

Regular patterns of discourse tend to form systems of discourse in which cultural norms lead to the choice of certain strategies for face relationships. These face relationships lead, in turn, to the use of particular discourse forms. Those different discourse forms imply certain modes of socialization which complete the circle by predetermining cultural norms. In chapter 6 we introduce the concept of the Utilitarian discourse system, which plays out in the field of discourse the philosophical position of Utilitarian economic and political ideology.

Having provided the background in the preceding chapters, chapter 7 then turns the focus directly on the broadest form of interdiscourse communication, intercultural communication. The approach we take is to emphasize the need both to share knowledge and to assume that miscommunication will occur and will need to be dealt with. In chapter 7 the question of culture is raised. There are many aspects of intercultural communication which have been brought up in the research literature. We discuss history and worldview, the functions of language, and non-verbal communication. The pernicious problem of binarism and stereotyping is shown to be one which arises when someone knows enough to contrast two cultural groups or discourse systems, but remains unaware of further dimensions of contrast and commonality.

Chapters 8–11 then take up the question of the different kinds of discourse system. Chapter 8 begins by presenting an outline guide for the study of discourse systems. It then takes up the first of two goal-directed discourse systems, the corporate discourse system. Chapter 9 considers a second goal-directed discourse system which cuts across the corporate system, the professional discourse system. Chapters 10 and 11 then use two involuntary discourse systems, the generational discourse system and the gender discourse system, to illustrate how problems of interpretation arise in discourse because of our different interpretive frameworks. Chapter 11 concludes by pointing out that each of us is simultaneously a member of multiple discourse systems which may make competing demands on us for membership and identity.

We believe that the most successful professional communicator is not the one who believes he or she is an expert in crossing the boundaries of discourse systems, but, rather, the person who strives to learn as much as possible about other discourse systems while recognizing that except within his or her own discourse systems he or she is likely to always remain a novice. We believe that effective communication requires study of cultural and discourse differences on the one hand, but also requires a recognition of one's own limitations.

2

How, When, and Where to Do Things with Language

A: Bill, that's a great idea. Could you write up a one-page summary for tomorrow's board meeting?

B: Of course, Mr Hutchins. Should I have it translated?

A: You'd better ask Jane. She'll know just who will be there.

Such a dialogue seems quite ordinary in business communication and it probably does not require much imagination to understand what these two speakers are talking about. We know, for instance, that Bill has just said something which Mr Hutchins thinks is a good idea. We know that there will be a board meeting on the day following this conversation. We also know that Bill is in some way a subordinate of Mr Hutchins. Their way of addressing each other tells us that. Mr Hutchins feels free to use the first names of others (Bill and Jane) but Bill is apparently in the position of needing to use the designation of "Mr" when speaking to Mr Hutchins.

In chapter 1 we said that language is always ambiguous. This dialogue is no exception. In spite of the things we know from this dialogue, there are quite a few things we cannot discover from the words alone. As an example of this ambiguity, even though we know that the board meeting is the next day, we do not know when this dialogue took place. The word "tomorrow" is relative to the time when it is spoken. If we do not know when this dialogue occurred we cannot know when the board meeting occurred.

In this short dialogue both speakers understand what is going on by relying on assumptions they make about the situation they are in, about the person they are speaking to, and about the relationship that exists between them (as well as about many other things). They "read between the lines" of their speech in order to make inferences about what is meant.

If language was unambiguous there would be no need to make such inferences. And even if perfectly clear and explicit language was possible, it does not seem all that attractive an option. For example, if we were to take this dialogue and to rewrite it to make explicit just those parts of it that we have mentioned above, it might sound like this:

A: William Smith, my subordinate, that which you have just told me is a great idea. Since I am your superior I require you to write up a one-page summary for the meeting of this company's board meeting which is on Tuesday, December 8, 1994.

B: Of course, Robert Hutchins, my immediate superior. Should I have it translated?

A: You'd better ask Jane Pollard, the vice-president and colleague of equal rank to me. She'll know just who will be there.

One reason we would not want to try to be explicit is that we could never entirely succeed. For each step of increased explicitness we would add new elements, to interpret which we would have to read between the lines. For example, we replaced "board meeting" with "this company's board meeting," but "this company" would also have to be replaced with the specific name of the company.

The second reason, however, that we could not be entirely explicit is that in becoming more explicit about these matters we become cloudier about others. For example, we have changed the terms "Bill" and "Mr Hutchins" to make the relationship between these two speakers more explicit. But in doing so too much attention is focused on their relationship and it begins to sound rather distant and hostile. It does not make it sound more friendly and familiar to turn it into the following:

A: William Smith, my subordinate with whom I feel an easy familiarity . . .

B: Of course, Robert Hutchins, my immediate superior, with whom I also feel an easy, though respectful familiarity . . .

Such an explicit statement of the relationships actually makes it seem less familiar and friendly. In fact, we have a very effective system for saying all of that. We do it the way these speakers did it in the first place: A calls B by his first name "Bill," and he, in turn, calls the other "Mr Hutchins." Both of these speakers understand this system in which they exchange such forms of address, so they can use it as a kind of code for exchanging comments about their relationship while they get on with the business of writing up the summary for the board meeting.

Shared knowledge is the basis on which these speakers read between the lines of their conversation. We will consider two different types of shared knowledge in this chapter and the chapter which follows:

1   shared knowledge of actions and situations (chapter 2);
2   shared knowledge of relationships and identities (chapter 3).

In this chapter we focus on the scenes or venues in which our communicative actions and activities occur. These communications can be understood as happening in acts, events, and situations among participants at certain times and places for particular purposes. The dialogue above can be easily interpreted by both participants partly because they share knowledge about what a board meeting is, when and where it is likely to take place, and what sorts of thing will happen when it occurs. And although they do not themselves know who the participants will be, they know that who the participants are is a significant question and that their colleague, Jane, is knowledgeable about who will be participants. Shared knowledge about these components of such communicative situations is the framework in which successful communicative action takes place.

Sentence Meaning and Speaker's Meaning

A: Can you tell me what time it is?
B: Yes, I can.

If this conversation took place under normal circumstances such as in an office or at a bus stop, A would consider B's answer to be very strange. The answer which B gives in this dialogue is grammatically correct and yet it is completely wrong. A is not asking about B's ability to tell time at all. He or she is asking B to tell him or her the time. The problem with B's answer is that it is responding to the sentence meaning but not to the speaker's meaning.

In chapter 1, we used the similar sentence, "What time is it?," as an example of the way in which the speaker's meaning can change depending on the context in which a sentence is used. When you are asking for the time on the street, "What time is it?" conveys a speaker's meaning very close to the sentence's meaning. But when a teacher uses this same sentence in a classroom the speaker's meaning is very different. The speaker (the teacher) really means, "I want you to tell me the time so that I can see if you know how to do it correctly." When the student responds by saying, "Two o'clock," that also means something different from what it appears to mean. What it means is something like, "I know how to tell the time correctly which I will show you by saying the correct time."

Understanding both sentence meaning and the speaker's meaning requires two kinds of knowledge. Sentence meaning depends on knowledge of grammar, speaker's meaning depends on knowledge of context. Our purpose in this chapter is to examine the concept of context.

Speech Acts, Speech Events, and Speech Situations

When you ask for the time at a bus stop with the sentence, "What time is it?," your meaning (the speaker's meaning) is that you want to know the time. This speech act takes place within a speech event which could be called *asking for the time*. Such an event is very brief and usually has three speech acts: asking the time, giving the time, and thanking. We could outline this speech event as follows:

Asking for the time	(speech event)
What is the time?	(speech act 1)
The time is X.	(speech act 2)
Thanking.	(speech act 3)

Your knowledge of communication in English includes both the sentences you need to accomplish the three speech acts and the knowledge of this three-act speech event.

When a teacher asks an elementary student what the time is, this is a very different speech event. We could call it *testing for the concept of telling the time*. It normally consists of three speech acts as well: asking the time, giving the time, and the teacher's evaluation. We could outline this speech event as follows:

Testing for the concept of telling the time		(speech event)
(teacher):	*What is the time?*	(speech act 1)
(student):	*The time is* X.	(speech act 2)
(teacher):	*Evaluation.*	(speech act 3)

The main difference between these speech events lies in the third speech act. There is also a difference in the participation structure. We could not have the student take the role of the teacher and the teacher take the role of the student in the normal use of this speech event.

Speech acts can be expressed in many different ways. The person on the street could accomplish speech act 1 with quite a few different sentences. Any of the following sentences would accomplish essentially the same speech act:

What time is it?
Could you tell me the time?
Excuse me, do you know the time?
Pardon me, do you have a watch?

In each case part of the meaning (the sentence meaning) is given by the sentence used and part of the meaning (the speaker's meaning) comes out of the fact that the interlocutors know the speech act of *asking for the time*. In the example we gave at the beginning, the problem was that the person responded to the literal sentence, not to the speaker's meaning. When A asked B, "Can you tell me what time it is?," B responded not with speech act 2 ("The time is X") but with a literal answer to the sentence. In such a case A might conclude that B is ignorant of the speech event *asking for the time*, B is being uncooperative, or B is, perhaps, joking. Since we do not usually joke with strangers on the street, that explanation can be ruled out.

We can interpret the meaning of sentences by understanding the context of the speech events in which they occur. In the same way, speech events take place within the larger context of speech situations. To give another example taken from a business meeting: within the conduct of a meeting the chairman of the meeting might be asked for a point in reference to a preceding meeting. He might then turn to the secretary of the meeting and begin the following dialogue:

> *Chairman*: Do you have the minutes?
> *Secretary*: Yes, here they are. I think 2.4.3 is what you will need.

Within this speech event which we might call a business meeting, the question, "Do you have the minutes?," probably conveys the speaker's meaning, *"Please find the relevant point and indicate that to me."* Both the chairman of the meeting and the secretary understand their participant roles. His role includes such aspects as to conduct the meeting, to gather in the points of view of the members, and so forth. The secretary's role is to provide an accurate record of the meeting, to provide references to other meetings, and to handle such administrative affairs as are needed by the members of the meeting.

This is knowledge of the speech event of the business meeting which all of the members share. As a result the fairly simple sentence, "Do you have the minutes?," conveys in polite language quite a complex set of speech acts. Some of them might be as follows:

> *Take out the minutes of the last meeting.*
> *Find the relevant point within the minutes.*
> *Show me the relevant point.*

We can see that the meaning of this sentence depends upon its placement within a speech event by placing it within a different but very closely related speech event, the pre-meeting informal discussion. We can imagine most of the participants of the meeting have come into the conference room. They are casually chatting with each other while they wait for the chairman of the meeting to call the meeting to order. During that period of casual conversation the chairman turns to the secretary and we have the following dialogue:

Chairman: Do you have the minutes?
Secretary: Yes, here they are.
Chairman: Good. Thanks.

In this case the same sentence, "Do you have the minutes?," would be understood as a much more literal question regarding whether or not the secretary had brought the minutes to the meeting.

This speech event, which we could call *pre-meeting preparation*, is very similar to the longer speech event which follows but can also be clearly distinguished from it in various ways. We would expect many of the members to speak to each other casually, often on topics not related to the purpose of the meeting. There would be much simultaneous speaking, in contrast to the meeting, in which we would expect one person to speak at a time. Such differences in topics and in participation structures show that there are really two quite separate events within a larger speech situation.

We could outline the structure as follows:

Speech situation: Business meeting
Speech event: Pre-meeting preparation
Speech act: Asking if the secretary has the minutes
Speech act: Confirming that the secretary has the minutes
Speech act: Thanking the secretary
Speech event: Meeting
Speech act: Asking the secretary to find the point under consideration in the minutes
Speech act: Indicating point 2.4.3 in the preceding meeting's minutes
Speech event: Post-meeting discussion

Grammar of Context

We understand the meanings of sentences in part because we know the grammatical rules by which they are constructed. Of course, much of our knowledge of those rules is not conscious. Nevertheless, we follow regular patterns in our use of subjects and predicates and in our selections of vocabulary items, which makes it possible for others to interpret our sentence meaning, even if that interpretation is often very ambiguous.

In the same way, we interpret the meanings of speakers because we know the rules by which contexts are constructed. We could call this a kind of grammar of context, which we use to interpret the meanings of speech acts within speech events which occur within speech situations.

In the example we have given above, a number of the features of this grammar of context have been mentioned. We know about participants and their roles. The chairman has a different role from the secretary and both of them have roles which are again different from the members of the board or committee. We also know that the meeting has specific rules for conduct so that we can tell when it has begun and when it has ended. That, in turn, tells us what belongs in the pre-meeting speech event or in the post-meeting speech event. Both of those events have different rules for participation and topics compared with the meeting itself.

The shared knowledge of grammar is well known to be essential for effective communication, and language teaching has focused primarily on helping students to develop that kind of knowledge. Our purpose is to emphasize the shared knowledge of context which is required for successful professional communication. We do so because, on the one hand, it is this knowledge which is essential for the interpretation of speaker's meaning and, on the other hand, because one major aspect of becoming educated as a professional communicator is learning the very specialized contexts of business and other professional work environments. In a real sense a professional communicator earns that designation because he or she has invested the time and effort directly in the study of the contexts of professional communication.

There are many different theories of grammar and many different schools of thought about how it should be taught. The same is true of what we are calling the grammar of context. For some researchers the term "sociolinguistics" covers this area of study. For others the preferred term would be the "ethnography of speaking." While we follow the latter scheme, we do so in a non-dogmatic way. For our purposes the most important point is that there are many aspects of context which are relevant in interdiscourse professional communication, and we need some common vocabulary for talking about them.

The outline which follows summarizes the main components which we believe are necessary for the student of professional communication to study.

Seven Main Components for a Grammar of Context

1 Scene:
   (a) Setting:
       – Time
       – Place:
           Location
           Use of space

(b) Purpose (function)
(c) Topic
(d) Genre
2 Key
3 Participants:
(a) Who they are
(b) Roles they take
4 Message form:
(a) Speaking
(b) Writing
(c) Silence
(d) Other media:
  – Video
  – Overhead projection, slides
  – Amplification
  – Recording
5 Sequence:
(a) Set agenda
(b) Open agenda
6 Co-occurrence patterns
7 Manifestation:
(a) Tacit
(b) Explicit

These seven components of a grammar of context along with their sub-components should not be thought of as fixed categories. They should be used to stimulate your thinking about the elements of which speech situations and speech events are composed. Some speech situations such as business meetings and university lectures are relatively fixed in the constellation of components which make them up. For example, a business meeting will most often have a regular scene – a conference room in the main office of the company at a regular morning hour, etc. University lectures are speech situations which quite predictably take place in lecture halls. Other speech situations are more notable for the variability of the components of which they consist. A friendly conversation might take place in a range of settings from the hallways of an office to the crowded interior of a commuter train.

To make the distinction between the concept of the speech situation and the components of a grammar of context clear, perhaps we could think of the speech situation as an answer to the question, "What are they doing?" The components of the grammar of context are an answer to the question, "How are they doing it?"

Scene

The most obvious aspect of context is probably the setting in which speech situations and events occur. We will use the word "scene" to include the setting as well as topic, genre, and purpose, since they are all so closely related.

The setting is first of all a physical location. For example, the setting for a business meeting is likely to be a conference room located in the office spaces of the company or the organization holding the meeting. In fact most businesses are set up to have prearranged settings for many of their functions. There are general offices in which clerical staff keep the main records and do the main clerical work of the business. There are conference rooms, offices for various members of the staff, storage rooms, computer or data-processing centers, and often lunchrooms or lounges for staff. Many businesses also have separate public spaces such as lobbies or sales or display rooms.

Our shared knowledge of scene includes knowing which spaces are most appropriate for which purposes, and so purpose can hardly be separated from the knowledge of setting. While there is usually some leeway in the purposes for which physical settings can be used, it would be seen to be strange behavior to conduct a high-level management meeting in the customers' waiting room of a large corporation. Or it would be seen as unusual for administrative staff to be typing up memos while seated at a conference table at which a sales presentation was being made. Generally speaking we have some well-defined idea of how to relate the purposes of speech events to conventionally appropriate locations.

Setting includes not just the physical location, however; time as well is a crucial aspect of setting. If we know that a meeting has been called to discuss a new personnel policy we can assume that the meeting will be held sometime during normal business hours. The internationalization of business and government over the past few decades has combined with rapid air transportation so that more and more the meaning of "normal business hours" has come into question. For example, it is not unusual for those who trade stock to gear their working hours to the hours in which major stock exchanges are open for trading. The "normal working hours" of stock brokers in Honolulu correspond with the actual hours during which the New York Stock Exchange operates. Because of the location of Hawaii, that makes their "normal" day begin at four o'clock in the morning. Other businesses such as newspapers or television production operate on schedules that are geared to production deadlines. One major aspect of knowing the setting for speech events within such professional contexts is knowing what "normal working hours" means.

We also know, regarding the spaces in which speech events are held, that position in spaces is an important aspect of communication. We expect the chair of a meeting to sit in a position which will be seen as the "head" of the table, for example. We know that people of higher authority have more freedom to occupy more space and to move about freely within it than those of lesser authority. The president of a company might be seen to walk about a room giving a presentation of a new development plan to which all of his or her subordinates sit quietly at a conference table listening. For each kind of speech event or speech situation there are likely to be pre-established norms for the places where they will be held, for the use of space within those places, for the times they will occur and the duration of those events. All of these will be considered to relate to the purposes of the events.

Most communicative events carry some expectations regarding topics. In a letter of credit issued by a company for the import of foreign-made goods one would expect the topics to include such things as the amount of money concerned, the quantity of goods involved, some indication of effective dates for payment and delivery and so forth. One would not expect to find a discussion of a movie the author had seen on television the night before. In fact one of the main features that indicate a change in speech event is a change in topic. In shifting from a pre-meeting speech event to the main agenda of the meeting the chair is likely to say something like, "Perhaps we should get down to the business on our agenda." It will be understood by everyone present that from then on casual or irrelevant topics should no longer be introduced and that it is time to focus on the topics introduced by the agenda only.

"Genre" is a term borrowed from literature to refer to different conventional forms of speech events. For example, jokes, lectures, business meetings, textbooks, memoranda of agreement, sales letters, product brochures, tables of organization, contracts, evaluation reports, advertising copy, business lunches, and so forth are all different genres found in professional communications. By genre we mean any speech event, whether it is spoken or in writing, which has fairly predictable sets of speech acts, participants, topics, settings, or other regularly occurring and conventional forms. Much of the education that now exists for professional communication focuses on the forms of a small set of the genres normally in use. We see literally hundreds of books which present the forms of business letters. That, of course, is reasonable since the genre of the business letter takes up a large portion of the written communication between one business and another. There are also many books on phone calls, which are another very frequent genre of professional communication.

The focus on the internal content and structure of genres is not the whole story, however, since to use any genre of communication effectively requires knowing just when it is appropriate to use it. In recent years, for example, it has become an unwritten rule of public speaking in North American business environments that the speaker should include a few jokes at the beginning of a talk. This expectation of public speakers had become so generalized that it came to affect the annual address to Congress given by the president of the United States. By the time of the State of the Union address in 1992 the president began this significant and formal ceremonial occasion with a sequence of several jokes. While at one time the inclusion of this genre in public ceremonial occasions would have been considered a terrible breach of decorum, in the business-dominated environment of that particular administration the jokes seemed to convey sympathy with the conventions and practices of the business world.

Key

"Key" is a term borrowed from music to refer to the tone or the mood of a communication. A businesswoman the authors know once took her young daughter with her to a business meeting. She had told her daughter that they were going to attend a meeting and that she would have to be quiet and behave herself. As it had turned out the meeting had developed a very relaxed key and there was much free conversation and laughing. Afterwards the child said to her mother, "That wasn't a meeting; it was a party." When she was asked why she said that, her answer was that meetings were to be serious and parties were for laughing. This young child had understood a significant aspect of two typical speech situations in our culture: that a business meeting and a party normally differ in key.

One very interesting aspect of professional communication, especially when it occurs in an international environment, is that there is so much variability across cultural groups in their expectations about key and about how and when different keys should be expressed. It is well known and, perhaps, even stereotypical that Asians tend to smile or laugh when they are embarrassed. While it is true that many others including Americans and Australians also "laugh nervously," it is equally stereotypical that Americans and Australians are always laughing or joking with each other or with their business partners. Yet in spite of the stereotypical nature of these observations there is a serious potential for the misreading of key in communications between North Americans or Australians and Asians. A key of embarrassment or difficulty might be expressed by Asians in such a way that their counterparts would read it as indicating a key of relaxation or enjoyment. Such a misreading could equally well be conveyed in the opposite direction where Asians might misread a relaxed, joking tone as hiding embarrassment. In either case the failure to correctly interpret the key being conveyed by one's business partners could lead to serious misinterpretation of the speakers' meanings.

Participants

Two aspects of participants need to be taken into consideration in reading the contextual grammar of speech situations: who they are and what roles they are taking. Naturally, of course, the sheer number of participants is a significant aspect of any communicative situation.

To begin with number first, any speech event needs to take into consideration the number of participants even if just to know how to prepare the setting. A meeting of 200 people cannot be easily held in a conference room. It is equally true, but for a very different reason, that a meeting of twenty people cannot be held in a large auditorium. In arranging for an event such as a lecture or a sales presentation, most professional communicators would prefer to arrange to have a space just a little larger than the number of people would require. If the space is too small, people are made uncomfortable since not everyone will be able to sit well or to see the main speaker or presenter. On the other hand if the space is very much too large, people will tend to be seated widely apart from each other and that will create a sense of isolation and social coldness.

Yet number is a relatively minor aspect of the study of participants. It is much more important to know who the participants are and what roles they take. It is well known, for example, that most governments have protocol offices whose job is to make sure that all participants in government functions will be given just the right treatment. Seating at state dinners, for example, is an important matter of correctly signifying the relative positions of power and authority among the invited guests.

A second aspect, of equal importance, is to understand not just who the participants are but what roles they are taking within the speech event. It is quite common, for example, for someone who is of major importance within a company or some other organization to have what is an apparently insignificant role in an actual speech event. Often major decisions are made behind the scenes and the business which is conducted more openly is only done to legitimate or ratify decisions made elsewhere. We have often seen in companies, for example, cases where a junior company position is occupied by someone who is related to the owner or is, perhaps, held in high esteem by someone much more powerful in the company. In actual business events that person may appear to have a fairly insignificant role and nevertheless be more greatly empowered to make decisions than his or her official role would indicate.

One final point on the question of participant roles is important to make. While generalizations are dangerous, of course, it is perhaps safe to say that the tendency is for North American and other western companies to give a great deal of power to the individuals who represent them in international negotiations. There are two aspects to this power. It is often true that people higher up in the institutions are used to undertaking such negotiations. In addition, westerners tend to be less tied to their companies as individuals than Asians are to theirs. As a result, when westerners enter into a negotiation they know that if the negotiations fall through and they lose their position within the company as a result, they can always just leave the company and find another job elsewhere. Asians, on the other hand, are often put in the position of negotiating on behalf of someone else who actually holds the power to make decisions. This is for several reasons. It is probably true that decisions are made higher up in Asian companies than in North American companies. At the same time, in international negotiations it is usually people lower in the company structure who have a more agile command of intercultural communication and of English, and so they are given the position of conducting negotiations.

The result of this difference in the authority given to negotiators is that Asians are somewhat more restricted to just giving and taking information in such meetings than their North American counterparts, who are in the position of making their own decisions right there on the spot. This difference in participant roles is not likely to be known or very well understood by both parties. The result is that each assumes the other party has equivalent status and therefore cannot understand or cannot easily interpret the speakers' meanings of the sentences exchanged. The North American is likely to speak in terms of "I": "I will offer so much for a certain quantity." The Asian is likely to speak in terms of "we": "We cannot say immediately whether we can meet that price or that deadline." The North American's role may sound like exaggeration or egocentrism to the Asian. The Asian's role may sound like resistance or non-cooperation to the North American. In either case the problem stems from the lack of understanding of differences in participant role structure.

Message form

One of the most important aspects of professional communication is to know what is the most effective medium to use for communication. A wily educational administrator in the Yukon Territory of Canada once told one of the authors, "Whoever prints the program determines the content." It is well known in business and in governmental communications that whoever makes the agenda for a meeting has already had the strongest voice in how the meeting will come out before it has even begun.

In every field of professional communication it is important to choose the form of the message carefully. In marketing there is an enormous range of possibilities including television and radio commercial advertisements, newspaper advertisements, direct mailings, brochures, leaflets, word of mouth, testimonials of well-known people, bus-side and train placards, and virtually every other form in which messages can be conveyed.

The decision of which medium to use is not just a question of medium; it is also a question of contents and of social structure, even of law. An advertising campaign that prints a paragraph of text in a newspaper advertisement might have only two or three words of text in a television spot but emphasize the use of visual symbolism and sound instead. A radio spot would, of course, have only sound. The result is that the contents themselves would be considerably different.

To look at the legal question, in most cases agreements made face to face or over the phone have little or no legal status. They become legally binding only when they are written, signed, and in some cases witnessed as well. Faxes apparently have no legal status since they are considered copies of documents, not the documents themselves.

One result of the more official status accorded original written documents is that it becomes a significant aspect of negotiation whether something is given written status or not. As we will discuss below, one major aspect of the grammar of context is that some things are explicitly known and some things remain tacit or unexpressed. A business conducting questionable business practices, of course, will want to keep as few written records as possible so that legal authorities cannot check up on its activities. But even for completely legal activities it is often felt desirable or necessary to keep some aspects of institutional knowledge tacit.

Almost every organization in which professional communicators work has an official organization chart which shows who holds which position of authority and what the normal lines of communication are to be. At the same time, as we have mentioned above when we were talking about participant status, it is often the case that unofficial lines of authority and of communication exist within that organization. Such lines are virtually always kept out of writing. They remain part of the oral tradition of companies and of institutions. One important aspect of shared knowledge is not only knowing what those lines of communication are, but also knowing that they are not to be made explicit, especially not in written form.

Sequence

Speech situations have important internal structures which determine the order in which events can occur. Knowing this structure is essential to being able to interpret just which speech event is happening. For example, in the pre-meeting speech event we discussed above the sentence, "Do you have the minutes?" was understood to mean that the chair was asking if the secretary had brought them to the meeting. Within the meeting, however, the same sentence was understood to mean that the chair wanted the secretary to consult the minutes. At that time we said that this was because one occurred within the meeting and the other occurred before the meeting, but how did we know that? There were several indications, one of which was participant structure and topic selection – people were freely talking to each other about general topics and then the chair called the meeting to order. That still does not tell us, however, how the participants knew that the meeting had not started. The answer to that question is that part of their shared knowledge, part of their grammar of contexts, told them that meetings have several events and those events come in a normal sequence. The first is a transitional event that takes place while everyone gathers at the meeting place and prepares for the meeting. Since they knew that sequence of events, they knew they could talk freely until the chair called the meeting to order and started it formally.

Across cultures there is a particular problem with understanding events, often because most aspects of the events are similar and only the order will be changed. North Americans eat their salads before their main courses while the French eat theirs after the main courses. Many a westerner has eaten too much during the first few courses of a Chinese dinner because it has not been apparent to him or to her how many courses would be coming or that, indeed, there would be any further dishes served at all. A North American dinner party would most likely begin with a short period of conversation (and perhaps drinks) before dinner, then dinner, and then after dinner the main evening's entertainment. A Cantonese dinner party, however, disperses as soon as the meal is eaten. If there is entertainment it will happen before dinner. This difference in sequencing causes considerable confusion when Cantonese and North Americans have dinner together.

The more formal a speech situation is the more likely it is to have a formal agenda. This is because sequence is so important in defining participation in speech events. As we have said above, it is well known that whoever controls the agenda has a major voice in the outcomes of speech events.

There are two sides of sequencing as part of the grammar of context. On the one hand it is part of our shared knowledge, which helps us to interpret meanings if we know the conventional sequences in which things happen. On the other hand it is part of our ability to create meanings, to be able to manipulate the sequences of events to achieve the greatest effectiveness.

Co-occurrence patterns, marked and unmarked

We have presented these components of a grammar of context as somewhat isolated. Nevertheless, we have had no choice but to mention a number of co-occurrence patterns among them. For example, the genre of jokes in most cases occurs together with the humorous key. That does not mean that it is impossible to use a joke in a non-humorous key. For example, someone might be very offended by a joke and find it not funny at all. In telling a friend about it he or she might tell the joke but in a key of having been affronted.

Such a predictable co-occurrence as a joke in a humorous key would be called unmarked whereas a joke told in an affronted way would be considered to be marked. All that this means is that the unmarked configuration would be thought to be quite unremarkable. It is something nobody would really notice unless they were studying the phenomenon. On the other hand something which was marked would be surprising or unexpected. This does not mean that it does not happen; it just means that when marked events or collocations of these components occur, we notice that something is different and that we have to pay particular attention to interpret them correctly.

We have given a number of examples of unmarked speech events or genres above. A board which meets in a conference room during normal business hours and which has an agenda would be unmarked. There is little unexpected about that. If that same meeting was to be held in an underground vault deep in the basement of corporate headquarters, it would be very marked and we would be looking for an explanation of why something so marked was happening.

Manifestation

To close this presentation of the components of communication events and situations, we want to bring up again a point made above. Some of the components of communication are manifested in very explicit form. Other components remain tacit, that is, unexpressed. In the example we mentioned above, the official authority structure of a business or a corporation is almost always presented in an organizational chart or a table of organization (TOE). That is an explicit manifestation of the structure of the organization. At the same time the unofficial power structure or authority structure by which decisions are often directly taken or at least influenced is normally not explicitly given; it remains tacit.

There are at least two reasons why not all components of communication are made explicit. The first reason is simply because that is often very difficult to do, because we do not really know how they work. Much of our activity as human beings remains out of our conscious control and so it is not surprising that much of our communicative activity should also remain out of our conscious awareness.

The second reason that many aspects of communication remain tacit is that we prefer for them to do so. It is a major component by which the grammar of context is constructed for some of them to be tacit and some of them to be explicit. Again, perhaps, we should ask what the reasons are that we prefer for some aspects of communication to remain tacit. Some of the reasons are fairly positive aspects of human communication, others are not usually looked upon so favorably.

In chapter 1 we discussed how Deborah Tannen, in her book *You Just Don't Understand* (1990a), has pointed out that at least in North American society women prefer to be indirect or inexplicit about their wants and their needs. From this point of view a man can show a woman he loves how much he loves her not by being explicit about it but by choosing gifts for her which show that he knows what she really values. In such a case the meaning of the gift is completely destroyed if the woman's wants have been explicitly expressed. In other words, in human communication it is valuable to say less than is required, because only in that way is the other person given the opportunity to show his or her involvement by reading one's tacit or unexpressed intentions or wants. This is the more positive side of the reasons why tacit or inexplicit human knowledge is important to us.

In professional communication a similar dynamic is at work. When a person comes up for promotion, for example, it will be considered a very strong recommendation to see that this person has "read between the lines" of his or her professional requirements and gone beyond that to do what is best for his or her organization. In fact it could almost be thought of as a negative recommendation to say that a particular person has always done exactly and only what was explicitly required. And so, if it is considered valuable for a person to go beyond what is required, it is necessary to never explicitly say everything that is required.

The negative side of this same aspect of communication is that such unstated and tacit understandings can be held against a person, and that person has no recourse where this happens. To take the idea of promotion again, if it is never stated on what basis a person will be promoted, then it is always very easy to say that person has not done enough to deserve promotion.

It is for this latter reason that so many attempts to correct social injustices and inequalities have taken the form of trying to make all the rules completely explicit. While the motives for wanting everything to be explicit are laudable – who could say that they really want injustice? – it is unfortunate that this position shows a great misunderstanding of human communication. Human communication is always ambiguous, as we have said. One way of rephrasing this statement is to say that in human communication it is impossible to make every aspect explicit. For professional communication, the main point is not to fret over the injustices which occur but to try to understand how communication is structured through a grammar of context which gives us the basis for interpreting the speaker's meaning.

3

Interpersonal Politeness and Power

Communicative Style or Register

On Nathan Road in Tsim Sha Tsui, one of Hong Kong's most crowded tourist and shopping areas, two men passed by a vendor of imitation Rolex watches.

> *Vendor* (to first man):   Eh! Copy watch?
> *Vendor* (to second man):   Rolex? Sir?

Both of the passers-by were Americans. The first was apparently a sailor from a US Navy ship in port at that time. This man was together with several other men who also looked like they might be American sailors. The second man the vendor of copy Rolexes spoke to was in his mid-fifties and dressed much more formally in a suit coat.

In speaking to these two men the vendor of copy Rolexes made a shift in register or communicative style. When he spoke to the first man (who was quite a bit younger than the vendor) he used a very informal or familiar style. He addressed him with, "Eh!," and referred to the item for sale as a "copy watch." When he spoke to the second man (who was quite a bit older than the vendor) he used a more formal or deferential form of address, "Sir!," and referred to the item for sale as a "Rolex."

In this case the vendor used somewhat limited linguistic resources to signal that he had perceived a social difference between these two potential customers. This is very much like the example we gave above at the beginning of chapter 1, when Mr Hutchins referred to his subordinate as Bill.

Linguists have used many different terms to refer to such shifts in linguistic form when those shifts are used to indicate changes in components of speech events or speech situations. Among linguists, the term "register" tends to be associated mostly with particular scenes, and "communicative style" tends to be associated with participants, though these are not clear distinctions in many cases. For example, a greeting might be given in a very informal way if you meet a friend casually on the street, but much more formally if the two of you are participating in a board meeting. While the participants remain the same, the greeting will vary in register because of the different setting.

"Communicative style" is the term we prefer for this chapter on interpersonal politeness and power because it is a more general term than "register" used by most sociolinguists to refer to either personal identities or interpersonal relationships among participants. We would not say, for example, that Rebecca has an interesting register but we might say that she has an interesting communicative style. On the other hand we could say that Fiona is very good at choosing the appropriate register or communicative style for any situation. In other words, the term "communicative style" is less restrictive and can include the concept of register.

Face

The question of human psychological identity is a complex issue that goes beyond the study of communication into psychology, sociology, and philosophy. Nevertheless, there is an important aspect of identity that has been recognized as an essential element in all communication. In chapter 2 we said that there were two aspects of participation which are important to consider: who the participants are and what roles they are taking. At that time we were referring mostly to the places that participants occupy in an institutional or a social structure on the one hand, and on the other hand, the particular position they were taking in some speech event. Now we want to take up a third and more deeply personal aspect of this component of participation: the interpersonal identity of the individuals in communication.

The concept of face is not new to Asian readers, who will recognize the term *mianzi* in Mandarin (*minji* in Cantonese, *mentsu* in Japanese, *chae myon* in Korean), where it carries a range of meanings based upon a core concept of "honor," but perhaps the way it is used in contemporary sociolinguistics and sociology will be somewhat different. The concept first was introduced by the Chinese anthropologist Hu in 1944, though the term had been used in English for at least several centuries before that. The American sociologist Erving Goffman based much of his work on interpersonal relationships on the concept of face.

One of the most important ways in which we reduce the ambiguity of communication is by making assumptions about the people we are talking to. As the simplest example, when we begin talking to someone we try to speak to them in a language we know they will understand. In a mono-lingual speech community that is rarely a problem, but in the increasingly multilingual international business community it is becoming a major issue, to be solved right at the outset of communications.

We also make significant assumptions about what kind of a person the other person is and what kind of a person he or she would like us to think of him or her as being. When Mr Hutchins called his subordinate colleague by his first name, Bill, he projected the assumption that there was a difference in status between them and he also projected that they both would agree to that difference in status by simply using the name Bill without further comment. Bill, in turn, projected that he accepted that difference in status and ratified that by calling his employer Mr Hutchins.

Many aspects of linguistic form depend on the speakers making some analysis of the relationships among themselves. The choice of terms of address is one of the first of these recognized by sociolinguists. The watch vendor in Tsim Sha Tsui also recognized that different forms of address, "Eh!" or "Sir!," were appropriate in trying to catch the attention of two different potential customers. The study of face in sociolinguistics arose out of the need to understand how participants decide what their relative statuses are and what language they use to encode their assumptions about such differences in status, as well as their assumptions about the face being presented by participants in communication.

Within sociological and sociolinguistic studies face is usually given the following general definition: "*Face is the negotiated public image, mutually granted each other by participants in a communicative event.*" In this definition and in the work of sociolinguists the emphasis is not so much on shared assumptions as it is on the negotiation of face. For our purposes we want to keep both aspects of face in mind. We believe that while there is much nego-tiation of face in any form of interpersonal communication, participants must also make assumptions about face before they can begin any communication.

We do not have to figure out everything from the beginning every time we talk to someone. Mr Hutchins and Bill do not need to open up negotiations about their relationship each time they speak to each other. Just the fact that Mr Hutchins is Bill's employer is sufficient information to know that they differ in status. Knowing that difference in status and how it is normally expressed in English, we can predict fairly accurately that Bill will say "Mr Hutchins," and Mr Hutchins will say "Bill."

Participants make certain unmarked assumptions about their relationships and about the face they want to claim for themselves and are willing to give to the other participants in any communicative situation. In addition to these unmarked assumptions, participants also undertake a certain amount of negotiation of their relationships as a natural process of change in human relationships. For example, if a person wants to ask a rather large favor of another person, he or she is likely to begin with the assumed relationship, but then he or she will begin to negotiate a closer or more intimate relationship. If such a closeness is achieved then he or she is likely to feel it is safer to risk asking for the favor than if their negotiations result in more distance between them.

In the field of sociolinguistics this combination of unmarked assumptions about the participants and their relationships with the negotiations about those assumptions is called the study of face. Such study also goes by the name of politeness theory.

The "Self" as a Communicative Identity

One reason the term "face" is attractive in communicative studies is that it leaves open the question of who is the "real" person underneath the face which is presented in communication. That deeper question is ultimately a question of psychology or, perhaps, philosophy, and we will not go further into it. Nevertheless, it is important to point out now that there may be significant cultural differences in the assumptions made about the "self" that is involved in communication. The idea of "self" which underlies western studies of communication is highly individualistic, self-motivated, and open to ongoing negotiation. We believe that this concept of the "self" is not entirely appropriate as the basis for Asian communication. There is reason to believe that the "self" projected by Asians is a more collectivistic "self," one which is more connected to membership in basic groups such as the family or one's working group and which is taken to be more strongly under the influence of assumed or unmarked cultural assumptions about face.

The Paradox of Face: Involvement and Independence

Face is really a paradoxical concept. By this we mean that there are two sides to it which appear to be in contrast. On the one hand, in human interactions we have a need to be involved with other participants and to show them our involvement. On the other hand, we need to maintain some degree of independence from other participants and to show them that we respect their independence. These two sides of face, involvement and independence, produce an inherently paradoxical situation in all communications, in that *both* aspects of face must be projected simultaneously in any communication.

The involvement aspect of face is concerned with the person's right and need to be considered a normal, contributing, or supporting member of society. This involvement is shown through being a normal and contributing participant in communicative events. One shows involvement by taking the point of view of other participants, by supporting them in the views they take, and by any other means that demonstrates that the speaker wishes to uphold a commonly created view of the world.

Involvement is shown by such discourse strategies as paying attention to others, showing a strong interest in their affairs, pointing out common in-group membership or points of view with them, or using first names. As we will indicate below, we might say such things as, "Are you feeling well today?," or, "I know just what you mean, the same thing happened to me yesterday," or, "Yes, I agree, I've always believed that, too." Any indication that the speaker is asserting that he or she is closely connected to the hearer may be considered a strategy of involvement.

Many other terms have been used in the sociolinguistic literature to present this concept. It has been called positive face, for example, on the basis of the idea of the positive and negative poles of magnetism. The positive poles of a magnet attract, and by analogy involvement has been said to be the aspect of communication in which two or more participants show their common attraction to each other.

Involvement has also been called solidarity politeness; again, for the reason that sociolinguists want to emphasize that this aspect of face shows what participants have in common. Any of these terms might be acceptable in some contexts, but we feel that the term "involvement" is clearest and creates the fewest analytical complications for the reader.

The independence aspect of face emphasizes the individuality of the participants. It emphasizes their right not to be completely dominated by group or social values, and to be free from the impositions of others. Independence shows that a person may act with some degree of autonomy and that he or she respects the rights of others to their own autonomy and freedom of movement or choice.

Independence is shown by such discourse strategies as making minimal assumptions about the needs or interests of others, by not "putting words into their mouths," by giving others the widest range of options, or by using more formal names and titles. For example, in ordering in a restaurant we might say, "I don't know if you will want to have rice or noodles," or in making the initial suggestion to go out for coffee we might say, "I'd enjoy going out for coffee, but I imagine you are very busy." The key to independence face strategies is that they give or grant independence to the hearer.

Independence has also been given various other names by researchers in sociolinguistics. It has been called negative politeness, as an analogy with the negative pole of a magnet, which repels. We prefer not to use this term, because technical or formal contrast between "positive" and "negative" can easily be forgotten and readers can too easily begin to think of "positive politeness" as good and "negative politeness" as bad.

Another term which has been used as an attempt to get around the potential negative aspects of "positive" and "negative" politeness has been "deference politeness." We have used "solidarity" and "deference" in earlier writings, but find that some readers have a strong preference for one type of strategy or the other and, again, miss the point that *both* aspects of face must be projected simultaneously in any communication.

The most important concept to remember about face is that it is paradoxical. By that we mean the concept of face has built into it *both* aspects; involvement *and* independence must be projected simultaneously in any communication. It is always a matter of more or less, not absolute expression of just one or the other. A speaker must find just the right way of saying something which shows the degree to which he or she is involving the other participants and the degree to which he or she is granting independence to them.

The reason involvement and independence are in conflict is that emphasizing one of them risks a threat to the other. If I show you too much involvement, you are likely to feel that your independence is being threatened. On the other hand if I grant you too much independence, you are likely to feel that I have limited your involvement.

Any communication is a risk to face; it is a risk to one's own face at the same time it is a risk to the other person's. We have to carefully project a face for ourselves and to respect the face rights and claims of other participants. We risk our own involvement face if we do not include other participants in our relationship. That is, if we exclude others, while that may increase our own independence, it at the same time decreases our own involvement. At the same time, if we include others, we risk our own independence face.

Looking at it from the other person's point of view, if we give too much involvement to the other person, we risk their independence face. On the other hand if we give them too much independence, we risk their involvement.

The result of the double risk, the risk to involvement face and the risk to independence face of both the speaker and the hearer, means, therefore, that all communication has to be carefully phrased to respect face, both involvement face and independence face. This could be said another way: *"There is no faceless communication."*

Politeness Strategies of Involvement and Independence

Now that we have given you a general introduction to the concept of face in interpersonal communication, we hope that we can make this discussion clearer by giving a number of examples of actual linguistic strategies which are used to communicate these different face strategies.

The most extreme contrast between involvement and independence is the difference between speaking (or communicating) and silence (or non-communication). Any form of communication at all is somewhat on the side of involvement. In order to communicate at all, the participants must share some aspects of symbolic systems which they can interpret in shared ways. If I speak to you and you are able to answer me, we have already shared some small degree of involvement. As a result we would classify speech on the side of involvement, and silence (or better still, non-communication) on the side of independence.

Perhaps it is important to clarify that there are silences which can be interpreted as high involvement as well. We know that two people who share a very intimate situation can communicate to each other a high degree of involvement while remaining completely silent. That is why we have rephrased "silence" as "non-communication" above. It is the silence of non-communication to which we refer when we say it is at the independence end of the continuum. One grants (and claims for oneself) the highest level of independence by having no communication with the other.

Taciturnity and volubility are somewhat lesser extremes of non-communication and communication. Taciturnity means, simply, not talking very much. Volubility is the other side of the coin, "talking a lot." Both of these are highly relative terms. There is no absolute amount of speech which can be classed as taciturn or as voluble. The same is true for individuals; there are no absolutely taciturn or voluble individuals. Likewise there are no absolutely taciturn or voluble groups, or societies, or cultures.

Nevertheless, one aspect of the grammar of context is expectations of the amount of speech. For example, many religious rites or ceremonies are very restricted in the amount of incidental conversational or non-formal speech expected. In such a situation, a person who was speaking at all might be perceived as being very voluble. On the other hand, at a friendly dinner party among close friends, a person who was speaking, but not to any great extent, might be considered to be taciturn, because the expectations are for a good bit of conversational exchange.

Psychological studies of conversational exchanges and formal interviews have shown that the more talk there is, the more these exchanges are perceived as "warm" or "affiliative." In contrast, the less talk there is, the more they are perceived as "cold" or "non-affiliative." On the basis of this designation of "affiliative," we believe that it is best to consider more talk, volubility, to be an involvement strategy, and less talk, taciturnity, to be an independence strategy.

From the point of view of face relationships, we have said above that any communication is based on sharing a symbolic system, and that such a sharing is already to some degree an expression of involvement. Therefore, the question of what language to use is a crucial one in international business and government relationships as well as within bilingual or multilingual speech communities. If negotiations are conducted among participants using different languages (but, of course, with translators), this is a situation of lesser involvement or of higher independence than if negotiations are conducted using the same language. Therefore, it is a question of face relationships to decide whether discussions should go on in separate languages mediated by translators or whether they should go on in a common language. Naturally, of course, if the negotiations go on in the native language of one of the participants (or group of participants) that will tip the balance of involvement toward their side. It will give the other participants a sense of having their own independence limited, perhaps even unduly. At the same time, an insistence on the use of separate languages to overcome this problem can produce a sense of too great an independence, which can be felt as hostility or unwillingness to come to a common ground of agreement. The choice of language in discourse is not simply a matter of practical choice governed by efficiency of communication of information. Every such choice is also a matter of the negotiation of the face of the participants.

Linguistic strategies of involvement: some examples

There are many ways in which involvement can be shown through linguistic form. The examples which follow are just ten types which have been selected from English. While there is some disagreement among researchers about exactly which linguistic forms will be used in different languages to indicate these strategies, the examples here will give you a general idea of what we mean by linguistic strategies of involvement. (In these examples the letter "H" represents the "Hearer" to whom one is speaking, and "S" represents the "Speaker.")

1   Notice or attend to H:
    "I like your jacket."
    "Are you feeling better today?"
2   Exaggerate (interest, approval, sympathy with H):
    "Please be careful on the steps, they're very slippery."
    "You always do so well in school."
3   Claim in-group membership with H:
    "All of *us here* at City Polytechnic . . ."
4   Claim common point of view, opinions, attitudes, knowledge, empathy:
    "I know *just* how you feel. I had a cold like that last week."
5   Be optimistic:
    "I think we should be able to finish that annual report very quickly."
6   Indicate S knows H's wants and is taking them into account:
    "I'm sure you will all want to know when this meeting will be over."

7   Assume or assert reciprocity:
    "I know you want to do well in sales this year as much as I want you
    to do well."
8   Use given names and nicknames:
    "Bill, can you get that report to me by tomorrow?"
9   Be voluble.
10 Use H's language or dialect.

Linguistic strategies of independence: some examples

As in the case of involvement, there are many ways in which independence
can be reflected linguistically. The ten types below have been selected from
among the most common used in English. Again, "H" refers to the "Hearer"
and "S" to the "Speaker."

1   Make minimal assumptions about H's wants:
    "I don't know if you will want to send this by air mail or by
    speedpost."
2   Give H the option not to do the act:
    "It would be nice to have tea together, but I am sure you are very
    busy."
3   Minimize threat:
    "I just need to borrow a little piece of paper, any scrap will do."
4   Apologize:
    "I'm sorry to trouble you, could you tell me the time?"
5   Be pessimistic:
    "I don't suppose you'd know the time, would you?"
6   Dissociate S, H from the discourse:
    "This is to inform our employees that . . ."
7   State a general rule:
    "Company regulations require an examination . . ."
8   Use family names and titles:
    "Mr Lee, there's a phone call for you."
9   Be taciturn.
10 Use own language or dialect.

Politeness (or Face) Systems

We have said above that face relationships between and among participants
consist of two elements: an unmarked set of initial assumptions and a series

of negotiations in which those unmarked assumptions are either ratified or altered in some way. Under normal circumstances, face relationships remain fairly stable and negotiation of the overriding relationship is relatively minor. When the assistant manager of a sales department meets with his or her manager, the relationship is not likely to change from meeting to meeting. Once it has been established at the beginning of employment in that position, it is likely to remain the same until one or the other moves to a different position.

We could describe such general and persistent regularities in face relationships as politeness systems. For example, Mr Hutchins can be expected to always address Bill by his first name and Bill is likely to always say "Mr" when speaking to Mr Hutchins. Such a regular relationship indicates what we would call a politeness system, because both speakers in the system would use a certain fairly regular set of face strategies in speaking to each other.

There are three main factors involved which bring such a politeness (or face) system into being: power, distance, and the weight of the imposition.

Power (+P, –P)

In discussions of face or politeness systems, "power" refers to the vertical disparity between the participants in a hierarchical structure. In other words, Mr Hutchins is above Bill in the hierarchical structure of their company. We would describe their relationship as +P (plus power) because Mr Hutchins has special privileges (and, of course, responsibilities) over Bill and Bill owes certain duties to Mr Hutchins. In most business and governmental structures, the organization chart shows quite explicitly what the +P relationships are. As a result the language used between such participants is relatively predictable.

In contrast to such a situation, where there is little or no hierarchical difference between participants, we would consider that to be –P or an egalitarian system. Close friends generally share a –P relationship, since neither one is considered above the other. But the relationship does not have to be among close friends. Two people who have equivalent ranks in their own companies or their own organizations might have a –P relationship even though they do not know each other at all. In international protocols in both business and government, most communications are attempted at the same level so that –P relationships can be achieved. Company presidents talk to company presidents, assistant sales managers deal with other assistant sales managers, ambassadors talk to ambassadors, and clerks talk to clerks.

Distance (+D, −D)

The distance between two participants should not be confused with the power difference between them. Distance can be seen most easily in egalitarian relationships (−P). For example, two close friends would be classified as −D because of the closeness of their relationship. On the other hand, two governmental officials of different nations are likely to be of equal power within their systems but distant, +D.

Even within a single business organization, power (P) is not the same as distance (D). The head of the personnel office and his or her staff will have a hierarchical relationship (+P), but most likely will have a close (−D) relationship because they work together daily. Those same employees will have a hierarchical difference *and* a distance between them and the head of, say, the quality control department within the same company (+D, +P), because they rarely have contact with each other.

Weight of imposition (+W, −W)

The third factor that will influence face strategies is the weight of the imposition. Even if two participants in a speech event have a very fixed relationship between them, the face strategies they will use will vary depending on how important the topic of discussion is for them. For example, if Bill is talking to Mr Hutchins about a routine daily business matter, their face strategies will be quite predictable. On the other hand, if Bill has decided that today is the day to approach Mr Hutchins about getting a promotion, he is likely to take on an extra-deferential tone and use a much higher level of independence strategies than he normally uses. Or on the other side of it, if Mr Hutchins has to approach Bill with some rather bad news, perhaps that his position is going to be eliminated, he will use a much lower level of involvement than he customarily uses.

In other words, when the weight of imposition increases, there will be an increased use of independence strategies. When the weight of imposition decreases, there will be an increased use of involvement strategies.

From this you should be able to see that in relatively fixed interpersonal relationships, such as those within a business or some other organization, power (P) and distance (D) are not likely to change very rapidly or very frequently, and what is mostly under negotiation will have to do with the weight of imposition (W).

Because our focus is now on politeness or face systems and not on individual situational relationships, weight of imposition will not be a major factor in the discussion which follows. We will focus primarily on systems which develop through the variations in power and distance.

Three Politeness Systems: Deference, Solidarity, and Hierarchy

Three main types of politeness system can be observed in many different contexts. These are based primarily on whether there is a power difference (+P or −P) and on the distance between participants (+D or −D). We have called them the deference politeness system, the solidarity politeness system, and the hierarchical politeness system.

Deference politeness system (−P, +D)

If a university professor named Dr Wong from Hong Kong meets a university professor from Tokyo named Dr Hamada, they are likely to refer to each other as "Professor Wong" and "Professor Hamada." In such a system they would treat each other as equals and use a relatively high concentration of independence politeness strategies out of respect for each other and for their academic positions. Such a system of mutual but distant independence is what we mean by a deference politeness system.

A deference politeness system is one in which participants are considered to be equals or near equals but treat each other at a distance. Relationships among professional colleagues who do not know each other well is one example.

The characteristics of this system are that it is:

1   symmetrical (−P), that is, the participants see themselves as being at the same social level;
2   distant (+D), that is, each uses independence strategies speaking to the other.

Such a face system can be sketched as in figure 3.1.

Speaker 1 < ═══════════════════ Independence ═══════════════════ > Speaker 2

[+D = Distance between the speakers]

Figure 3.1   Deference politeness system.

One could find deference politeness anywhere the system is egalitarian but participants maintain a deferential distance from each other. Much international political protocol is based on this system, where equals from each government meet but are cautious about forming unnecessarily close ties.

Solidarity politeness system (–P, –D)

When two close friends have a conversation with each other they exemplify a solidarity face system. There is a high level of involvement politeness strategies. There is no feeling of either a power difference (–P) or distance (–D) between them.

The characteristics of this solidarity face system are that it is:

1 symmetrical (–P), that is, the participants see themselves as being in equal social position;
2 close (–D), that is, the participants both use politeness strategies of involvement.

Such a face system can be sketched as in figure 3.2.

Speaker 1 < = involvement = > Speaker 2

[–D = Minimal distance between speakers]

Figure 3.2   Solidarity politeness system.

One could find solidarity politeness anywhere the system is egalitarian and participants feel or express closeness to each other. Friendships among close colleagues are often solidarity systems. For example, Professor Wong, who calls Professor Hamada "Professor" or "Doctor," might call a colleague in his own department with whom he works every day by some much more familiar name. Those familiar with North American business will recognize this pattern as one Americans adopt very quickly in business relationships, especially in sales and marketing.

Hierarchical politeness system (+P, +/–D)

The third politeness system is hierarchical. In such a system the participants recognize and respect the social differences that place one in a superordinate position and the other in a subordinate position. This is the system of face in which Mr Hutchins speaks "down" to his employee Bill and Bill speaks "up" to his superior, Mr Hutchins. The main characteristic of this system is the recognized difference in status, for which we are using the designation +P. It may be of much less significance whether or not there is distance between the participants. For our purposes we have considered this system to be either close or distant, +P or −P.

In such a face system the relationships are asymmetrical. By that we mean that the participants do not use the same face politeness strategies in speaking to each other. The person in the superordinate or upper position uses involvement strategies in speaking "down." The person in the subordinate or lower position uses independence strategies in speaking "up." Calling someone by his or her surname and title (Mr Hutchins) is an independence strategy. Calling someone by his or her given name without a title (Bill) is an involvement strategy.

The characteristics of this hierarchical face system are that it is:

1   asymmetrical (+P), that is, the participants see themselves as being in unequal social position;
2   asymmetrical in face strategies, that is, the "higher" uses involvement face strategies and the "lower" uses independence face strategies.

Such a face system can be sketched as in figure 3.3.

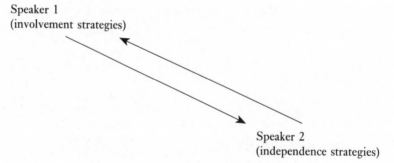

Speaker 1
(involvement strategies)

Speaker 2
(independence strategies)

Figure 3.3   Hierarchical politeness system.

This sort of hierarchical face system is quite familiar in business, governmental, and educational organizations. In fact, it could be said to be the most common sort of organizational relationship, as indicated in tables of organization.

A sociolinguistic survey of many different communicative systems shows that the factors of power (or hierarchy) and distance may arise for many different reasons. In some societies or at some times in history, power differences (+P) arise based on differences in age, gender, wealth, hunting prowess, ability to entertain, education, physical strength or beauty, membership in particular families, or color of hair or skin. In fact, almost any element of human life which can be easily perceived by others has at some time or other been the basis for making hierarchical distinctions.

In the same way, distance (+D) can arise for perhaps all of the same factors. Members of one's family might be close (–D) while all others are distant (+D), or family members of one gender are close while those of the other gender might be distant. It has been said that Alpinists in Germany switch from the distant forms of the pronouns for "you" (the so-called V-forms) to the close forms (the so-called T-forms) of the pronouns when their climb brings them above the tree line. In some Asian business circles, late-night entertainment might bring out strategies of involvement indicating little distance (–D) which will then be reversed to the more normal distant (+D) strategies of independence in the next working day in the office.

We are most concerned that the reader understand the main properties of these three systems of face. Two of them are symmetrical: the deference system and the solidarity system. One of them is asymmetrical: the hierarchical system. In the first, all participants use on balance a greater proportion of independence face strategies. In the second, all participants use on balance a greater proportion of involvement face strategies. In the hierarchical face system, however, because it is asymmetrical, the participants use *different* face strategies; involvement strategies are used "downward" and independence strategies are used "upward."

Miscommunication

We have a friend who in learning Spanish could never get right the differences between the familiar set of pronouns and the formal set of pronouns. He found it difficult to remember when he should say, "*Usted*" ("you" formally), and when he should say, "*Tu*" ("you" informally). He simplified the whole system by just insisting on using the T-forms.

This, of course, presented a major problem for Spanish speakers in Mexico, where he was living at that time. As a foreigner he was expected to use the formal terms, the "*Usted*" forms of politeness. In other words, he was expected to use independence strategies of politeness. But he was not using them; he was using the T-forms, the involvement forms. In Mexican social terms there were only two contexts in which he could use the involvement forms: either if he was a very good friend or if he was trying to pick a fight (that is, if it was an attempt to assert power over the other). In other words, the solidarity system is used only among intimates.

Remember that when one participant uses involvement face strategies and the other uses independence strategies, the one using the involvement strategies is the *higher* of the two. When someone addresses you as Mr

Schneider and you answer back, "Juan," whatever your intentions might be, what he hears is the same thing we read above between Mr Hutchins and Bill: we hear one person taking a higher position over the other. In the interpersonal world of Mexican conversations this sounded like trying to put someone down or to insult him or her by taking a superior position.

Our friend had thus presented our Mexican friends with a problem. Within their cultural interpretation of these face strategies, they expected a deference politeness system. When he used an involvement strategy, they had only two choices: (1) they could hear it as an insult, or (2) they could hear it as an expression of close and longstanding friendship. It should be noted that within that segment of Mexican society, at least at that time, it was quite normal for people to be relatively good friends for quite a few years before moving on to the stage of using the familiar pronouns or other involvement strategies. Those were reserved for close and old friends.

It is not surprising that our friend ran into both solutions to this problem. Many people befriended him, taking into consideration that his poor ability with the language was the cause of his misuse of pronouns and understanding that he only intended to show warmth and friendship. On the other hand, from time to time someone he did not know well took offense, and more than once he found himself with bruises as the result.

The point we wish to make with this anecdote is that miscommunication often arises, especially across the boundaries of discourses or discourse systems, because it is difficult to know in a new group, in a new language, or in a new culture how to express these rather subtle differences in face values. This analysis of face also tells us what sort of miscommunication arises. We can state it as a general rule: "*When two participants differ in their assessment of face strategies, it will tend to be perceived as difference in* power." If I use involvement strategies I expect to hear either reciprocal involvement (if I think it is a solidarity system, that is, −P−D) or independence (if I think it is a hierarchical system and I think I am in the higher position). If I think it is a solidarity system, and you use independence strategies, it sounds to me like you are putting yourself in a lower position and giving power over to me.

If I use independence strategies, I expect to hear reciprocal independence strategies (if I think it is a deference system and we have a level of mutual respect). But if you use involvement strategies back, what I hear is that you are trying to exert power over me.

To put it in the terms of our dialogue between Mr Hutchins and Bill, if Bill answers back to Mr Hutchins, "Sure, Jack, I can have it ready," we are certain that Mr Hutchins will feel that something has gone wrong. And it is not just "something" that has gone wrong. He will feel that Bill is being insulting, trying to rise above his position, trying to usurp authority, or in some way trying to deny the authority structure.

We have said that face relationships consist of two elements: the initial unmarked assumptions and the ongoing negotiation in the interaction. Now we can say that where two or more participants fail to agree on what sort of face system they are using, they will feel the negotiation to be one over the dimension of power (P). This could also be worded conversely: where two or more participants fail to agree on the initial system of hierarchy (P), they will find it difficult to set a comfortable level of face strategies in their communications. Or to put it one final way: the calculation of the appropriate level of face strategies (or the appropriate face system) is always inextricably tied to the expression of the hierarchical system of relationship between or among the participants. We said earlier that there is no faceless communication. Now we would like to add to that there is no *non-hierarchical* communication. That is because any difference in sense of hierarchy gives rise to difficulties in selecting face strategies, and any miscalculation in face strategies gives rise to feelings of power differences.

It is for this reason that we have entitled this chapter "Interpersonal Politeness and Power." The characteristics of the communication of face make it inevitable that power (that is, hierarchy) is interrelated to politeness levels.

4

Conversational Inference: Interpretation in Spoken Discourse

We began by saying that language is always ambiguous. Language has at least two major kinds of ambiguity, which we might call external and internal. External ambiguity has to do with knowing the contexts in which meanings are to be interpreted. In the preceding chapters we have showed two of the means we have to interpret the speaker's meaning through an analysis of context: sharing knowledge of actions and situations (chapter 2), and knowledge of relationships and identities (chapter 3).

The second problem of ambiguity in communication is not entirely or exclusively a question of context, however. It is the more internal problem of knowing which pieces go together to form a continuous whole, and how we signal that to each other. This is the study which was originally called discourse analysis, though as we will see below, the idea of discourse analysis has been considerably extended in recent years. The original main focus of discourse analysis was on how we form units of communication that are larger wholes than just words or sentences.

Unfortunately, the word "discourse" is not used in the same way by everyone who studies discourse. For some analysts the main focus is on the logical relations among sentences in texts (or, of course, conversations). For others the focus is more on the processes of interpretation we use in understanding discourses. A third group is concerned with discourses which take place over many years or across many societies, such as the discourse of modern medicine or the discourse of foreign exchange. Finally, many analysts are beginning to study the ways in which discourses are used to establish and reinforce ideological positions in society.

Our interest is in professional communication between members of different groups or discourse systems, not directly in discourse analysis as such. Therefore, we will bring in ideas, terms, and methods from different schools of discourse analysis to try to create a broader framework for the analysis of professional communication.

We begin by asking how we understand discourses of a conversational nature. Even though written communications are a major aspect of any professional communication, we believe that spoken communication is more fundamental. For example, we know that in applying for a position in a company there is almost always some form of a written résumé, an application form with significant details of a person's life, education, and experience, and even examples of a person's work. Nevertheless, in most cases these written materials serve a preliminary screening function to select the most likely candidates for a position. Then the crucial decisions about hiring are usually made based upon an oral interview and, perhaps, also an oral presentation. Along with those formal oral presentations will also be informal conversations, which often seem quite incidental and yet create a major impression of one's abilities, competence, and likelihood of success in the position. As we will argue, the processes of inference we use in ordinary conversation are an essential aspect of how we interpret the communications of others.

How Do We Understand Discourse?

First speaker: Should I have it translated?
Second speaker: Yes, here they are.

Most readers should find the "dialogue" above impossible. We also think that most readers can understand perfectly well what each of the separate sentences means. In fact, both of these sentences come from samples in preceding chapters and, in that context, we believe that the speaker's meaning in each of these sentences was made clear by the context.

The problem that we are trying to understand in this chapter is: how do we know that these two sentences do not belong together in this case and how did we know that they did fit into the preceding dialogues? The word most often used for this aspect of discourse is "coherence," which is the characteristic of having cohesion. Coherence in discourse can be loosely defined as whatever tells the participants that all of the pieces go together.

In the first case the original dialogue was as follows:

A: Bill, that's a great idea. Could you write up a one-page summary for tomorrow's board meeting?
B: Of course, Mr Hutchins. Should I have it translated?

Even if we know nothing more about the speech event within which this dialogue took place, we can infer that the word "it" in Bill's sentence refers back to "one-page summary" in Mr Hutchins's sentence. This property of reference is one form of cohesion in discourse. Some analysts would call reference a cohesive device. This is a general term to cover any aspect of language or context that a speaker (or, of course, writer) can use to indicate a connection among elements. The use of pronouns such as "it" as a replacement for the longer, full noun phrase "one-page summary" shows the listener or reader that what one is saying is connected to what has just been said.

That is one reason why the second sentence in our false dialogue does not feel like it is connected to the first speaker's sentence. The pronoun used is "they." It is very difficult to imagine any situation in which "they" could refer to the same thing as "it" in the preceding turn in the dialogue.

In that case the original dialogue was as follows:

Chairman: Do you have the minutes?
Secretary: Yes, here they are. I think 2.4.3 is what you will need.

"Yes" indicates a response to the preceding question. The word "minutes" is plural and so it seems quite natural that it would be replaced with the pronoun "they" as a cohesive device to link the dialogue together into a piece of a longer discourse.

And so to return to our original question, "How do we understand discourse?," we can say that at least part of the answer lies in the use of such lexical and grammatical cohesive devices.

A second aspect of our ability to give discourse coherence has already been discussed to some extent in chapter 2 as part of the grammar of context. The same sentence, "What time is it?," took on different speaker meanings depending on the speech event in which it was used. In both *asking for the time* and in *testing for the concept of telling the time* the first two turns are very similar. They could be identical. What is different is the third turn. In *asking for the time*, the first speaker is expected to thank the second speaker. In *testing for the concept of telling the time*, the first speaker is expected to evaluate the second speaker's response to the question. Such regular, recurring sequences of expected turns have been named "adjacency sequences." Adjacency sequences are one form of learned, predictable, or regular expectations of patterns which bring coherence to discourse. Such regular patterns have been considered one form of schema or script. Together they form a second major source of coherence in discourse.

The third source of coherence in oral discourse is really what makes oral discourse oral; it is what we call prosodic patterning. By that we mean to include such aspects of the discourse as are, in fact, oral: intonation and timing. For example, let us look at the following dialogue:

A: Can you have the report on overseas sales ready for the meeting this afternoon?
B: *This afternoon?* I thought that wasn't due until Thursday.

B says *this afternoon* in a higher pitch and perhaps also draws it out a bit. By this (as well as by the cohesive device of repetition) he shows a connection to the preceding speaker's turn as well as calling into question speaker A's assumption that the report can be finished.

We include such emphatic uses of intonation as well as timing under the general category of prosodic patterning.

The fourth major source of coherence in discourse is neither a learned form nor a logical or cognitive structure. It is what John Gumperz (1977) has called conversational inference. This process, which was briefly introduced in chapter 1, works one turn at a time as participants move through a face-to-face interaction. At each turn they simultaneously interpret the preceding discourse, give an indication of their own inferences drawn from that discourse, and make their contribution toward the continuation of the discourse. This complex process of inference is both an essential aspect of communication and a major source of miscommunication.

Taken together, cohesive devices, schemata, prosodic patterning, and conversational inference make up the four major means by which we produce and interpret coherence in spoken discourse.

Cohesive Devices: Lexical and Grammatical

No linguist or sociolinguist would attempt to make a complete list of all the possible lexical and grammatical cohesive devices in any one language, let alone as a general statement intended to cover all languages, and it is not our goal to try to do this either. Our goal is just to indicate the means participants have for giving coherence to discourse, not to explicate all of the ways this is done. Halliday and Hasan's *Cohesion in English* (1976) is a full, book-length discussion to which the reader may refer for an extended discussion.

For our purposes it will be sufficient if the reader understands that there are many different kinds of cohesive device available for participants in discourses. We will give a few examples of just two, reference and verb forms, and a somewhat longer discussion of just one other formal cohesive device, conjunction.

Reference

Reference is one of the most frequently used cohesive devices. Perhaps it is impossible to imagine a sentence which does not make reference in some form, and in most cases those references will perform a function of providing discourse cohesion. In addition to pronouns, the use of the definite article "the" is frequently used for discourse cohesion. For example, in the sentence above, "Do you have the minutes?," "the" makes reference back to the minutes both participants know they have been talking about. Of course, the chair could have said, "Do you have the minutes of the last meeting?" In that case, the reference is forward to the words "the last meeting?" In either case, "the" is used to make a connection within the discourse.

Verb forms

All languages have some differences in verb forms which are used to produce cohesion. In English, it is the tense system which most often carries out this function. The dialogue about the minutes takes place in the present and this use of tense is maintained across the turns of the two speakers. It would make an odd contrast and a violation of cohesion if the speakers had used different tenses, as in the following:

Chairman: Do you have the minutes?
Secretary: Yes, here they were. I thought 2.4.3 is what you will need.

On the other hand, a shift in tense could indicate a cohesive discourse but with a somewhat different meaning. It might have been as follows:

Chairman: Do you have the minutes?
Secretary: Yes, here they are. I thought 2.4.3 is what you would need.

In this latter case, the secretary's shift to "I thought" from "I think" indicates a cohesion or continuity with his or her planning for the meeting which took place *before* this speech event. By using these verb forms the secretary is able to indicate to the chairman that it is not any accident that those minutes were available just at that moment.

Conjunction

We have chosen to focus more closely on conjunctions for two reasons: conjunctions are rather widely taught as a part of formal instruction in English as a second language and so our readers are likely to be somewhat more familiar with these cohesive devices, and in addition to that, conjunctions have been found in a number of research studies to be particularly problematical for Asian speakers and writers of English.

For example, in one study researchers found that conjunctions such as "but" and "and" were used in such a way that the result was a sense of general confusion and incoherence in the overall structure of the lectures given by Korean, Japanese, and Chinese speakers of English. Very similar findings have been reported for Cantonese writers of English in Hong Kong. Cantonese writers of English in one study used conjunctions more frequently than native speakers and writers of English, and they used those conjunctions more frequently in the marked sentence-initial position.

Conjunctions are lexical items (or words) which are normally placed between two clauses and which show the relationships between those two clauses. Halliday and Hasan (1976) analyze four major kinds of conjunction of clauses in English:

1 additive (typically marked with "and");
2 adversative (marked with words such as "but");
3 causal (marked with "because" or "so," etc.);
4 temporal (markers such as "and" or "and then").

An additive conjunction indicates that the following clause adds to or completes what came before.

> Harvey is good at making oral presentations and he also writes very well.

An adversative conjunction shows that the following clause opposes in some way the idea presented in the preceding discourse.

> Harvey is good at making oral presentations, but he is terrible with written reports.

A causal conjunction indicates that the second clause is in some way a logical cause or a result of the preceding clause.

> Harvey is good at making oral presentations, because he took a training program in presentations last year. (*Cause*)
> Harvey is good at making oral presentations, so the boss always asks him to do them when we have foreign clients. (*Result*)

Finally, a temporal conjunction relates two clauses in time.

> Harvey gave a good oral presentation, then he ruined his chances with a bad written report.

The causal conjunction "because"

We said above that conjunctions normally stand between clauses and show the relationship between them. While this is generally true, and therefore forms the unmarked structure in English, some conjunctions may also occur at the beginning of the two clauses which they relate. The conjunction "because" is a common example of this. The problems begin with deciding whether or not to take the conjunction "because" to be relating the sentence before it to the sentence following it.

There are two main structures in which "because" is used in English. In the most common or unmarked structure it is as follows:

X because Y

where Y is taken to be the cause of X or the explanation of X. That is to say, X is what you are saying, and Y is the explanation.

X = Harvey is good at making oral presentations
because
Y = he took a training program in presentations last year.

In the marked structure the order of the clauses is reversed as follows:

Because Y, X

That is to say, Y is what you are saying and X is the result.

Because Harvey took a training program in presentations last year, he is good at making oral presentations.

It is important to realize that the causal or explanatory relationship is the same in both cases; in either case it is the training program which is the cause of Harvey's skill in making oral presentations. What is different is the focus on Harvey's skill in oral presentations in the unmarked order and the focus on the training program in the marked order.

We will return to this particular conjunction, "because," in our discussion of conversational inference which follows, since it is one which causes particularly acute problems in real-time processing. This is especially so where there is any ambiguity in the use of the conjunction. For now we only wish to point out that conjunctions are among the more significant of the formal, lexical cohesive devises which speakers can use to give coherence to their discourse.

Cognitive Schemata or Scripts

In an American coffee shop there is a regular pattern of activities which with minor variations is like the following:

1 You find a seat.
2 You determine your order.
3 You place your order with the waiter or waitress.
4 You receive your food.
5 When you finish eating, you pay your bill at the cashier's.

Part of normal life and normal knowledge for many westerners is this expected sequence of activities, which has been called a schema or a script. The role of such patterns in interpreting discourse is that, even where not all of the details are mentioned, a listener who knows the script can reconstruct the event from a combination of what is said and his or her knowledge of the script.

For example, we might tell a short narrative like this:

> Yesterday I saw Eleanor at the coffee shop, but since I had just paid and she was just ordering I told her we'd get together tomorrow.

Those who know this script will know that the speaker was just leaving the coffee shop and that Eleanor had just taken her seat, though the narrator has not actually mentioned either of these details.

One of the authors on his first trip to Japan discovered that in at least some cases the coffee shop script is somewhat different, even though it has very similar elements. In that case the script was as follows:

1 You determine your order.
2 You pay for your order at the cashier's.
3 You find a seat.
4 You place your order with the waiter or waitress.
5 You receive your food.
6 You eat, and leave when you have finished.

Although many of the elements are the same, a direct translation of the little narrative about meeting Eleanor above would not carry the same meaning against the background of this script. In the Japanese coffee shop script, if the narrator had just paid and Eleanor was just ordering, the two participants would be very near each other in their progress through this script. There would be little reason why they could not sit together and talk. His or her justification for not speaking just then to Eleanor, which is clear in the American script, would be less justified in the Japanese script and need further clarification.

The concept of cognitive schemata or scripts is very useful in coming to understand how people interpret meanings in discourse. Unfortunately, the concept is generally rather vague as it has been used and often covers several quite different phenomena. A fuller study than we are able to present here would require a much more detailed account of the many different kinds of schema. For our purposes we have decided to put together into this category three general types of knowledge which people use to interpret discourse: scripts, world knowledge, and adjacency sequences.

World knowledge

By "world knowledge" we mean something that is vaguer than scripts as such. An example of the sort of thing we mean was given earlier, in chapter 1. When we say, "There's a taxi at the door," our knowledge of the world includes knowing that the taxi will have a driver. As a result there is nothing odd about using the definite article in making reference to this driver, as in the following discourse:

There's a taxi at the door. Shall I ask the driver to wait a few minutes?

It is from our general world knowledge that we are able to interpret to whom this "the" refers quite unambiguously in this case.

A friend of the authors has told them of his friend who went into business largely because when he was in college he did not know what it meant to have a major. As some readers will know, in American colleges and universities one takes a group of general courses which are required for all degree programs, and then, in addition to those, one specializes with a concentration in one particular discipline. That specialization is called one's major.

Our friend's friend did not know this when he first went away to college. From time to time people asked him what his major was, but he was unsure about how to answer. As a solution, he listened to what others said when that question was asked. The next time he heard the question asked of someone, that person answered that his major was "business." Not too long after that when he was discussing his program with his counselor, the counselor asked him what he planned to have as a major. He answered that it was business. The result was that he was directed into a concentration in business courses and remains in business today.

In such a case, the knowledge of the world is knowledge of the general procedures of an institution like a college or the general requirements of completing an American degree program. Unlike a script, it does not form any particular sequence of elements necessarily. This sort of "encyclopedic" knowledge of one's world is the sort that often causes confusion or miscommunication in intercultural communication.

Adjacency sequences

The speech events *asking for the time* and *testing for the concept of telling the time* are examples of a kind of schema which occurs very frequently in day-to-day discourse. If someone initiates one of these sequences with the first turn, "What time is it?," it is very predictable that the second turn and then the third will follow. Such predictable sequences have been called adjacency sequences by discourse analysts.

Second-language learners are all quite familiar with the adjacency sequences called "greetings." Westerners who walk down the street in Taiwan or Korea or Hong Kong while children are going to school or coming home from school will hear, "Hello, how are you?," almost every day from children who have learned this greeting in school.

Adjacency sequences have been quite intensively studied by discourse analysts. There are greetings of many kinds, such as face-to-face or by telephone; such greetings may be different depending on the time of day – morning, mid-day, and afternoon or evening – and they may vary in key from lighthearted morning greetings among colleagues in an office to somber greetings at ritual events such as weddings and funerals. Departures also depend on such things as the time of day (with special last departure-of-the-day formulas – the difference between "Good evening" and "Good night"), situation, and key. Many textbooks for language learners have been written which focus on just such adjacency sequences, or as they have sometimes been called, "gambits."

There are several questions relating to the interpretation of meaning in discourse which arise in thinking about adjacency sequences. The first of them is that they definitely ease communication by giving a regular and predictable order to the discourse. Even if you do not know English well, when you hear, "Good morning, how are you?," you can feel quite safe in giving the discourse cohesion by saying, "Fine, thank you." In short, adjacency sequences are formulas for cohesion.

It should not be surprising, then, that the great majority of adjacency sequences are used at transitional points in discourse. They are used at the beginnings (greetings), ends (departures), topic changes (such as "by the way," "not to change the subject"), and other points where a change in the participant roles is potentially disruptive of cohesion.

On the other hand, adjacency sequences present two problems, one to the participants in a discourse and the other to the analyst of discourse. The problem for participants shows up quite acutely for learners of a language. It is not too difficult to master a small set of quite efficient adjacency sequences. One can learn how to greet people, how to depart from them; one can learn how to ask for clarification or for repetition – "What does X mean?," or, "Could you please say that again?" These adjacency sequences can give to non-native speakers a certain level of fluency which can easily give an exaggerated impression of their overall ability in discourse. The authors have often had this experience in learning a new language. You actually become hesitant to use adjacency sequences because once you have engaged the attention of a speaker of the language you find that you are out of your depth and have little ability to continue the conversation once it has begun.

While we have phrased this as a problem, we should point out that we do not mean that learners of a language should not try to learn adjacency sequences. They remain one of the more important aspects of achieving discourse competence.

The problem that adjacency sequences pose for us in our analysis of discourse is that in several decades of study, analysts have now come to agreement that there are virtually no such sequences of more than a few turns. Perhaps four or five turns are the outer limit of regular adjacency sequences. That means that although these sequences are of considerable importance in achieving discourse cohesion and in knowing how to interpret meaning in discourse, they cannot be used to account for any aspects of discourse cohesion beyond just a few turns.

Prosodic Patterning: Intonation and Timing

Prosody is a general term for the study of speech rhythms. In our analysis of conversational inference we feel it is most useful to divide the subject into two main sub-topics: intonation and timing. Naturally, in practice it is very difficult to separate these two aspects in the ongoing flow of a conversation.

Intonation

Spoken English makes relatively little use of pitch alone to make meaningful differences. Usually it is more useful to talk about stress, which is a combination of factors such as higher pitch, louder volume, lengthening, and even a difference in the vowel quality. For example, the difference between the two words, *con*tent ("what is inside") and con*tent* ("satisfied") is ordinarily described as a difference in stress with a higher pitch on the stressed syllable, a slight lengthening of the stressed syllable, and, perhaps, an increase in volume, as well as differences in the two vowels in the words. In other words, stress is a phenomenon which applies to single syllables on the whole, even though other syllables in the vicinity of the stressed syllable might be affected in secondary ways.

Tone contour is the result of the pattern of stressed and non-stressed syllables, the indication of declarative, emphatic, or question function, as well as of the termination or non-termination of a speaker's turn. In practice, it has proved to be anything but simple to accurately describe tone contours in English, and any single analysis has had to be modified for dialectal, regional, and register differences.

In order to understand cohesion in professional discourse it is probably not essential to know and understand all of these aspects of intonation in English. We believe that as long as the reader has a clear conception of how stress is used (or misinterpreted) and how tone contours are used (or misinterpreted), it will be clear how these aspects of discourse are used in achieving coherence in discourse.

Imagine this conversation:

A: Have you paid these invoices yet?
B: Yes, I've paid *those* invoices.

The use of the word "those" tells us several things. For one thing it indicates a reference back to "these invoices" in the preceding turn. That is simply a matter of the choice of the pronoun and indicates cohesion of the sort we discussed above under reference. The emphasis on "those" tells us something additional. It suggests that while "those" invoices have been paid, there are others which have not been paid.

This sort of stress has generally been called contrastive stress; it is used to indicate that something other than the expected situation is being alluded to. In other words, one of the most important aspects of contrastive stress is to indicate that the speaker recognizes the unmarked assumptions being made, and that those unmarked assumptions do not entirely hold true.

All of the following sentences could be used to indicate somewhat different questions about the unmarked assumptions:

Yes, *I've* paid those invoices. (That is, I've filled out the proper forms, but, perhaps, payroll hasn't put them through their process yet.)
Yes, I've *paid* those invoices. (But, perhaps, I haven't finished with recording them or filing them properly. Or, in a second interpretation: And don't tell me I haven't paid them!)
Yes, I've paid those *invoices*. (But I haven't gotten around to paying other bills in the same pile.)

Naturally, we could not be writing about this if it were not possible to transform this aspect of oral discourse somehow into written discourse. In this case, we have used *italics* to indicate emphasis, and we expect the reader to fill in the correct actual pronunciation on the basis of his or her knowledge.

What will be most important for our analysis, however, is to remember that while we are able to use typography in written English to transcribe stress from oral English, normally we would use a different linguistic form to accomplish the same task.

For example, in written form the question might be put in a memo as follows:

> Have the attached invoices been paid?

The answer would most likely be written back something like:

> Yes, I've done the attached invoices, but the others are yet to be completed.

In other words, the written form is likely to be more explicit about the attention being called to the unmarked assumptions and to the fact that there is some variance from those assumptions. In oral discourse, contrastive stress is more likely to be used, partly because it is available in speaking and it is not so easily available in writing, and partly because oral discourse tends to work one turn at a time. If a question does arise from the use of contrastive stress, the other speaker is likely to check it out in the next turn. Since writing does not allow such rapid feedback between participants, there is usually a greater degree of explicitness, especially where there is likely to be some question about assumptions.

Suppose a secretary would like to know if his or her boss has completed drafting up an important report. He or she might ask, "Finish that report?" or perhaps the same secretary is telling the boss the list of things he or she planned to do next. He or she might say, "Call Frankfurt. Write the memo to Purchasing. Finish that report." Now, perhaps, the secretary is talking to his or her assistant who is word processing this same report. He or she might say, "Finish that report."

In all three cases, this same string of words, *Finish that report*, would be said with quite different overall tone contours. In the first case, it would be given a questioning intonation; in the second case, it would be said with a non-emphatic final intonation contour; and in the third case, it would be said with an emphatic intonation contour indicating an imperative. Any native speaker of English would recognize the difference in meaning among these three intonation patterns, though the exact description of such contours is far from being a simple matter.

If we go back to the second example, we can isolate the most important of these contours for conversational inference. In the list of things the secretary planned to do, he or she gave three activities,

> Call Frankfurt. Write the memo to Purchasing. Finish that report.

We have said that the third of these sentences will have final intonation contour. Here we want to notice that the other two will have non-final intonation contour. It is difficult to describe this contour exactly because there are several different patterns for it used by English speakers. In one pattern, the non-final contour has a slight rise in pitch on the last syllable. In another pattern, the non-final contour has a slight fall in pitch on the last syllable. In either case, what makes it different from the final contour is that it does not fall away to a low and very soft pitch.

The reason intonation contour is so important to spoken discourse cohesion is that participants use their reading of intonation contours in deciding whether or not it is their turn to take over the floor. In the example above, if the boss had intervened after the sentence *Write the memo to Purchasing*, with its non-final contour, we would expect that he would make some apology for interrupting and the conversation might be more like this:

Secretary: Call Frankfurt. Write the memo to Purchasing . . .
Boss: Excuse me a moment. Is that the one I dictated this morning?
Secretary: Yes, that one.
Boss: OK, go on.
Secretary: Finish that report.

As we will see below, the interpretation of when it is one's turn to speak is one of the most crucial aspects of conversational discourse, and much of that interpretation depends on a correct understanding of final and non-final intonation contours.

Timing

In the short dialogues we have used as examples, we have usually written the speech of one participant and then put a space between that person's speech and the next person's speech. This is a way of representing typographically the small pause that occurs between turns as one speaker gives up the floor and another takes over the right to speak. Much has been written about these interturn pauses. Our own research interest in them comes from their role in giving rise to interpersonal judgements of competence. We have found that even very small differences in the timing of interturn pauses can lead conversationalists to develop negative attitudes toward each other.

Disfluencies in discourse often produce an apology. This is because we have a strong feeling that conducting a smooth discourse which both is coherent and changes smoothly from one speaker to another is an important aspect of how we conduct our social affairs. The problem of negative attitudes arises because interturn pauses are not just simple silences between turns; they are points at which each speaker must make a quick judgement about what to do next, and that judgement must be based on what he or she assumes the other is likely to do.

This is how it happens: when a person finishes a turn at speaking, he or she pauses a moment for the response of the other speaker. The end of the turn is actually a rather complex phenomenon to analyze, but it is indicated by such things as changes in tempo, intonational contours (often a drop in pitch), and the completion of syntactic units. With these and other gestural clues one speaker shows another that he or she is finishing a point and expects the other speaker to respond. Normally, then, the other speaker may take the floor to comment, to extend the point, or even to change the subject. At the very least a feedback response, such as saying, "Uh huh," or even a simple nod, is required to confirm that the point has been taken.

If the first speaker reaches one of these turn exchange points and the second speaker responds as expected, everything progresses smoothly. If, on the other hand, the second speaker does not respond, the first speaker has a problem. There are many reasons why the second might not have responded. He or she may not have noticed the cues or may have been daydreaming. Whatever the reasons, the first speaker is left holding the conversational bag. He or she needs to decide whether or not to continue and assume the point was taken, or back up and repeat the point either literally or in paraphrase.

These conversational disfluencies are actually quite rare, even though in ordinary conversations such transitional points come up as often as once a second.

This comment masks a considerable analytical difficulty. One issue is the typology of pauses. There are at least four kinds of pause: those taken for time to think (cognitive), those taken so that the other conversationalist may take over the floor (interactive), those taken so that the other may give feedback without actually taking the floor (backchannel), and those caused by other factors such as a cough. In actual conversation it is never entirely certain what sort of pause any particular pause is until it is over, that is, retrospectively. For instance, if one speaker pauses for feedback but the other speaker takes the floor, a feedback pause has been transmuted into an interactive pause. Or, if one pauses to think a moment and the other takes the floor, a cognitive pause has become an interactional pause. The pauses in a conversation are as much in need of ongoing interpretation and reaction as the words, clauses, and sentences. Our comment here is meant to imply only that such points of ambiguity arise typically about once a second.

In fact as we speak we are constantly monitoring our listeners for signs of their response to our speech, and when these responses are absent or disfluent we are thrown out of our rhythm. The results are repetition, paraphrasing, stuttering, and usually embarrassment, if not a sense of some hostility toward the other person.

Unfortunately, there are many non-grammatical factors which can influence our timing in such points of transition in a conversation. While our timing varies widely during a single day and one person varies widely in his or her timing from one day to the next, if any two conversationalists are different in their expectations about the appropriate length of these interturn pauses, the results can be disastrous. When the faster person is speaking, he or she will get to a turn exchange point and pause a moment for the response of the other. Since he or she expects a shorter pause than the other, he or she will decide to either move on or repeat before the other person has had a chance to respond. This pattern will be repeated again and again, until cumulatively the result will be that the faster speaker is doing all of the talking, constantly repeating himself or herself, paraphrasing, and finally coming to the conclusion that the other person either has nothing to say or is linguistically incompetent.

On the other side of the interaction, the person who moves through the encounter at a somewhat slower pace will find himself or herself constantly frustrated in trying to get the floor to speak. After waiting a slightly longer time to take a turn, he or she will begin to speak, only to realize that the other has already begun to rephrase a prior comment or is now going on to something new. In any event, the slower of the two now will feel somewhat confused and begin to develop a sense that he or she is being conversationally bullied. It does not take long for this person to develop a defensive or even hostile reaction to the conversation, if not to the other person as well.

There are many factors which contribute to a person taking longer or shorter interturn pauses. Interpersonal face relationships, as we discussed them in chapter 3, are among the most important. Generally, longer pauses are associated with independence politeness strategies, while shorter pauses are associated with involvement politeness strategies. As a result, in a solidarity face system, the pauses tend to be shorter; in a deference face system, the pauses tend to be longer; and in a hierarchical face system, there is a difference in the use of pauses by the person in the higher position and the person in the lower position.

This latter point is quite significant, as we will see below. The situation can be described in the opposite manner: we can also say that where one speaker uses shorter pauses and the other uses longer pauses, there will be a tendency for the system to develop into a hierarchical system, whether the participants intend that outcome or not. In other words, if one speaker takes shorter interturn pauses than another, there will be a tendency for that first speaker to come to dominate the interaction, if not to dominate the other person as well.

The issue for interdiscourse professional communication is that there are differences in expectations about pauses both within and across different groups. There are also significant differences in expectations about face relationships. Asians appear to be among the world's quicker speakers when speaking in their own languages: such as Chinese, Japanese, and Korean. Hayashi (1988), for example, has written about the rapid and elegant conversational dance of the Japanese, which foreigners can hear but so rarely join. It is, of course, impossible to judge such things impressionistically, and a more accurate, research-based comparison would immediately run foul of the problem that the linguistic means of indicating turn transitions differ importantly from language to language. What is important to us is not how Asians speak in Chinese, Japanese, and Korean, but how they speak in contexts of professional communication in English.

In professional communications which take place in English between Asians and westerners, an Asian faces many barriers in the way of turn exchange fluency. The most obvious one is simply that he or she is using a second language and is likely to still be a language learner. That almost by definition slows one down. Compounded with a second-language user's lower levels of ability in the language, however, are the factors we have outlined above; such an Asian assumes initially that deference is the proper attitude to take in relation to a stranger, and deference is normally associated with longer turn exchange pauses, if not complete silence.

On the other hand, the westerner in most cases uses English as a native language and has a high level of fluency. In addition to this, the westerner is most likely to assume that interpersonal relationships should progress to a system of symmetrical solidarity as quickly as possible, and so is likely to emphasize involvement politeness strategies, including shorter interturn pauses. Consequently, everything conspires to produce a significant difference in the length of interturn pauses between Asian English users and their western counterparts in business or government.

Unfortunately, if everything else conspires to produce a difference in pause length, that difference will lead the faster speaker, the western person, to dominate the conversation, even if it is his or her intention to create highly fluent, interactive discussions. Quite unconsciously he or she will find himself or herself repeating things, paraphrasing prior statements, simplifying, and linguistically backing and filling to account for the conversational gaps and arrhythmia. Where the westerner possesses much energy and great goodwill he or she will press on; where this is not the case, unfortunately, he or she may come to the conclusion that the Asians are less competent linguistically (and intellectually) than they really are.

Metacommunication

We can now come back to the question with which we started: how do we understand discourse? This may not be a crucial question in ordinary, day-to-day life, since we just go about communicating without paying undue attention to how we do it. For professional communicators, on the other hand, it is a crucial question. Professional communication depends on being able to understand not just when and where to communicate what, but also how it is done. Only by explicitly analyzing the process of communication can a professional come to communicate effectively.

In trying to answer the question, "How do we understand discourse?," we have introduced the idea of cohesive devices and cognitive schemata. We could think of the first as the resources we use in bringing cohesion to discourse and to our interpretations of discourse. We could think of the second as the broader conceptual frameworks within which discourse is set. Nevertheless, knowing both cohesive devices and cognitive schemata is not sufficient to come to an understanding of how we understand discourse. We need to also understand the process of interpretation itself. This process is called conversational inference.

The anthropologist Gregory Bateson (1972) pointed out some years ago that every communication must simultaneously communicate two messages, the basic message and the metamessage. The idea of the basic message we are familiar with. The metamessage is a second message, encoded and superimposed upon the basic, which indicates how we want someone to take our basic message. The prefix "meta" is from Greek and carries the meaning of higher or more general. Bateson also pointed out that this was not just a question of human communication. When we play with a dog, the dog may pretend to bite us. We can tell from the basic message that the dog is biting. The metamessage is conveyed by the dog making its bite quite gentle and at the same time wagging its tail and other such gestures.

Human communication is no different. According to the anthropologist John Gumperz, each successful message carries with it a second metamessage which tells the listener how to interpret the basic message. A basic message by itself cannot be interpreted. Gumperz (1977, 1982, 1992) uses the term "contextualization cues" for the ways in which we convey metamessages in ordinary conversational discourse.

As it stands, this way of talking about communication is simply another way of saying what we have said repeatedly throughout this book: to interpret not just the sentence meaning but also the speaker's meaning, we must make reference to the context. The problem with this statement as it stands is that it does not take into consideration real-time processing. The process of making inferences about spoken discourse is an ongoing process, in which we must be constantly interpreting the immediately preceding discourse at the same time as we are moving on to subsequent stages of the discourse.

The consequence of real-time processing is that every communication that takes place in real-time must simultaneously deal with at least three forms of coherence:

1   the basic message (what the speaker is saying);
2   the metamessage (how the message is to be taken);
3   the discourse contextualization (confirmation of the preceding metamessage).

To put it in a more ordinary way, to maintain a coherent discourse, each speaker needs to keep the discourse going while at the same time confirming to the others that he or she has followed what has gone on up to that point.

Sometimes a discourse can go on a bit with both (or all) participants not knowing that they have gone off the track. For example, we can look at the short dialogue we used above:

A: Bill, that's a great idea. Could you write up a one-page summary for tomorrow's board meeting?
B: Of course, Mr Hutchins. Should I have it translated?

We can imagine this as a somewhat different dialogue as follows:

A: Bill, that's a great idea. Could you write up a one-page summary for tomorrow's board meeting? And could you also be sure the agenda is typed?
B: Of course, Mr Hutchins. Should I have it translated?
A: No, I don't think we usually translate them.
B: Oh, I'm sorry. I meant the summary; should I have it translated?
A: Oh, I see. You'd better ask Jane about that.

When Bill says, "it," there is an unclear reference. Mr Hutchins takes the pronoun to mean the agenda but Bill had intended the summary. He only discovers his error when Mr Hutchins uses, "usually," and, "them." The summary is a unique event whereas the agenda is a regular, recurring aspect of board meetings. From this world knowledge of meetings and from the use of these cohesive devices of reference, Bill is able to guess that Mr Hutchins has misunderstood his question and they undertake the adjacency sequence usually called a repair sequence, where they go back to straighten out the mistake.

This shows the real-time nature of the structure of coherence in spoken discourse. It is worked out as it goes, and requires constant confirmation among the participants that they are understanding the same things and in the same way.

When Bill and Mr Hutchins discover their mistake in the example we have just discussed, they simply go back and make the necessary correction. There are two things to be observed in this rather simple case. The first is that it is quite simple and does not involve a major misinterpretation of meaning. The second is that even though it is simple, Bill feels obliged to apologize. Successful conversational discourse requires that the participants not only maintain cohesion or relevance, but that where there are breaks in the cohesion they go back and repair them. Cohesion in discourse is not only a convenience or even a simple communicative necessity, it is also a social and interpersonal obligation. One has and feels the obligation to maintain a smooth and coherent discourse, and if one has been responsible for a break it is taken as a disruption of good interpersonal relationships.

Smooth discourse depends so strongly on shared knowledge that when there is a break or disruption, the most immediate reaction is that the culprit must be a member of a different group. To put this another way, smooth discourse is one of the most significant means humans have of demonstrating who is an insider in any particular group and who is an outsider. Most of us are quite conscious of different pronunciations or of different words used by members of other groups, but in day-to-day practice it is cohesion in discourse which provides the strongest and most emblematic forces for group identity.

Non-sequential processing

Most conversational repairs can be handled as the one shown above was, with a brief side-sequence of two or three turns. The participants go off to one side conversationally while they straighten out their confusion, and then return to the main path of their topic. This is because oral discourse tends to be structured one turn at a time. Even within turns, oral discourse tends to be structured a sentence at a time or even a clause at a time. Cohesive devices tend to be placed between two clauses or sentences to show the relationship between the clauses on the two sides.

The reason for this is that real-time processing requires not only the forward movement of saying the next combined basic message plus metamessage, but also the backward-looking confirmation of what has gone before in the preceding turns. It becomes a rather complex problem of processing to load too many messages together into the same utterance.

Nevertheless, there is a sort of conversational overloading when confusion arises for some reason. To give a specific example, let us go back to the conjunction "because." We said earlier in this chapter that the unmarked use of this causal conjunction was:

X because Y

This is the order in which oral discourse normally indicates a logical relationship between two clauses or sentences. There is also the marked usage in which the form is:

Because Y, X

While there is nothing grammatically incorrect about this usage, in real-time discourse it can present a problem.

We might think of an ordinary stretch of one speaker's turn as having a sequence of sentences, *E F G*. Without any further indication, we would take each of them to stand alone. Of course, in actual discourse we would want to analyze the prosodic features of these clauses. That would include the features we have mentioned above, such as their intonation or timing, which would give significant clues about how to interpret the sequence. We will return to the question of the prosodic patterning below.

The logical or sequential problem arises with a cohesive device like "because," since it can stand either in between the two clauses it relates, or *before* the two clauses it relates. In that case, the logical relationship is also taken to be in the reverse order. In other words, we might have the following sequence:

E because *F G*

If we do not have any further information to clarify this, we would expect the speaker to mean

[*E* because *F*] *G*

This is because the unmarked order assumes that "because" is relating the clauses between which it stands. On the other hand, it is possible that the speaker means

E [because *F, G*]

The point we are making is that it is difficult for a listener to know until the speaker gets to *G* which of these orders is the one he or she intends.

Imagine the sequence, *E F G*, corresponds with the following three sentences:

He had lunch.
He was so hungry.
He ate at the staff canteen.

It would be difficult to know if the speaker meant to say

He had lunch, because he was so hungry. He ate at the staff canteen.

Or if the speaker actually meant

He had lunch. Because he was so hungry, he ate at the staff canteen.

The meanings of these sequences would be quite different. In the first case, the focus is on the hunger and on having lunch. The business about eating at the staff canteen seems quite incidental. In the second case, having lunch seems almost a background detail, whereas the focus seems to have shifted to eating at the staff canteen. We would expect the speaker to go on and talk about the staff canteen. In the first case, we would expect the speaker to go on to talk about the hunger of the person in the story.

As we have said, inferences which are drawn in discourse are drawn as definite conclusions and they are drawn very quickly. By the time the listener, the potential second speaker, had heard the third clause he or she would have come down on the side of one or the other of these interpretations and settled that was what the first speaker was talking about. The problem is that it has not yet been confirmed by the first speaker which of these two inferences is the correct one, and the second speaker has not spoken yet. One can easily imagine, somewhat later in the conversation, hearing the second speaker saying, "But I thought you said he went to the staff canteen because he was hungry." And one can imagine the first saying, "No, I didn't say that."

It is what happens at this point that becomes a problem in cumulative ambiguity. It is likely that neither of the participants in this discourse could say exactly what had been said so that it could be clarified. What would most likely happen is that the listener would begin to feel that the first speaker was vague or confused, or did not tell a clear story. It is also likely that the storyteller would come to think that the listener had not been paying attention. His or her attention would begin to shift away from the communication of the story, and come to focus more on the conversational partner's discourse capacity. In extreme cases, it is likely that he or she would begin to accuse his or her conversational partner of failing to co-operate, or even of illogicality.

What happens in this case is that the difference in these two possible interpretations of *E because F G* has not been confirmed at the time it came up in the discourse, because neither participant realized there was any problem. They have simply carried this ambiguity forward and acted as if each of their separate interpretations were the correct one.

Right at the beginning of this book we quoted a Chinese businessman using the marked structure *because Y, X*, and showed how this resulted in some confusion about the topic. Studies of the use of conjunctions by Asian speakers of English have shown that there is a tendency for such speakers to use more conjunctions than native speakers of English. Other studies have shown that this particular construction, *because Y, X*, is very commonly used by Asian speakers of English in ordinary spoken discourse; indeed, at a much higher frequency compared with native-speaker oral discourse. While this form alone is hardly sufficient to explain all the occurrences of confusion and miscommunication between Asians and westerners in conversation, it does give an indication of how processes of conversational inference function in real time to produce miscommunication between Asian speakers of English and native English speakers.

Before going on, we want to make one final note on how this sort of confusion arises even in oral discourse, where prosodic patterning would normally be sufficient to make it clear which of the interpretations was the correct one. In intercultural discourse, prosody is often the most ambiguous feature. Even among native speakers of English, for example, there is much disagreement about just how final intonation should be indicated.

Furthermore, non-native speakers of English often have accents in their pronunciation of English words. Most often this accent amounts to unclear placement of stressed syllables. Final and non-final intonation contours are based upon the stressed syllables of words. Where there is any doubt about the pronunciation of words, it will most often produce some ambiguity in the placement of stress. That, in turn, carries over into doubt about the larger intonation contours. Since sentence and clause boundaries are indicated by such prosodic contours, it is sometimes quite unclear just where the sentence and clause boundaries are intended to be placed.

If a non-native speaker of English uses the ordinary, unmarked structure we have described above, there is not much of a problem because that is the structure expected by the native speaker. On the other hand, if he or she uses the marked structure and places "because" before the two clauses, it is likely that the native English speaker will be unsure whether this has been done for two reasons, not just one. It both will be the marked form and is likely to be prosodically not entirely clear that this is the speaker's intention. Consequently, there is no solution but to wait until the next clause is finished, balance the two possibilities against each other as to which might be the most convincing interpretation, and then go on to the next point in the discourse.

Interactive Intelligence

The term "conversational inference" was introduced to sociolinguistic studies by John Gumperz in a 1977 paper to capture the fact that as people communicate with each other, the process of interpretation moves through real time from utterance to utterance in an ongoing process of interpretation. As we have indicated above, participants in ordinary conversation are constantly in a state of uncertainty, which is normally resolved through making tentative inferences and then acting upon them until further notice. The most important sources of these inferences beyond the grammatical system of the language itself have been outlined above, namely, cohesive devices, cognitive schemata, and prosodic patterning.

As we have said, communication is fundamentally ambiguous. Nevertheless, it is central to all human activity. Therefore, we can begin to understand that it is the fundamental nature of the human interpretive process to seek resolutions to this ambiguity. This interpretive process is what the sociolinguist Stephen Levinson (1990) calls interactive intelligence – the innate human capacity to draw inferences from ambiguous information.

This interactive intelligence is an essential aspect of human intelligence. As such it is brought to bear upon any communicative interpretation. This process seems to work very successfully, in fact, when conversationalists share common histories, cultures, and life experiences. The inferences they draw by assuming others think just as they do are generally safe. Problems are encountered, however, especially in the complex environment of international communication in English, when participants in a conversation hold different assumptions because of membership in different groups. Among the groups which can be significant are culture or ethnic groups, professional and corporate groups, generation groups, or gender groups. The problem is, of course, exacerbated when communication is across more than one group boundary such as culture and gender.

Later we will turn to the discussion of communication across such groups, or, as we will call them, discourse systems. As we will see, conversational inference is a fundamental aspect of interactive intelligence and should be thought of not as a problem to be eliminated in communication, but rather as one of the most fundamental of human cognitive processes.

5

Topic and Face: Inductive and Deductive Patterns in Discourse

What Are You Talking About?

Successful discourse depends on knowing what your discourse partner is talking about and making sure your discourse partner knows what you are talking about. Whether it is professional discourse or ordinary conversation with friends, discourse can hardly proceed without some idea of what the topic under discussion is. We started this book with an example in which a Cantonese-speaking businessman put his supporting arguments first and then concluded with his main point.

His main point was that he wanted to delay in making a decision until after Legco had made their decision. We call this line of argument inductive, because it places the minor points of the argument first and then derives the main point as a conclusion from those arguments. The structure could be sketched out as:

Because *A*, and because *B*, and because *C*, therefore *D*

This pattern contrasts with the deductive pattern, in which a topic is introduced at the beginning of a discourse and then the minor or supporting arguments are presented afterwards. In chapter 1 we gave a short narrative in which a Mr Wong and a Mr Richardson failed to understand each other because one, Mr Wong, was giving primary attention to the end of the conversation (inductive pattern), and the other, Mr Richardson, was giving primary attention to the beginning of the conversation (deductive pattern).

An American businessman was asked what he thought was the most important aspect of business communications. His answer was, "All you need is the five Ws and one H: what, who, where, when, why and how. Nothing else. If it's too long, you lose money." This American businessman would certainly favor the deductive discourse pattern. In this discourse style of "five Ws and one H," which is widely favored among American and other western businessmen, the idea is to get the topic out onto the conversational floor right away so that you know what you are discussing. Details can then be worked out deductively as they are needed. This pattern forms a strong contrast with the pattern used in the first example above, and this contrast can easily lead to confusion about what is the topic under discussion.

Before going any further in this discussion, we want to point out that both of these patterns are available to either Mr Wong or Mr Richardson. That is to say, there is nothing inherently Asian or western about these patterns. Nevertheless, if two (or more) people in a discourse approach the discourse with different assumptions about which pattern will be used, they are likely to have the problems of misinterpretation we have mentioned above.

Both the inductive (topic-delayed) and the deductive (topic-first) patterns of discourse are used for the same main purpose. That purpose is to reduce the overall ambiguity of the discourse. In the inductive pattern, the point is to make it quite clear why the speaker is coming to that particular conclusion. This is done by outlining the arguments and by testing the other participants for potential acceptance of the topic before introducing it. In the deductive pattern, the topic is introduced at the beginning so that it will be clear what the relevance of the supporting arguments is. While the intent is the same, the strategies are starkly contrasted.

Having said above that there is nothing inherently Asian or western in either of these patterns, since, as far as we know, both patterns are used in all societies, nevertheless there is a strong probability that such a broad discourse pattern will emerge in east west discourse as a significant area of cultural difference and even stereotyping. The purpose of this chapter is to resolve these problems: what is the cause of longer, fixed patterns in discourse; and, more specifically, what causes the differences between the so-called Asian (inductive) and western (deductive) patterns for the introduction of topics in discourse?

We begin with a discussion of the factors of interpersonal relationship which lead to the choice of one or the other of these rhetorical strategies. Since the introduction of a topic is in itself a face politeness strategy of involvement, this question is ultimately a question of interpersonal face politeness.

Topic, Turn Exchange, and Timing

On the surface of it, the western or deductive pattern of introducing the topic at the beginning of a discourse seems quite natural, at least to westerners in professional discourse. The businessman tells one, "Introduce your topic. Nothing else. If it's too long, you lose money." In saying this he is saying that this pattern is entirely natural in the business environment. We believe, however, that the situation is somewhat more complex than this business-man is ready to recognize or understand. As we will argue below, we do not believe this is a generalized pattern or a schema for discourse. The deduc-tive discourse pattern arises as a result of a complex interplay among other factors. The most basic factor is face politeness. This factor we will take up last. The other factor which produces this typical discourse pattern is an interaction among an adjacency sequence, turn exchange, and timing.

The call–answer–topic adjacency sequence

In a bookstore we might hear a telephone call which would begin as follows:

A: (Telephone rings)
B: Hello, Scollon Books.
A: Yes, do you have a copy of *Intercultural Communication?*

There is nothing very remarkable about such a conversation. When the telephone rings, you pick it up and say something like, "Hello." In some cases, you might identify yourself. The caller will ask to speak to a particu-lar person, or, perhaps, he or she recognizes from your voice that you are the person being called for. In any case, once it has been established you are the right person, the caller says why he or she has called. The rest of the conversation follows from there.

One of the best established adjacency sequences was first noted two decades ago in research on telephone calls. This sequence has three main turns (though there are possible side-sequences) in which the caller and the answerer are identified:

1   the call, accomplished through the ringing of the telephone;
2   the answer;
3   the introduction of the caller's topic.

As is the case with other adjacency sequences, there are strong expectations governing each of these turns, and we will take them up in order.

The call

On the telephone this turn is accomplished mechanically through the ringing of the telephone. As this research has been extended, the call has come to be understood as any form in which one person calls for the attention of another. This may be accomplished by knocking on a door or by pushing a doorbell or buzzer. We may call someone by saying such things as, "Excuse me," or, "Say, Bill." In any event, the call consists of any means we might use for indicating that we intend to start a discourse.

The answer

Observations of answers in many situations, not just in telephone calls, shows that the most important characteristic of the answer is that it is open-ended. By that we mean that the person who answers does not limit the caller's freedom to introduce the topic. The caller is granted freedom to introduce the topic in his or her next turn. The most important aspect of this limitation on the answer is that the answerer may not introduce a topic, but he or she must show openness for the topic of the caller.

In the phone conversation example we have given just above, it is not possible for the answerer to answer as follows:

A: (Telephone rings)
B: Hello, Scollon Books. We would like you to buy a copy of *Intercultural Communication*.

In other words, the answerer may not introduce a topic, but must say something quite non-committal, such as, "Hello," or "Good morning." In normal business or office environments the answer is usually the name of the company or office and the person answering: "Scollon Books, order department, Ron speaking."

The introduction of the caller's topic

The third move in this adjacency sequence is the caller's move, and this is to introduce the topic. In recent years, the rapid development of direct telephone marketing has shown that there are almost no limits on what topics may be introduced by the caller. The only way the answerer can really avoid the caller's topic is to avoid answering at all. This is, perhaps, the main reason that anyone who can afford to do so has a secretary or a receptionist placed between himself or herself and such callers. Although the original research was based on telephone calls, this pattern (with only minor variations) has been shown to be the prevailing one throughout much of western society for not only telephone calls, but all initiations of conversations.

It should be obvious that this adjacency sequence is the sequence by which a deductive discourse pattern is started. This does not mean, however, that the answerer may never introduce a topic. Once the original caller's topic has been developed, the answerer may then bring up a topic of his or her own. There are many formulas or gambits with which the answerer may introduce a topic. These are all of the "by the way" sort, in which explicit mention is made of changing of the topic which is currently on the floor.

One might even go so far as to say that the deductive topic belongs to the caller and the answerer must then resort to an inductive pattern of topic introduction. In other words, the second speaker (the answerer) must follow along with the topic of the first speaker while looking for the means to introduce his or her own topic. It is preferable for this topic to appear to arise inductively out of the caller's topic. The gambits to cover such inductive introductions are ones like, "You know, that brings to mind something I wanted to tell you."

To summarize, the most important aspect of the "call–answer–topic" sequence is that the topic belongs to the caller, and therefore, the discourse will be started on the first speaker's topical home ground.

Deductive Monologues

One question which often arises in intercultural communication is, "Why do deductive discourses so often become monologues?" There is no inherent reason why a person who is granted the right to introduce his or her topic at the start of a conversation should be granted the additional right to produce a long-winded monologue, and yet, this has often been observed to be the result.

For the answer to this, we need to recall our discussion in chapter 4 of interturn pausing. There we said that if two speakers (or more) differ in the length of the pauses they take between turns, the speaker with the shorter pauses will come to dominate the conversation. This is because at each point where turns might be exchanged, the faster speaker recaptures the conversational floor. While there are many reasons why one person might have shorter turn exchange pauses than another, some of which are non-linguistic, shorter interturn pauses are an involvement politeness strategy; longer interturn pauses are an independence politeness strategy. Introducing one's topic is also an involvement politeness strategy. As a consequence, the person whose topic is being discussed will have at least some slight tendency to use shorter turn exchange pauses in consonance with their control of the topic.

The combination of these factors is what produces the monologues or dominated discourses so often associated with the deductive discourse pattern. One person speaks first and thereby gains the right to introduce his or her topic. Then that same person tends to use shorter turn exchange pauses. As a consequence, he or she continually regains the floor at each point of possible transition. The combined result is that one speaker will tend to continue to speak about his or her own topic for an extended sequence of turns. The net effect of these combined factors amounts to practically a monologue, even though it is constructed one turn at a time as the participants move through the discourse.

The Inductive Pattern

One problem we are trying to resolve in this chapter is why there appears to be a western preference for a deductive pattern for the introduction of topics and an Asian preference for an inductive pattern for the introduction of topics. We have now detailed how the deductive pattern arises in western discourse as a combination of the call–answer–topic adjacency sequence coupled with such factors as turn exchange patterns and timing. We now want to turn to the so-called Asian inductive pattern to see what factors can account for its prevalence in much Asian discourse.

We have already given several short examples in which intercultural miscommunication arose because of the delayed introduction of a topic by an Asian participant. The pattern is known well enough, at least by those with intercultural experience in Asia or with Asians. The problem this pattern poses for discourse analysis is that we know adjacency sequences have never been established for turn exchanges extending beyond, at most, a few turns. We find it hard to believe, for example, that someone using this pattern has in mind to begin an interaction, but to delay the introduction of the topic until, say, turn 57 or turn 23. No such fixed point for the later introduction of topics has ever been demonstrated, and this is the point: we can say the topic will be introduced later, but, until it is introduced, neither participant could say when it would be introduced.

In this it is quite unlike the "call–answer–topic" sequence, in which all participants know that whoever has initiated the interaction has the right (and, in fact, the obligation) to introduce the main topic with which the discourse begins. In the "call–answer–facework–topic" pattern, the only thing we can be sure of saying is that the person who initiates the communication has the right to introduce the topic, but we cannot say when that will be on the basis of this adjacency sequence alone.

In order to clarify the elements of the inductive pattern, we will need to look more closely at the ethnographic description we have made of the Chinese inductive pattern. We ask the reader to remember that, labelling apart, we do not mean that this pattern is either restricted to Chinese (or other Asians) or that it is the only pattern available in Chinese (or other Asian) discourse.

When we first described the Chinese inductive pattern in Taiwan, we described it, as we did above, as the "call–answer–facework–topic" pattern. By this we meant that, just as in the western pattern, the first speaker introduces the topic, but the topic will be delayed until after a period of facework. Asians often expressed agreement with this description. They said that delaying the topic was somehow necessary so that they could get a chance to feel the mood or the position of the other participants. We called this period of getting warmed up to each other "facework," loosely following Goffman's (1967) concept of facework. The point we wanted to make was that a Chinese person, even if that person had the right to introduce the topic, might want to be rather sensitive to other participants by delaying the introduction of the topic until the moment was right for it.

This description, however, does not square with two frequent exceptions. Our students said, for example, that this was not the case at all when they talked among themselves. They said that they felt entirely free to just call up a friend and say, "Let's go to a movie," or to come across a friend on their college campus and say, "Let's go have coffee." This quick introduction of the topic seemed very much like the western pattern of immediate topic introduction.

The second exception to the pattern we had described was in situations such as calling a taxi, paying an electric bill, or buying a bus ticket. In such cases, there was, if anything, even less preliminary communication than in typical western exchanges. In such cases, the pattern appears to be simply topic, without any preliminary call or answer. This latter exception has often been noticed by foreigners visiting Asia, who are confused by the contrast between the elaborate facework and deferential delay of topics in some situations and the very abrupt introduction of topics in other cases.

Inside and outside encounters

To deal with the latter pattern first, we found that the cases of very abrupt topic introduction were all of a kind we came to describe as outside or service encounters. In these encounters, such as buying tickets for a museum, depositing money in a bank, getting a seat in a restaurant, or buying vegetables in a market, the relationship between the participants is considered to be an outside relationship. By that we mean that the participants have no dealings with each other besides in this single transaction.

In an outside encounter the topic is really already known; you are going to buy a ticket or you would not be standing at the ticket window. All that remains to be learned is just which ticket you want. In this sense, outside encounters are highly conventionalized, culturally established encounters which require very little interpersonal negotiation. This would be true in most cultural settings. In Asia, it is fair to say that there is a quite strong cultural sense of division between outside and inside interactions. The outside interactions receive little attention or interest.

Inside relationships, in contrast, are much more important in Asia than is characteristic in the west. While most of Asia should be described as post-Confucian, that is, once having been influenced by the Confucian ethical system but no longer directly participating in it, nevertheless, there is a strong carry-over from Confucianism in interpersonal relationships. Generally speaking, Asians feel that such relationships as those within the family or between people who have frequent and longstanding relations with each other should be governed by careful propriety. That careful propriety in inside relationships includes careful concern for face relationships among participants in speech events.

Hierarchical Confucian relationships and topic introduction

It has been said by some ethnographers that all relationships in Asia are hierarchical. Perhaps that statement is extreme, especially in such highly modernized international centers as Tokyo, Taipei, Hong Kong, or Singapore. Nevertheless, it is certainly accurate to say that hierarchy in relationships is much more consciously observed than it is in the west. The carry-over from Confucianism means that even today, most Asians are quite conscious in any interaction who is older and who is younger, who has a higher level of education, who has a lower level, who is in a higher institutional or economic position and who is lower, or who is teacher and who is student. They are especially conscious of such relationships within extended family structures, with each person carefully placed with a kinship term which tells all participants to which generation they belong in relation to others.

As a result of discussions with Asians on the question of topic introduction, we came to realize that the crucial question was not so much who spoke first; the crucial issue is who is in the higher position and who is in the lower position. In the Asian discourse system, the person in the higher position has the right to introduce the topic and that right supersedes the question of who speaks first in the interaction.

We were then faced with a further question: if the person in the higher position has the right to speak first, and he or she also has the right to introduce the topic, why does that person not simply introduce his or her topic at the beginning of the conversation? Why is the topic delayed?

One answer we received to this question is that in many, perhaps most cases, the person in the lower position was required to greet the person in the higher position. School children in Taiwan, for example, are expected to chime in with, "*Lao shi hao*" ("How are you, teacher?"), when the teacher comes into the classroom. Nevertheless, when asked, many said that they could not always freely greet their superiors, especially when their superiors were clearly occupied.

This leads us to recognize that the first turn, the call, is often not speech at all in Asian discourse, but rather, some gesture or facial expression that shows an openness to being greeted. The call is then answered with a greeting, followed by a pause in which the person in the lower position waits to see if he or she is expected to continue in the discourse.

The description we have given of the Asian patterns for the introduction of topics is based on our ethnographic research in Taiwan, Hong Kong, Zhongshan (Guangdong), Korea, and Japan. After we had first written about this research we read the *Li Ji* or *Li Chi*, the *Book of Rites* (Chai and Chai, 1966). This ancient book from the third and second centuries BC gives a description which fits very closely with the contemporary pattern, though of course it is described in ancient ways.

This ancient Confucian code lays down quite clearly a set of appropriate behaviors in interpersonal communication, which corresponds quite closely with Asian communicative practice in the twentieth century. Our evidence is that Asians are not conscious, on the whole, of these ancient rules of etiquette. The close correspondence with contemporary behavior seems to arise not out of study of the *Li Ji* itself, but rather out of the Chinese sense of role relationships and their implied sense of self.

While there is much more which could be said on this topic, it is clear that under ordinary circumstances it is quite inappropriate and therefore quite uncomfortable for a student to introduce a topic of his or her own in a communication with a teacher. More generally, it is quite unusual for a person in the lower position to introduce his or her own topic without first receiving the right to do so from the person in the higher position. While the *Li Ji* does not use the term, it seems clear that this is a description of the inductive pattern for the introduction of topics in a discourse.

The false east–west dichotomy

In spite of all of this evidence from both ancient and contemporary sources that the inductive pattern is widely approved of and used in contemporary Asian communication, we believe that it is quite wrong to consider this an

Asian pattern. There are two reasons for this, which come down to the same thing: *both* inductive and deductive patterns are used in both Asian and western communications.

If we take up the Asian side of this false dichotomy first, we should return to the observation made by our students in Taiwan and in Hong Kong as well. In ordinary conversations among friends, the deductive pattern is most commonly used. One calls up a friend and says, "Let's go shopping at the night market," or when you come across a friend on the street you can easily say, "Let's go have a cup of tea." In other words, where people are in a close relationship to each other and of relatively equal status, in both east and west the normal pattern is the deductive pattern.

Some commentators have felt that this use of the deductive pattern for the introduction of topics is an adoption of "westernization" in the conversational styles of the younger generation of Asians. Of course, western influence is not unlikely, given that so many Asians see western films, watch western television, and read western fiction. Nevertheless, we believe that the deductive pattern has been in use in Asia for as long as we have records. For example, we believe it would be very hard to classify the dialogues between Confucius and his students as anything but deductively organized, though often sections show inductive organization. Most frequently, in fact, the dialogues are introduced by a topic which is raised by a student.

As for the use of the inductive pattern in the west, all we have to consider is the situation in which one is going to a friend with the intention of borrowing some large sum of money or asking for some other big or embarrassing favor. In such a situation the person would understandably be reluctant to come out with his or her topic at the outset of the conversation. We can be certain there would be an extended period of facework in which the would-be borrower would feel out the situation for the right moment in which to introduce his or her topic.

We believe that even though a superficial observation indicates a strong preference for the inductive pattern in Asia and for the deductive pattern in the west, this apparent cultural difference lies not in a cultural template for the introduction of topics in discourse, but in differences in the cultural structuring of situations and participant roles. It is this difference in expectations on participant roles, or face, which leads to the frequently observed differences in the introduction of topics in Asian and western discourse.

Face: Inductive and Deductive Rhetorical Strategies

In speaking of the practice of introducing the topic at the beginning of a discourse and comparing that with delaying the introduction, we have used a somewhat vague language. We have called these two ways of introducing topics "patterns," "discourse patterns," or "patterns of discourse." We have been intentionally vague, because we have been concerned not to create the idea that there was behind these patterns anything as formal as a schema or a script as we have used these terms in chapter 5. It is true that the deductive pattern is closely associated with a particular adjacency sequence, the "call–answer–topic sequence." Nevertheless, we are inclined to believe that the sequence is derived from some deeper aspects of discourse, such as cultural expectations about face or the purposes and functions of discourse, and should not be treated as causal in itself.

Now we are prepared to argue that a more accurate way of speaking of these two phenomena is to refer to them as rhetorical strategies, which, therefore, are more appropriate in some situations than others to achieve particular purposes, as we will discuss below. We will show that the use of these strategies is directly related to the three systems of face which we presented above in chapter 3. For our purposes now, the most important aspect of the three systems of face which we discussed in chapter 3 is the distribution of the strategies of involvement and of independence.

Readers who have studied Euclidean geometry may remember that the proofs you studied were presented deductively. That is to say, first you had a theorem, in other words, you had a conclusion; then you set about to prove that conclusion, starting from what was well known and obvious and moving on through logical steps until the conclusion with which you started seemed inevitable. In rhetoric, deductive strategies are usually used in cases of proofs or logical arguments where the goal is to show the reader or listener how one has arrived at a foregone conclusion.

In ordinary discourse, the deductive rhetorical strategy is used for basically the same purposes. It is the unmarked way in which one presents an idea that is taken for granted, or if the idea is not taken for granted, it is taken for granted that the speaker has every right to hold or to advance that idea and does not need to convince the listener of that right. In other words, when the speaker assumes that he or she has the right to advance an idea or when he or she believes that what is being said is true and only needs to be demonstrated to be understood, or when there is less emphasis on the listener taking action than there is on the listener understanding and acknowledging the truth of one's proposition, the most effective choice is the deductive rhetorical strategy.

A handbook on effective rhetorical skills points out that the inductive rhetorical strategy works by presenting the evidence one has first, and progressively leading the listener (or reader) to the conclusion one would like him or her to accept. This strategy works best, this handbook says, when your conclusion is one which you believe your listener (or your reader) is likely to resist.

In other words, the inductive rhetorical strategy works in the situation opposite that for the deductive rhetorical strategy. It is best to use the inductive approach when it is not clear that the speaker has the right to advance a particular topic, when it is unclear that the listener will accept the speaker's conclusion, or when the purpose of the discourse is to exhort the listener to action.

Earlier research on face politeness strategies has made no mention of these rhetorical strategies in light of the two types of face strategy. Here we would like to argue that the deductive rhetorical strategy is, in fact, a face politeness strategy of involvement, whereas the inductive rhetorical strategy is a face politeness strategy of independence. We believe this follows from the descriptions we have given above of their respective roles in discourse.

Involvement strategies emphasize what the participants have in common; they assert the speaker's right to advance his or her own position on the grounds that the listener will be equally interested in that position and in advancing his or her own position. The most extreme strategy of involvement has been called "bald on record," in other words, simply stating one's position. This is, we believe, simply another wording for advancing one's own topic. Such strategies of involvement are particularly effective where the other participants do not wish to assert their independence from the speaker and show themselves quite willing to be accepted within a group of common membership.

Independence strategies emphasize the independence of the participants in a discourse from each other. They are particularly effective when the speaker wishes to show that he or she does not wish to impose on the other participants. We argue that the inductive rhetorical strategy is most effective in just such a case, where the speaker is being careful to avoid assuming that his or her listener will automatically agree with his or her position.

Topics and Face Systems

The conclusions follow quite naturally from this description. In a symmetrical deference politeness system, both speakers (or all participants) prefer strategies of independence. What this means is that all speakers will use inductive rhetorical strategies. To put this in plain terms, all speakers will avoid the direct introduction of their own topics. They will prefer to let their own points of view arise out of the ongoing discourse as inevitable conclusions from what has been said. Discourses will consist of indirect points which lay the foundation for conclusions (the topics of speakers). Such conclusions may, in fact, never need to be directly stated, because they will follow inevitably from what has been said.

This description of topic avoidance in discourse, by the way, matches almost exactly the ethnographic observations we have made of the discourse of the Athabaskan people (Scollon and Scollon, 1981). The extreme of good Athabaskan conversation is, in fact, silence. People enjoy having a good, quiet sit together with no topics being raised at all. While such an extreme is rare among the cultures of the world, of course, it does match our experience of the discourse of foreign diplomats, for example, in which each word is carefully chosen (we hope) and new topics are broached with great care.

In a symmetrical solidarity politeness system, on the other hand, both (or all) speakers will prefer face politeness strategies of involvement. As a result, each participant will feel quite free to introduce topics on the assumption that both speakers and hearers share membership in the same social, or at least discourse, group. If we remember that shorter turn exchange pauses are also a strategy of involvement, we can see that in extreme examples of such symmetrical solidarity there will be a very rapid set of exchanges with many topics being introduced.

This is the sort of system of conversational interaction which Tannen (1984) has described for New Yorkers. She has described not only rapid introduction of topics, but much conversational overlapping, finishing of the sentences of other speakers, and other such forms of involvement face politeness.

Finally, an asymmetrical (hierarchical) politeness system will show a rather complex set of possibilities. As we have said above, the person in the higher social position would use involvement strategies of politeness. This would mean that it would be most appropriate to use the deductive rhetorical strategy and for this speaker to introduce his or her own topic. On the other side of the interaction, the person in the lower position would follow an inductive strategy, and avoid introducing a topic in the first case, or put off bringing up his or her topic until it followed naturally from the preceding discourse.

To stand this analysis on its head, we can now ask how we interpret these rhetorical strategies as they occur in discourse. If we do not know in advance what the relationship is between ourselves and others, we will hear the inductive rhetorical strategy as one of two things: expression of mutual deference among equal but distant participants, or expression of subordination to our own superior position. As we have argued above in our discussion of conversational inference, we cannot, in fact, be certain what the other participant's intentions are until we have confirmed them. Nevertheless, in order to proceed we must choose some position from which to continue the discourse. If we have interpreted the inductive rhetorical strategy as equality with distance, we will reciprocate by also avoiding the assertion of our own topics. In other words, we too will use the inductive strategy.

On the other hand, if we have interpreted the other speaker as intending to show deference to our higher position, we will respond to the inductive rhetorical strategy with the deductive rhetorical strategy. In other words, we will introduce our own topic. The other participant, then, will have to respond to our own interpretation. If his or her intention was, indeed, deference to our higher position, there will be no problem. On the other hand, if he or she has assumed mutual deference, our introduction of our own topic will sound like an assertion of authority or power or as an attempt to take control of the discourse inappropriately.

This is what the philosopher Nietzsche had in mind when he wrote, "The familiarity of the superior embitters, because it may not be returned" (1990: 494) The mismatch of inductive and deductive strategies is a major source of miscommunication about what the topic of the discourse is, but it is not only that; it can also be the source of bitterness and other negative attitudes when participants fail to come to agreement about their interpersonal relationship.

We started this chapter by saying, "discourse can hardly proceed without some idea of what the topic under discussion is." Now we can see that our original statement is really too simple. It is not just a matter of stating what the topic under discussion is, because which rhetorical strategy you should use for stating the topic is also undergoing negotiation. The American businessman's strategy of the five Ws and the one H (what, who, where, when, why, and how) is the most effective rhetorical strategy if you are either in a close and equal personal relationship with the other participants, or in a position of power over others to whom you are communicating. If you are not equals, not close, and not in power, his advice is bad advice indeed. The result of such a deductive rhetorical strategy in those latter circumstances would be to sound aggressive, domineering, or inconsiderate.

The businessman who emphasized this deductive rhetorical strategy to the authors is, in fact, in a position of considerable power. He may well be in the situation of the boss who tells his staff a joke and thinks he has been very funny because everyone laughs. They have hardly any other choice but to laugh. He forgets that the acceptance of his discourse strategies is the result of his position, not the result of his own personal merits or stylistic skill.

Face Relationships in Written Discourse

We have based our analysis of the structures of discourse on the idea of conversational inference. We have argued that when people talk to each other, they have the continual ongoing problem of interpreting what other participants are saying at the level of the information, but also they must interpret what face positions other participants are taking in the relationship. Even such aspects of discourse as when, where, and how you introduce a topic are based on this process of conversational inference and face relationships.

On the surface of it, none of this is true when the discourse takes place in writing. In writing, one person (or perhaps a group of people) composes a text which is then read by its reader or readers at another time and most likely in another place. There is limited feedback overall, and no feedback at all in the composition of the text. In other words, a spoken discourse represents the joint product of all of the participants in the situation, but a written discourse represents the one-sided product of a discourse by the participants who compose the text. The other participants, the readers, can more or less take it or leave it in their interpretation of the text, but they cannot manage an alteration in the basic structure of the text.

Of course, there are many variations in the nature of written texts and we could not possibly take them all into consideration at this time. For example, some texts are really much more like individual turns in a face-to-face interaction. Around an office, for example, many short notes are exchanged. The following three notes are actual notes in an office which were written on small memo pads, but they are not very different from three successive turns in a face-to-face conversation:

A: Would it be possible for us to meet sometime to discuss my project? I need to get on to the next step and could use your advice. I am free Tuesday any time after 11 or after 3 on Wednesday.

B: Would 12 o'clock Tuesday be OK?

A: Tuesday at 12 is fine. See you then.

Where the discourse is like this series of exchanges, it is relatively easy to see that processes of interpretation which are very much like those of conversational inference come into play in interpreting these messages. We can see from the first memo that A is in a lower institutional position than B. A is introducing the topic somewhat inductively by saying that she would like to meet to discuss it, leaving open the possibility that B might not have the time or the interest to do so. She gives a wide range of options for a time to meet so that B is not unduly restricted in setting up an appointment. B, in turn, confirms that he is willing to let her introduce her topic, but narrows the range of options open quite considerably.

We could compare this with what it might look like if A and B were in the opposite institutional positions. Such an exchange might look like this:

A: I need to talk to you about my project. Would you be free at 12 o'clock Tuesday? Otherwise, let me know what other time might work.

B: Tuesday at 12 is fine. I'll look forward to learning about your project.

In this case the person in the higher position is much more direct and much more limiting in the options available for an appointment. B, on the other hand, is a bit more expansive about his interest in A's project. In other words, this written exchange could be quite easily understood within the framework of interpersonal face relations as we have described it above. The person in the higher position uses strategies of involvement including the deductive rhetorical strategy for introducing his or her topic, while the person in the lower position uses strategies of independence.

The problem we want to discuss here is this: what happens when the written discourse is either quite extended in length or spans a large distance of either space or time between the participants of the writer and the reader? In such a case, is it still possible to talk about face relationships between the writer and the reader, even where little or no feedback is possible between them?

Essays and press releases

We could approach the problem of face relationships in written discourse from one of two directions; either we could analyze the face relationships between writers and readers, and then ask how topics have been introduced and which patterns of politeness and which rhetorical strategies have been used, or we could analyze texts asking which rhetorical strategies and face politeness strategies have been used, and then ask what the face relationships are in such cases.

Since texts are easier to get our hands on than face relationships, we prefer to start with two typical types of text, the essay and the press release. We have chosen these two because both of them are highly salient types of text in the lives of professional communicators; many professional communicators find that writing press releases is a major part of their work, and there is hardly a professional communicator in existence who has not achieved his or her position at least partly through writing successful essays in school and examinations.

The businessman we have now quoted so often was actually speaking of how you write a successful press release, though later he went on to say this applied to all business communications. He was only stating what is widely understood in professional communication as the most direct rhetorical strategy: "Say what you have to say and quit; nothing more."

We have said that this rhetorical strategy is the deductive rhetorical strategy and as such implies either a face system of symmetrical solidarity (in which both speakers use strategies of involvement) or a face system of hierarchy in which only the person in the dominant position uses such an involvement strategy. Of course, there are many different types of press release. In some cases, such as when a government issues a press release, it is clear that the writer is, at least officially, in a superior position to the reader.

The press release: implied writers and implied readers

Let us take up this case first. In actual fact, it is not the writer himself or herself who is superior to the reader, since the reader is actually unknown in any specific case and includes everyone who might read the press release. In fact, the actual writer is likely to be someone in a very inferior bureaucratic position compared to the person or the office which has issued the information in the press release. And, furthermore, many of the readers of the press release will be people much higher in the official bureaucracy.

The point this brings out is that the relationship expressed in a press release is not between the actual writer of the press release and any particular reader. The relationship is more abstract than that. It is between the voice of the government (which is taken to be a person in this case) and the people. In other words, the use of the deductive strategy is appropriate since it is the government speaking, not the particular writer of the text.

To put this another way, in written discourse there are really two kinds of relationship we need to consider: the relationship between the actual writer of a text and the actual reader of a text on the one hand, and the relationship between the implied writer and the implied reader on the other hand. The actual writer of a governmental press release may have any of the possible face relationships with some of the actual readers of the press release. The writer may find that his or her text is read by friends, children, parents, work colleagues, strangers, members of the legislature or parliament, or almost any other imaginable real person. Nevertheless, as the writer writes the press release, he or she takes on a role, the role of the implied writer, speaking with the voice of the government in whose name the document is issued. Therefore, the actual writer ignores his or her own social position and composes texts from the point of view of the implied writer, the government.

The same applies to the reader of this text. The governmental press release may be published in a newspaper which might be read by people of many different social positions and statuses. The text does not alter its face relationships with each of those readers separately. It takes one kind of reader as the standard or the model for its implied reader. In the example of a governmental press release, the implied reader is assumed to be a law-abiding, interested, dutiful citizen.

In business environments, press releases are somewhat different in fact, though not any different in principle. When a business sends out a press release about a new product or service, for example, it makes certain assumptions about the implied reader of the press release, whether or not actual readers fit those characteristics. Naturally, in business, one wants to come as close as possible to the actual characteristics of those readers. In any event, a business press release takes the position that its readers are busy, active, interested co-participants in the enterprise of the business. It assumes that they are interested in engaging in commerce with the business which is making the press release, whether as co-partners, as customers of the product or service, or as stockholders in the enterprise.

In other words, the relationship assumed between the implied writer and the implied reader of a business press release is one of symmetrical solidarity, whether or not the actual writer and the actual reader are in that relationship to each other. Again, there is really no telling with written discourse who will read it and when or where. One must assume an implied reader, and that, in turn, means one must also assume an implied writer.

The essay: a deductive structure

We can probably assume that almost any reader of this book will be familiar with the preferred structure for an essay within the western tradition, since it is probably impossible to become an educated reader without having been asked to read many such essays as well as to write them. The structure of such an essay, or indeed of a book, has been laid out in many textbooks on composition. The general structure is as thoroughly deductive as one might find anywhere.

Textbooks on composition tell us that an essay (or a book) should have a thesis. A thesis is a straightforward statement of the main point the essay or the book has been written to advance. Such textbooks tell us that the thesis should be presented very early in the text. In a short essay of several paragraphs or several pages, that thesis should appear in the first paragraph. In a longer essay or in a book, the thesis might be delayed until after a bit of preliminary material, but in any event, the reader should be able to determine the main point within the first formal section of the text.

In the same way, each section of the essay or the book is expected to be treated deductively as well. Each paragraph, according to standard composition textbooks, should have a topic sentence, and that sentence should be the first sentence in the paragraph. Of course, in some cases a transition will be required; in those cases the topic sentence might be the second sentence. In any event, the main topic of the paragraph is generally said to be required at the beginning of each paragraph.

There is little question that the essay, as it is presented in standard composition textbooks, is a completely deductive rhetorical structure. What follows from this is that the relationship between the implied writer and the implied reader of the essay is one of symmetrical solidarity, as it is in the press release. In fact, you will find many examples of involvement politeness strategies in the language of essays within this western tradition of essays. In addition to the deductive introduction of topics, there are many phrases such as, "it will come as no surprise," "as we have seen above," and "it is obvious that," which express that the implied writer and the implied reader have the same point of view in approaching the text.

Just as in the case of the press release, in the essay it is assumed that the crucial face relationship is one of solidarity politeness between the implied writer and the implied reader. It makes little difference, actually, what the real relationships might be between the real writer and the real reader. Within the enclosed world of the essay text, it is assumed that a close, familiar relationship exists in which both parties are commonly pursuing a common goal. In most cases, of course, this unstated goal is the establishment of truth.

Limiting Ambiguity: Power in Discourse

Since language is inherently ambiguous, our main concern is with understanding how participants in communication are able to interpret each other. One main form of ambiguity in discourse is determining the topic. We began this chapter with a study of this question of topics in face-to-face discourse. We argued that even though conversational inference is the primary means by which we interpret each other in face-to-face discourse, conversational analysis alone cannot account for the structures which arise in discourse. In order to understand those structures, we have to take into account not only processes of conversational inference, including timing, schemata, adjacency sequences, and the rest, but also the face relationships among participants.

In order to understand how topics are introduced, given certain face relationships, we borrowed from studies of rhetoric the idea of two different and opposing rhetorical strategies, the deductive rhetorical strategy and the inductive rhetorical strategy. The first strategy, the deductive, is most effective when the topic is understood as given or when the authority of the speaker is unquestioned; the second strategy, the inductive, is most effective when the listener may question either the conclusion one wants to draw or the authority of the speaker to make such a statement.

Then we argued that the differences one might observe between Asian and western patterns for the introduction of topics were not really a matter of east and west, since both patterns are used widely in both societies. We argued that the use of these strategies depends most on the face relationships which exist between or among the participants in a discourse.

Finally, we have raised the question of how such interpersonal relationships are expressed in written communications, since in most cases there is little or no back-and-forth negotiation among the participants, the writer(s) and the reader(s). The conclusion we have drawn is that in some forms of written discourse, such as the press release and the essay, the relationships under consideration are not those between the real writer and the real reader, but those between the implied writer and the implied reader.

6

Ideologies of Discourse

Three Concepts of Discourse

We have reviewed many textbooks, professional tradebooks, and popular books on communication in business and professional environments. When these books directly express their philosophy of communication, it is never much different from the five Ws and one H of the American businessman we have quoted. In most cases these books explicitly state that the purpose of professional communication is to convey information, and the philosophy of communication which is explicitly stated is that information should be conveyed as clearly, briefly, directly, and sincerely as possible. Richard Lanham (1983), an English and rhetoric teacher at the University of Los Angeles, California, has called this the C–B–S style, for "clarity," "brevity," and "sincerity." This very focused form of communication is widely put forward as the most effective and even simply the "normal" form of professional communication by many, if not most, writers on the subject of communication. Such a philosophy of communication seems so obviously necessary and appropriate to writers of such books, as well as to people who work in professional communication, that it is rarely asked if this is really the standard which should be applied in all cases.

If you look closer at the actual examples used in these books on communication, you will find, as we did, that there are many exceptions to this principle. One textbook on business correspondence, for example, gives an example of the difference between what it calls a "friendly" business letter and a "cold" business letter. It advises that wherever possible one should compose friendly letters, because it makes the receiver feel better about doing business with your company.

What makes this case interesting is that the so-called friendly letter is quite a bit less straightforward and direct than the so-called cold letter. In other words, the authors of that text state a communication philosophy of the C–B–S style – never say anything beyond the necessary information; then the same authors give examples in which they urge the student to say a number of unnecessary things for the sake of warming up the tone of the letter.

There are two aspects to the problem we want to present in this chapter on systems of discourse: the first is that our stated philosophies of communication are often at variance with what we actually expect people to practice, and the second is that these divergences from reality are often very resistant to change. As we will see, there are important historical and ideological reasons for the communication philosophies people claim to follow. These communication philosophies tend to form what we call discourse systems, which then become a major factor in both organizational discourse and inter-discourse or intercultural communication.

The word "discourse" has been used in writing about language use in three somewhat different ways. In the most technically narrow definition of the word, the study of discourse has been the study of grammatical and other relationships between sentences. These relationships are often discussed as a problem of cohesion. This is the study of discourse which we developed in chapter 4. The purpose of such studies of discourse is to come to understand the inferential processes by which speakers communicate their meanings and by which hearers interpret what is said.

A more general use of the word "discourse" has been made to study broader functional uses of language in social contexts. Most of our book up to this point has been given over to this broader definition of the concept of discourse (chapters 1–3 and chapter 5). In such studies, the purpose is to come to understand how the language we use is based on the social environments in which we use that language. As we have argued, for example, the placement of topics in conversations depends on the development of relationships among the participants.

Now we have come to the broadest concept of discourse, which is the study of whole systems of communication. For example, we might study the language of dealers in foreign exchange, of public school teachers, or of members of the North American "Baby Boom" generation. Such broad systems of discourse form a kind of self-contained system of communication with a shared language or jargon, with particular ways in which people learn what they need to know to become members, with a particular ideological position, and with quite specific forms of interpersonal relationships among members of these groups.

To give a simple example to help to clarify this concept of a discourse system, we could consider what happens when a young person right out of school takes a position in a corporation. Liu Ka Men has just taken a job in an international corporation in Hong Kong. At first she feels somewhat out of place. This new company has many forms to be filled out, memos to be circulated, and locations of offices and people who are all new to her. In order to fit into the new situation she needs to start to learn this language (the forms of discourse), which is quite specific to this company.

There are two ways in which Ms Liu goes about learning her way through these new forms of discourse as she becomes socialized to this new work environment. On the one hand, the company provides various kinds of training. There are orientation classes for new employees as well as handbooks which outline company or office forms and procedures. On the other hand, Liu Ka Men is already beginning to learn a great deal from other members of the staff, who tell her just what is needed in particular circumstances. These forms of socialization to the new company, both formal and informal, have the result that over a period of time she starts to become more at ease and to sense greater confidence that she is beginning to fit into the new position.

Along with Liu Ka Men's socialization to the new company comes a sense of the company's "culture" or ideology. While in corporate circles this company ideology is now often referred to as the corporation's "culture," to avoid the negative connotations of the word "ideology," we prefer to use the word "ideology." By ideology we mean the worldview or governing philosophy of a group or a discourse system. The concept of power usually lies behind this word. That is to say, one aspect of the ideology of a group is whether or not it sees itself as more powerful or less powerful than some other relevant group.

Liu Ka Men gradually comes to identify with the attitude this company takes to its clients, its own history, and its future. Whether or not she really believes this position, there will be little doubt that success within the company will come with projecting the corporate culture in dealing with others.

This governing ideology will, in turn, have a considerable effect on interpersonal relationships (face systems) both within the company and between members of the company and their clients. Ms Liu begins to learn through subtle cues from older company members how to take the right attitude toward suppliers, toward various subsidiary companies, and toward the parent company of which her own company is a subsidiary. She learns very quickly which of the office employees should be addressed by given name, which by family name, which she might go out with for lunch, and which she should avoid in anything but strictly business matters.

Finally, these clusters of interpersonal relationships or face systems have a very strong effect on the forms of discourse which Ms Liu comes to use. Letters to subsidiary companies are likely to be written somewhat more directively than letters to the parent company, which will show a certain amount of deference. In telephone calls to colleagues she learns to nurture friendly relationships, but with clients she comes quite directly to the point.

There are four basic elements to this system of discourse into which Liu Ka Men has been introduced: the forms of discourse, the socialization, the

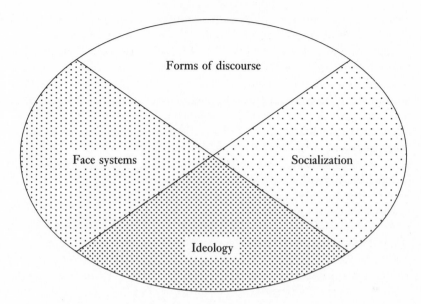

Figure 6.1   Discourse system.

ideology, and the face systems. Each of these four elements mutually influences the others, and so they come to form a rather tight system of communication or discourse, within which she becomes increasingly enclosed.
The more neatly she fits into this discourse system, the more she comes to
feel identified with it and the more others come to treat her as a full-fledged
member of the discourse system. A discourse system could be represented
as in figure 6.1.

When Liu Ka Men enters into this new company, of course, she does not
think of it as entering into a new discourse system and she would certainly
not think of her experience as dividing up into these four elements or
categories. We will use the conceptual construct of the discourse system
as a way of talking about what some other researchers have called simply
"discourses." Our purpose in using this construct is to bring to attention
the various elements or components of our experience of becoming a member
of a discourse. Furthermore, while we have presented these four elements
in this pattern, we do not mean that they might not be arranged in another
way. From the point of view of the study of discourse and communication,
it seems most useful to place the "forms of discourse" element at the top,
since it is those forms of discourse in which the student of professional
communication has the greatest interest. On the other hand, in our discussion
below of the Utilitarian discourse system, we will consider ideology first; in

that case we believe it is the ideology which is the strongest influence upon the other elements of the discourse system.

Although we could present them in any order, the four characteristics which will define a discourse system are as follows:

1 Members will hold a common ideological position and recognize a set of extra-discourse features which define them as a group (*ideology*).
2 Socialization is accomplished primarily through these preferred forms of discourse (*socialization*).
3 A set of preferred forms of discourse serves as banners or symbols of membership and identity (*forms of discourse*).
4 Face relationships are prescribed for discourse among members or between members and outsiders (*face systems*).

The Utilitarian Discourse System

The question we now want to consider is whether or not the C–B–S style constitutes or is part of a system of discourse. In order to answer this we will need to address several questions, such as those which follow:

1 Does this form or style of discourse arise out of a more complex pattern of ideology, socialization, and social organization or face systems?
2 Does the more complex pattern form a more or less coherent whole and do participants feel that they are members of a group as a result?

We could think of the analysis of systems of discourse as answering four basic questions:

1 What are the historical/social/ideological characteristics of the group? (*ideology*)
2 How does one learn membership and identity? (*socialization*)
3 What are the preferred forms of communication? (*forms of discourse*)
4 What are the preferred or assumed human relationships? (*face systems*)

The C–B–S style, which is so widely valued in professional communication as well as in academic communication and in so many other systems of discourse in contemporary society, is seen clearly in such forms of discourse as the essay, the press release, the newspaper article, the sales presentation, the job interview, as well as in many other genres of professional communication. In itself we would not say that the C–B–S style is a system of discourse; we would say that it represents the style of the preferred forms of discourse within a larger system which we will call the Utilitarian discourse system.

Ideology of the Utilitarian discourse system

Western writers did not always prefer clarity, brevity, and sincerity (the C–B–S style of the essay) in their writing and speaking. In the Middle Ages, for example, the preferred mode of presenting one's ideas was very inductive. One was to begin with all of the objections which might be raised to the position one planned to take; then, one moved on to the arguments in favor of the position; finally, one arrived at a statement of one's conclusion.

The historical question is this: when did we come to assume that communication should be analytic, original, move rapidly forward, have a unified thesis, avoid unnecessary digressions, and, in essence present only the most essential information? Most likely this preference for the C–B–S style began by the seventeenth century, and the Royal Society was most likely the leader. In 1667 Thomas Sprat, Bishop of Rochester, in writing his *History of the Royal Society*, commented on the approach to language taken by the Royal Society. He wrote,

> They have therefore been more rigorous in putting in Execution the only Remedy, that can be found for this *Extravagance*; and that has been a constant Resolution, to reject all the Amplifications, Digressions, and Swellings of Style; to return back to the primitive Purity and Shortness, when Men deliver'd so many *Things*, almost in an equal Number of *Words*. They have exacted from all their Members, a close, naked, natural way of Speaking; positive Expressions, clear Senses; a native Easiness; bringing all Things as near the mathematicall Plainness as they can; and preferring the Language of Artizans, Countrymen, and Merchants, before that of Wits, or Scholars (quoted in Kenner, 1987:117).

It seems clear enough that the preferred C–B–S style, or, as Sprat puts it, "close," "naked," and "natural" style, which is put forward in so many textbooks on business communication, is a style taken on quite self-consciously by the Royal Society as the preferred style for scientific deliberations. As science and technology have risen in the west to their current central position, business has risen together with them, and this preferred style has been carried with it into near total dominance in our thinking about effective communication. The businessman who urges the style of five Ws and one H is, without knowing it, giving a twentieth-century version of Thomas Sprat's warning against extravagance.

The Enlightenment: reason and freedom

The Enlightenment or the Age of Reason reached its high point in the eighteenth century. This movement arose as part of the reorganization of European thinking as the authority of the Christian church was declining. The central philosophers in their essays emphasized the rise of science as the new authority, and in doing so set the course for western and world development for the next two or three centuries.

We are certainly still under the primary influence of these writers. For example, Adam Smith's (1723–90) *An Inquiry into the Nature and Causes of the Wealth of Nations* (1990) laid the foundations for the modern concept of capitalist economic exchange. This book introduced the notion of the free exchange of goods within an open, unregulated market, which is still being argued in reference to such entities as the European Union (as well as NAFTA, ASEAN, and a number of others).

The concept of free economic market exchange cannot be separated from the concept of government by laws, which was first clearly articulated in the writings of Montesquieu (1689–1755). His book, *The Spirit of Laws* (1990), laid the cornerstone for the major state papers on which the new American government was founded: the Declaration of Independence, the Articles of Confederation, and the Constitution (*American State Papers*, 1990).

Immanuel Kant (1724–1804) was also a major figure in the development of Enlightenment thought. One essay, "The Science of Right" (1990), laid down the principles upon which the idea of intellectual copyright was established. In international negotiations today, this concept remains a hot point of dispute between nations.

All of these writings were based on the flowering of scientific and philosophical writing of the immediately preceding period. Sir Isaac Newton (1642–1727), for example, had laid down the principles for a completely rational concept of the physical universe. In Newton's science, the physical universe could be explained entirely through the application of physical laws and mathematics.

Writers such as John Locke (1632–1704) extended such studies of the physical universe by placing human beings within that universe as equally physical entities. For example, Locke (1990) described the human being as being born a *tabula rasa*, a blank slate, upon which the experience of the universe wrote a life.

This concept of the human being was a radical departure from the concept of the person upheld until that time in Europe, and, indeed, throughout most of the world. Before this, and elsewhere, humans have been thought of as deeply connected participants in a larger social and spiritual structure of society. The new Enlightenment concept of the human was to isolate each person as a completely independent, rational, autonomous entity who moves about through society according to society's laws, just like Newtonian physical entities move about according to natural laws. Newton argued that the universe could be understood entirely with just two concepts, entities and natural laws (including, of course, mathematics). Locke, Smith, Montesquieu, Kant, and the other Enlightenment thinkers reduced humans and human life to the same simple principles: isolated entities and social laws.

In light of this philosophical movement, it is not surprising that they would promote the C–B–S style as the most appropriate means of communicating, as they were modeling all human communication on the pattern of scientific writing.

Kant's view of the "public" writer

Humans are not as easily separated from their environments as elements, compounds, molecules, and atoms are, of course, and this posed a problem for Immanuel Kant. In an essay entitled, "What is Enlightenment? (1983)," he took up the problem of what it means for a person to have freedom of expression. His view was that a writer had freedom of expression only in his (or her) public self. By that Kant meant what we have called the implied writer. It is the implied writer who is the public person and who has freedom of expression, not the real writer.

In his essay on "The Science of Right," Kant (1990) then describes a written discourse as a kind of intellectual property which is owned by the original author (real writer), much in the same way as money is used as an abstract form of exchange. A real writer through an implied writer creates a discourse, which can then be sold in the form of a book. The physical book is not the discourse any more than the physical object of the bank note is the wealth it represents.

We believe it is important to understand that the connection between the concepts and language of financial exchange and the concepts and language of communication is not an accidental one. It is not just a matter of convenience that the C–B–S style has come to symbolize the communication of international business exchanges. Both the communication style and the economic principles were laid out together at the same time in history, the eighteenth and nineteenth centuries, and often by the same writers. They are products of exactly the same psychology, philosophy, and worldview.

Bentham and Mill's Utilitarianism

Jeremy Bentham (1748–1832) is an enigmatic figure in western thought. His writings were extremely influential in the development of contemporary western economic, political, and social life, and yet his name is not widely known outside the circle of historians and scholars who have studied the roots of modern politics and economics.

Bentham coined the term "Utilitarianism," which was what he called his philosophy. Utilitarianism grew out of the Enlightenment, and simplified even that rather oversimplified line of thought. Bentham's problem was to find an ethical principle to replace the idea that good was defined by the authority of God or the Christian church. Bentham argued that we should consider good whatever followed the "principle of utility":

> By utility is meant that property in any object, whereby it tends to produce benefit, advantage, pleasure, good, or happiness, (all this in the present case comes to the same thing) or (what comes again to the same thing) to prevent the happening of mischief, pain, evil, or unhappiness to the party whose interest is considered (Bentham, 1962:34).

This led to the most basic ideological concept of Utilitarianism – that something was good if it produced happiness, and therefore, the best society was the one which provided the greatest happiness for the greatest number of people.

This Utilitarianism was further developed by John Stuart Mill (1806–73) and has become the philosophical basis of the core of contemporary western social and economic life. While most people might never have heard of Jeremy Bentham or of J. S. Mill, if one asks an American, for example, what the purpose of government or of society is, one will hear a statement which embodies almost the exact words of these two political philosophers.

A second central concept of Utilitarianism is that progress is the goal of society. Of course, by "progress" is meant an ever increasing amount of happiness and wealth. As J. S. Mill understood it, progress was to be achieved by overcoming tradition and through the exercise of individual freedom of expression.

> The despotism of custom is everywhere the standing hindrance to human advancement, being in unceasing antagonism to that disposition to aim at something better than customary, which is called, according to circumstances, the spirit of liberty, or that of progress or improvement. The spirit of improvement is not always a spirit of liberty . . . but the only unfailing and permanent source of improvement is liberty, since by it there are as many possible independent centres of improvement as there are individuals. The progressive principle, however, in either shape, whether as the love of liberty or of improvement, is antagonistic to the sway of Custom, involving at least emancipation from that yoke; and the contest between the two constitutes the chief interest of the history of mankind. The greater part of the world has, properly speaking, no history, because the despotism of Custom is complete.

This is the case over the whole East. Custom is there, in all things, the final appeal; justice and right mean conformity to custom; the argument of custom no one, unless some tyrant intoxicated with power thinks of resisting. And we see the result. Those nations must once have had originality; they did not start out of the ground populous, lettered, and versed in many of the arts of life; they made themselves all this, and were then the greatest and most powerful nations of the world. What are they now? The subjects or dependents of tribes whose forefathers wandered in the forests when theirs had magnificent palaces and gorgeous temples, but over whom custom exercised only a divided rule with liberty and progress.

A people, it appears, may be progressive for a certain length of time, and then stop: when does it stop? When it ceases to possess individuality (J. S. Mill, 1990:300–1).

For the Utilitarians, free individual expression was the keystone of the development of their ideology. This freedom of expression was based on the third principle of Utilitarianism – their idea that the individual, not the community, was the basis of society. "The community is a fictitious *body*, composed of the individual persons who are considered as constituting as it were its *members*. The interest of the community then is, what? – the sum of the interest of the several members who compose it" (Bentham, 1962:35).

Of course, basing their concept of society on the individual, the Utilitarians needed to develop their concept of the individual. The fourth principle in this system is that humans are defined as logical, rational, economic entities. By that they meant that they assumed that humans would always choose their own greater happiness and wealth over all other considerations and that social action could be analyzed in terms of the value placed on goods and on human actions.

This emphasis on rational, individualistic, economic behavior led the Utilitarians to believe that technology and invention would be the key to the greatest happiness of the greatest number, as the fifth principle. The newly developing sciences as well as the discoveries in other parts of the world of major sources of raw resources for exploitation led them to believe that the society they imagined could actually be achieved.

From this set of ideological principles, it is not difficult to see that within the Utilitarian ideology, the creative, inventive (wealth-producing) individuals are thought of as the most valuable for society, since such individuals produce most of what the ideology considers its most valuable assets. This sixth principle provides justification for the sometimes greatly exaggerated social and economic differences found between members of what is otherwise supposed to be an egalitarian society.

Finally, one aspect of Benthamism or Utilitarianism which is not well known today is its emphasis on numerical calculations. The problem Bentham faced was how he could determine the greatest happiness for the greatest number of people. He developed what he called the "Felicific Calculus" or the "Hedonistic Calculus," which was a system by which he believed every pleasure and every pain could be given a numerical value and then, through a complex calculus, the relative value of all human actions could be detemined.

In this Felicific Calculus, everything, he imagined, could be given a numerical value, from the value of dinner to the value of parliament. Then if your arithmetic was good enough you could just run the calculations and find out what decision to take. This calculus was rejected by others as quite an impractical suggestion. At the time Bentham and Mill developed their Utilitarian thinking, there were no computers for them to use in doing their numbers. Nevertheless, methods were developed, which look very crude today, for taking massive counts of large populations of people. The idea of the census developed straight out of Utilitarianism, for example, and since the modern computer arose out of census taking, it is no stretch of the historical fabric to say that contemporary uses of computers for such functions as public opinion polls and market surveys are a direct realization of the thinking and the Utilitarian philosophy of Jeremy Bentham. This emphasis on quantitative measures of value forms the seventh principle of the Utilitarian ideology.

We can summarize the ideological position of the Utilitarian discourse system as follows:

1   "Good" is defined as what will give the greatest happiness for the greatest number.
2   Progress (toward greater happiness, wealth, and individuality) is the goal of society.
3   The free and equal individual is the basis of society.
4   Humans are defined as rational, economic entities.
5   Technology and invention are the sources of societal wealth.
6   Creative, inventive (wealth-producing) individuals are the most valuable for society.
7   Quantitative measures such as statistics are the best means of determining values.

Socialization in the Utilitarian discourse system

The question we want to discuss now is this: how does one become a member of the Utilitarian discourse system?

Later we will take up the question of education and socialization in more detail. Here it will be sufficient to point out that these two words are most often used to indicate a contrast between formal means of schooling through socially approved and controlled institutions (education) and informal means of bringing members into full participation in society (socialization or enculturation). In Europe, at least, this distinction between education and socialization arose in large part through the activities of the early Utilitarians.

J. S. Mill was one of the first and strongest advocates of the concept of government-supported and controlled public schooling. Up until that time, education for most people consisted of various forms of apprenticeships. Formal education in schools and universities was the privilege of a very few members of European society. For the rest, one picked up the trade of one's father or uncles, or mother or aunts, or one carried on the family farming. It was clear to the Utilitarians that the development of industrial society, upon which they pinned their hopes for the development of greater wealth for all, depended upon producing workers for those factories. These workers would have to be weaned away from their trades and apprenticeships and schooled in the skills and knowledge of the newly developing technologies.

The solution hit upon in both Europe and in North America was to develop government-controlled public schooling. In the period since about 1850, public schools have become the standard throughout all of the world dominated by Utilitarian thinking. These schools have two essential components – they are compulsory on the one hand and they are free (of cost) on the other. That is to say, it has come to be both a privilege and a legal requirement for students to attend these schools. Formal education has become a formal requirement of the Utilitarian discourse system.

This brings up two points regarding socialization: the value placed by the Utilitarians upon socialization (as opposed to education) and the nature of education (formal school) itself. In order to establish the concept of public schooling, formal education was given an exaggerated valuation while at the same time there was a powerful devaluation of non-formal types of learning. Within the Utilitarian discourse system, education through formal procedures has been considered the only really acceptable form of learning.

As to the second point, education in schools has taken over wholesale the ideological system of the Utilitarians. The seven principles we have given above could as easily be taken as the governing principles of schools throughout the European-based societies of the world. The emphasis in these schools is on the inventive and creative development of individuals who are seen to be in competition with each other. The goal is for them to become "productive members of society." There is an ever increasing emphasis on experimentation, rationalism, and technology. And evaluation is primarily based upon numbers (grades or marks). While there are, of course, many local variations upon these themes, the reader will certainly recognize that these Utilitarian themes have been used in the development of most public schools throughout the industrialized world.

Along with these aspects of public schooling has come an emphasis on the use of numerical or quantitative measures in all processes of enculturation.

Babies are weighed, measured for length, counted in multiple categories, given numbers, and registered in official archives upon birth, and through their early lives careful numbers are kept against which their development is determined to be "normal" or "abnormal." In 1904 Alfred Binet developed his now famous IQ test, which was further developed at Stanford by Terman as the Stanford–Binet IQ. This test or some variation is widely used to assess the creative or intelligence potential of virtually each individual who falls within the purview of the Utilitarian system.

In keeping with this view of the individual in Utilitarian society has developed the concept of the person as an empty container of the knowledge of society. John Locke first spoke of the person as a blank slate upon which experience writes his or her character or as an empty cabinet which experience comes to furnish. By the late nineteenth century, a child's mind had come to be taken as an empty container which it was the purpose of society and of schools to fill. The very influential book by the psychologist G. Stanley Hall (1844–1924) carried the title *The Contents of Children's Minds* (1883).

Along with the development of public schooling came a major shift in patterns of socialization within the home. The historian Robert Sunley (1955) has argued that there was a major shift in American and English societies from considering the father to be the moral authority for the family to the mother's taking on that role. The reasons underlying this shift in role had to do with the fact that men were increasingly becoming involved in business and other Utilitarian activities outside of the home. Ironically, these outside activities were seen as at least amoral if not immoral and, therefore, damaging to the moral authority of the men who engaged in them. As it was assumed that women would remain isolated within the confines of the household, it was inferred that their moral purity would remain unsullied.

Whatever the reality of these assumptions, the major shift is a social fact to be considered when we think of socialization into the Utilitarian discourse system. This discourse system has seen its appropriate place to be outside of the home, in public situations, that is, within business and governmental contexts, and also to be largely the domain of men. As we will see, this polarization of inside and outside (the home) and of women's and men's roles is only an ideological position, not the reality. Furthermore, it seems clear that this ideological system is now undergoing rapid change. Here our purpose is to point out the historical roots which are major factors in contemporary conflicts in interdiscourse system communications.

Forms of discourse in the Utilitarian discourse system

The question which we are now concerned with answering is this: what are the preferred forms of communication or discourse within the Utilitarian discourse system? In chapter 5 we pointed out that the essay and the press release manifest typical characteristics of the Utilitarian discourse system. Earlier in this chapter we have introduced the idea of the C–B–S style of discourse. Events (or genres), such as phone conversations, credit memos, management reports, or minutes to meetings, are all quite characteristic forms of discourse within the Utilitarian discourse system. In chapter 3 we presented the idea of face strategies and in chapter 5 we argued that the deductive rhetorical strategy might well be considered a face strategy of involvement which is characteristic of the same system.

When we use the term "forms of discourse" we mean to include all of the different ways in which discourse might take form – face strategies, specific genres and events, or preferred styles and registers. In chapter 8 we will go into more detail about the forms of discourse which might be preferred in other discourse systems. Here our purpose is to outline the six main characteristics of the forms of discourse preferred within the Utilitarian discourse system.

These forms have become the preferred ones for the expression of the ideology of that system we have discussed above. Furthermore, these forms – the essay is the most typical example – are also among the main ways in which new members are socialized into this discourse system. Naturally, not all of the characteristics which we will give below will be found to the same extent in each of the forms one might analyze. These are the ideals for discourse by which the system conveys its ideology, and they will be found to a greater or lesser extent in most instances of Utilitarian discourse. The six characteristics are that the discourse is:

1 anti-rhetorical;
2 positivist-empirical;
3 deductive;
4 individualistic;
5 egalitarian;
6 public (institutionally sanctioned).

Anti-rhetorical

We have quoted Thomas Sprat, Bishop of Rochester, in our introduction to this section. The Royal Society took a strongly anti-rhetorical position. By that we mean two things: speakers and writers tried to avoid obvious uses of rhetoric, and a new rhetoric developed in which the appearance of using no rhetoric began to develop. The dictum that one should use five Ws and one H is a rhetorical strategy of conciseness, but is disguised as saying not to use anything but fact.

Jeremy Bentham himself was a strong opponent of the use of such rhetorical figures as metaphor. He wrote, "Systems which attempt to question it [the principle of utility], deal in sounds instead of senses, in caprice instead of reason, in darkness instead of light. But enough of metaphor and declamation: it is not by such means that moral science is to be improved" (1988: 34). Quite typically for Bentham, after using a series of metaphors – "sounds," "senses," "caprice," "reason," "darkness," "light" – he then turns and denounces the use of metaphor and declamation.

In a study of academic writing, which we would consider a sub-system of the Utilitarian discourse system, Swales (1990) has pointed to this apparent non-rhetoric of Utilitarian discourse forms. "The art of the matter, as far as the creation of facts is concerned, lies in deceiving the reader into thinking that there is no rhetoric . . . that the facts are indeed speaking for themselves" (p. 112). A bit later in his discussion of research writing he writes: "We find the research article, this key product of the knowledge-manufacturing industry, to be a remarkable phenomenon, so cunningly engineered by rhetorical machining that it somehow still gives an *impression* of being but a simple description of relatively untransmuted raw material" (p. 125). The essence of this anti-rhetorical characteristic is that Utilitarian discourse forms should appear to give nothing but information, that they should appear to be making no attempt to influence the listener or the reader except through his or her exercise of rational judgement. This anti-rhetorical feature reflects ideological opposition to the use of authority while at the same time emphasizing the rational, scientific nature of human discourse.

Positivist-empirical

Utilitarian discourse considers scientific thinking to be the best model for all human thinking and for human discourse. Therefore, as its second characteristic, it emphasizes the features of positivist-empirical psychology while at the same time it plays down the contingent factors of human relationships. When the scientific community began to establish its procedures and practices in the sixteenth and seventeenth centuries, one problem the early scientists faced was how they might "prove" their findings to others. Traditionally, proof was based upon quoting authorities such as Aristotle, but the new scientists insisted that one should reject any evidence but the empirical and positive evidence of his (or her – though women were expected to play little or no role in science during this period) own observations.

Swales (1990) describes the problem faced by Robert Boyle. His experiments with gases required elaborate pumps and other equipment which could not be afforded by very many other observers. Therefore, it was unlikely that anybody else would be able to observe and replicate the experiments which he believed demonstrated the truth of his scientific findings. His solution was to donate the equipment to the Royal Society and to carry out his experiments there under the close observation of his scientific colleagues. He then asked them to sign a roster saying that they had agreed with him in his observations.

At the beginning, then, it was assumed that anybody who underwent the same procedures would find the same results, because it was believed that all reality was simply the interaction of the physical universe and universal laws of logic. It was assumed that the role of discourse was to simply state these observations and these results as clearly and directly as possible.

Nevertheless, it was only a short time before the practice which came to be called *virtual witnessing* came into play. In the first place, scientists had cut short the step of having separate individual researchers do the research themselves. Now scientists of the Royal Society and others cut short the step of conducting their experiments before other witnesses. They felt that if they simply narrated the experiment clearly, the logic of the narration would lead inevitably to the same conclusions one would reach if one had gone to the trouble of conducting the experiment oneself. Thus it began to develop that, in fact, the C–B–S style of discourse came to replace actual scientific experimentation.

The important aspect of this positivist-empirical characteristic is that the authority of the person or of personal relationships is played down and is replaced by the authority of the text itself. One believes what is said not because of who is saying or writing it but because of how the text is written. The positivist-empirical text came to replace the authority of even the scientist.

Deductive

We have said above, in chapter 5, that the use of deductive and inductive strategies for the introduction of topics depends on factors having to do with the relationships between the speaker and the listener, or between the writer (implied) and the reader (implied). When no relationship needs to be established or when the person speaking (or writing) does not need to call upon authority or does not need to establish his or her own authority, then a deductive strategy will be used.

Utilitarian discourse is fundamentally anti-authoritarian as well as anti-rhetorical. As a result, the relationships between members of this discourse system are played down and the text of the discourse itself comes to have primary authority, as we have argued just above. The result of this third characteristic of Utilitarian discourse forms is that there is an overall preference for the deductive rhetorical strategy for the introduction of topics.

There is something anti-rhetorical in this in that the deductive strategy is used whether or not relationships are really an issue. In other words, utilitarian discourse prefers to act as if human relationships were of little or no consequence. The use of the deductive rhetorical strategy is one effective way in which this apparent (though not necessarily real) situation can be communicated.

Individualistic

The fourth characteristic of Utilitarian discourse derives from the emphasis in Utilitarian ideology on the creative individual. J. S. Mill wrote that, "Over himself, over his own body and mind, the individual is sovereign" (1990:271). A major aspect of this sovereignty of the individual is that it should be demonstrated in discourse. That is, speakers and writers should avoid set phrases, metaphors, proverbs, and clichés, and strive to make their statements fresh and original. Obelkevich (1987) described this aspect of Utilitarian thought as a reaction to "a culture in which intertextuality was rampant; in which the notion of plagiarism (and the word itself) did not yet exist; in which there was no author's copyright, no property in ideas and no footnotes" (1987:56). The point we want to make here is that there are two sides to this individuality and creativity: on the one hand there is the insistence that communications must be free – that an individual may say whatever he or she wants – on the other hand there is the dictum that individual expression must be original. That is, not only may one be free from the restrictions of social discourse, one must continually show oneself to be free by producing original phrasings and statements.

Egalitarian

One consequence of the ideological position that individuals are the basis of society is that these individuals must be considered to be equal to each other. As we will discuss below under the topic of face systems, this egalitarianism of Utilitarian discourse is not applied to all human beings but only to "those capable of being improved by free and equal discussion" (Mill 1990:271–2). That is to say, this egalitarianism is applied only to members of the Utilitarian discourse system.

This fifth characteristic of Utilitarian discourse we have discussed in chapter 5. While actual speakers and hearers or writers and readers may have rather unequal positions in their organizations or in society, from the point of view of discourse, they are expected to take the stance of equals. In writing an essay, the implied writer and the implied reader are assumed to be equals. We will take up this point below in our discussion of the face systems of the Utilitarian discourse system.

Public (institutionally sanctioned)

Finally, the sixth characteristic of Utilitarian discourse forms is that they are largely seen as forms of public discourse. Above, we mentioned that Immanuel Kant argued that the term "public" discourse should be applied to those forms of discourse such as philosophical essays which are published. In his mind, freedom of speech should apply only to ideas put forward in such "public" discourse. J. S. Mill also put forward the same restriction on where the concept of freedom of speech should apply. In his essay *On Liberty* he wrote:

No one pretends that actions should be as free as opinions. On the contrary, even opinions lose their immunity when the circumstances in which they are expressed are such as to constitute their expression a positive instigation to some mischievous act. An opinion that corn-dealers are starvers of the poor, or that private property is robbery, ought to be unmolested when simply circulated through the press, but may justly incur punishment when delivered orally to an excited mob assembled before the house of a corn-dealer, or when handed about among the same mob in the form of a placard. Acts, of whatever kind, which, without justifiable cause, do harm to others, may be, and in the more important cases absolutely require to be, controlled by the unfavourable sentiments, and, when needful, by the active interference of mankind. The liberty of the individual must be thus far limited; he must not make himself a nuisance to other people (1990:293).

The consequence of this sixth characteristic of Utilitarian discourse is that constant checks have been placed upon discourse, so that only institutionally authorized discourses may get through the filter and become "free speech." Letters to the editor of a newspaper are screened by the editorial staff before publishing, and then they are only published in edited form. Academic articles and books are screened through a process of peer review so that only articles which meet the standards of colleagues will come to actual publication. Most institutions from schools to supermarkets have some process by which any notices which are to be put up for display are first screened by some authority for appropriateness.

This characteristic of the Utilitarian discourse system is often ignored in the enthusiasm for talking about freedom of speech. It should be borne in mind, however, that from the beginning in the seventeenth century down to the present, freedom of speech has meant and continues to mean not absolute freedom for any individual to speak or write to the public at large. It has meant that any individual has the right to submit his or her communications to the scrutiny of this very large array of institutionalized boards and review panels, and that where those communications are judged to meet the standards for "public discourse" they are then allowed to pass on to the public.

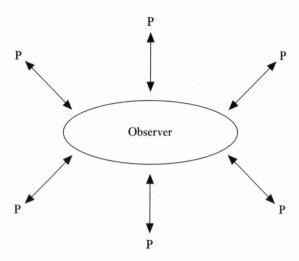

Figure 6.2   Bentham's Panopticon.

The Panopticon of Bentham

Now that we have dealt with the six characteristics of Utilitarian discourse forms, there still remains one final note on Jeremy Bentham that cannot be left out of this discussion. Bentham was excessively concerned with efficiency, including efficiency in settings for discourses of the broadest kind. In one case he turned his attention to the structure of buildings, such as the newly developing factories and the rapidly increasing number of prisons. He invented the concept of what he called the Panopticon. This was a structure in which one person could survey and control the work or activities of many individuals. In his ideal Panopticon the observer would be located in the center and surrounded by a ring of cells in which each individual could be seen by the observer in the center, but no individual could see the person on either side. Each individual's vision was limited to the observer in the centre, as indicated in figure 6.2. "P" in the figure represents the prisoner in Bentham's original Panopticon. In more recent configurations such as the lecture, however, it might be understood to represent the participants.

In actual usage, the most common form of Panopticon we know as the lecture theater. The speaker is elevated and stands alone where he or she can easily see everyone else in the room, and they can see him or her easily, but none of the participants has any communication except with those on either side. That structure is illustrated in figure 6.3.

Anyone who has taken a class in a school knows this structure. Although

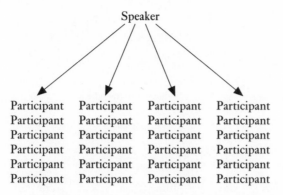

Figure 6.3 The lecture theater Panopticon.

in recent years it has been modified, with circles, centers, and other small-group distributions of students, the Panopticon remains the favorite structure for larger lectures, for after-dinner speeches, for sales presentations, for political conventions, and for so many other public and professional events that we hardly see that there is anything unusual or historical about it.

Our point in bringing up the Panopticon here is to show that even in the layout of the participant structures of communicative events, Utilitarianism has placed its stamp upon contemporary life. In every case, it is the same form. Communication should be highly focused with one or a few participants controlling the activities of the many; topics should be introduced deductively in a style that is clear, brief, and sincere; and all participants should participate as "public" entities subject to the constraints of being implied, but not real, communicators. In other words, one should in all communications be able and willing to take on this highly historical and highly constrained communicative role.

Face systems in the Utilitarian discourse system

We have already pointed out that the predominating ideology of the Utilitarian discourse system is one of individualism and egalitarianism. Now we need to clarify that while that ideology is widely expressed and practiced, nevertheless, there are two major exceptions which must be understood. In the first place, a distinction needs to be made between communications within the Utilitarian discourse system – that is, among members – and communications outside of the discourse system – communication with non-members. Then, with that consideration in mind, we will need to understand that within the discourse system there is also a major distinction

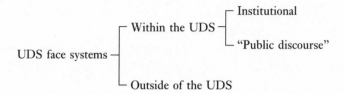

UDS = Utilitarian discourse system

Figure 6.4   Utilitarian discourse face systems.

between communications in "public discourse" and communications within institutional or bureaucratic structures. These multiple systems may be sketched as in figure 6.4.

Internal face systems: liberté, égalité, fraternité

There were two political revolutions which arose out of Enlightenment philosophy: the French Revolution and the American Revolution. Without going into these histories in detail, we only want to point out that the motto of the French Revolution, *"liberté, égalité, fraternité,"* captures the essence of the concept of the person as well as the concept of interpersonal face relationships. As it was essential for the Enlightenment and the Utilitarian concept of society for each individual to make free choices, it was also essential for each member to be considered an equal. The greatest happiness could not be achieved for the greatest number if some members of society were allowed to have a somewhat larger portion of happiness than others.

The American Constitution also established the legal basis for social equality, though, of course, it should be clear to the reader that two hundred years later the details of this social equality remain to be worked out in practice. The point we are making is that the Enlightenment established that a hierarchical system of social relationships was not consistent with its philosophy of free choice and rational, individual decision making. Over the two hundred years since then, this philosophical ideal has been transformed into a popular concept of universal symmetrical solidarity. In the most extreme forms, such as in various sub-cultures in North America and elsewhere, it is now taken as a major point of social development to eliminate any and all suggestions of hierarchy in any interpersonal or social relationships.

In the two hundred years since it first began to be developed, the Utilitarian discourse system has come to the position of the central and dominating discourse system throughout the western world. The forms of discourse preferred by this discourse system are the deductive rhetorical strategies of beginning a discourse with one's topic, and the use throughout of politeness strategies of involvement. The essay is the prototypical discourse form in academic or intellectual circles, and the press release or the business letter are the corresponding forms in general professional written communication. In spoken communication the C–B–S style is the preferred style. Say what you have to say, nothing more; you might lose money.

Throughout the culture, from talk shows on television to press conferences with political leaders, there is a reinforced emphasis on direct talk, on avoiding elaboration and extravagance, and on promoting close, egalitarian social relationships. The Utilitarian discourse system has little tolerance for hierarchical social relationships, and even where they exist, it is assumed they should be set aside in contexts of public communication. Within this system, everyone from presidents and prime ministers to corporation executives is expected to seem in their public communications just like "one of us". There is a great emphasis on popular appeal and commonness, even where these figures are known to live and move in social and financial circles to which the ordinary person would never have any form of access.

"Public" discourse

We have already pointed out that such egalitarian discourse is really only considered appropriate within the Utilitarian discourse system when, as J. S. Mill has said, one does not "make himself a nuisance to other people" (1990:293). In other words, the face system of symmetrical solidarity is taken to be appropriate only within contexts of socially and institutionally sanctioned public discourse. This, of course, is a much more narrowly restricted domain than it might at first have seemed to be. It is certainly a much narrower domain than is usually spoken of when people argue that their right to freedom of speech has been infringed.

Institutional discourse

The institutions of the Utilitarian discourse system are many. They include most western governments, virtually all western and international corporations, schools, private manufacturing and service businesses, professional associations, and so on. Communication within such institutions has long been established to be hierarchical – the face system we called asymmetrical or hierarchical in chapter 5. Virtually all such institutions have an organizational chart which shows the hierarchy of position, power, and decision making. From the time of Taylor's *Scientific Management* (1911) with its "span of control," it has widely been accepted that the most efficient organization or institution will operate along such hierarchical lines of the flow of power and communication.

Of course, there are many contemporary advocates of institutional re-organization who have taken issue with just these hierarchical concepts of organizational structure and communication. We feel, nonetheless, that it will be some time yet before any internal face system other than this asymmetrical or hierarchical system will come to dominate in the institutions of the Utilitarian discourse system.

What this means, of course, is that there is a dual system for corporate communications. There will be those for internal consumption, which will largely display patterns of involvement strategies downward to lower echelons of the corporate structure, with some more limited amount of independence strategies communicated upward – mostly in the form of "feedback" to higher-level directives. There will be another system of communication for outward consumption – for what we have called "public discourse." In those communications a stance of egalitarian communication or symmetrical solidarity will be displayed.

Outside discourse

This would be a good place to point out that J. S. Mill was not simply a political philosopher. He, like his father before him, was an officer of the British East India Company and, in his view, the major role of Europeans in relationships with the colonies was one of exploitation of resources on the one hand and of justified despotic leadership on the other. In this, J. S. Mill expressed the belief widely held within the Utilitarian discourse system that none of its principles of equality, individuality, freedom of expression, or rational thought need be applied to anyone who is not a member of the discourse system.

J. S. Mill put it as follows:

> Over himself, over his own body and mind, the individual is sovereign.
>
> It is, perhaps, hardly necessary to say that this doctrine is meant to apply only to human beings in the maturity of their faculties. We are not speaking of children, or of young persons below the age which the law may fix as that of manhood or womanhood. Those who are still in a state to require being taken care of by others, must be protected against their own actions as well as against external injury. For the same reason, we may leave out of consideration those backward states of society in which the race itself may be considered as in its nonage. The early difficulties in the way of spontaneous progress are so great, that there is seldom any choice of means for overcoming them; and a ruler full of the spirit of improvement is warranted in the use of any expedients that will attain an end, perhaps otherwise unattainable. Despotism is a legitimate mode of government in dealing with barbarians, provided the end be their improvement, and the means justified by actually effecting that end. Liberty, as a principle, has no application to any state of

things anterior to the time when mankind have become capable of being improved by free and equal discussion (1990:271–2).

This aspect of the Utilitarian discourse system recapitulates an old theme in western and other cultures in which members are treated as real, normal, and worthy of "civilized" treatment, and non-members are treated as "ethnics," "barbarians," and "pagans." In more recent terminology, members of the Utilitarian discourse system are judged to be "progressive," "democratic," "free," and "developed," and non-members are judged to lack these assumed qualities. One has only to consult the 1948 Universal Declaration of Human Rights to see that the ideology of the Utilitarian discourse system has been taken for granted as the natural and rightful state of human life on earth, thought it includes many aspects which had never or rarely been observed in human culture before the seventeenth century, except by the aristocracy, such as freedom of individuals, the right to own property, or the right to travel individually and freely throughout the world.

This is not a book on political philosophy and so it is not the place to develop further the theme of whether or not the ideology of the Utilitarian discourse system is or is not an adequate expression of universal human conditions and rights. The point we are making is that for members of this discourse system, the discourse system prescribes a face system of asymmetry and hierarchy with any and all non-members. The Utilitarian discourse system, while advocating equal rights for all members, quite specifically denies those rights of equality to those who do not show themselves willing to participate in the ideology of this discourse system. This is a point first made in J. S. Mill's essay *On Liberty*, quoted above, it is reiterated in the Universal Declaration of Human Rights, and it continues to be a major issue, in international discussions of such issues as the protection of intellectual copyright and international free trade agreements.

Multiple Discourse Systems

We have gone through all of the components of the Utilitarian discourse system. The ideology of this discourse system, its system of socialization through public education, its preferred forms of discourse such as the C–B–S style, deductive rhetoric, and its emphasis on egalitarianism in public discourse, and hierarchy in institutional discourse as well as in discourse with non-members of this system, have come to be self-evident to participants in this system. Political leaders, business people, teachers, and parents have all come to take them as the most natural way to communicate.

For professional communicators, this Utilitarian discourse system has all the more become the system which is taken for granted as the natural way to communicate. It is probably safe to say that the majority of professional communicators (novelists, poets, and song writers may be set aside in this discussion, even though they are certainly professional communicators) work in fields related to business or government. Since international business and government circles have generally taken the political and economic philosophies of the Enlightenment as self-evident, they have also taken this discourse system as self-evident. Virtually any textbook one might pick up on professional communication (with this book as really only a partial exception) will emphasize this discourse system. The task of the textbook is taken to be just to explicate the system, make it clear how to participate in it, and show how to produce most successfully the spoken and written forms of the Utilitarian discourse system.

If there were really no other competing discourse system, there would be no problem with this approach. Unfortunately, there are two flaws in it: it does not completely match reality, and there are a number of other, different, and competing discourse systems. We began this chapter by noting that even within a textbook that insists that one should present only the essential information and present it directly, there is found the advice to write warmer business letters by including non-essential information. In other words, at best this discourse system is held out as an ideal, but not always practiced by members of the discourse system.

The second problem is that there are also many other discourse systems in day-to-day social communication. Communications in the home, communications between men and women, communications of members of different generations, and communications among members of many ethnic groups all show major departures from the patterns of this discourse system. The self-evident nature of a particular discourse system tends to make those other discourse systems invisible. Within a particular discourse system, communications which are framed within another discourse system simply appear faulty or inefficient. One either does not interpret them or one interprets them within the discourse system one is using oneself. This latter problem is the central one of intercultural communication. Intercultural communication is interdiscourse system communication. Communications which cross discourse system lines are subject to being either not heard or misinterpreted.

We have shifted our understanding of the word "discourse" as we have moved in our discussion from a very limited concept with a concentration on the basic forms used for cohesion, such as conjunctions, to a meaning which now seems to enclose a very large portion of society and culture. This is not just a personal whim of the authors, but reflects a shift in the topics which discourse analysts have studied in the past two decades.

At first the focus of discourse analysis was cohesion, mainly within and between clauses in sentences. As analysts began to see that it was difficult, if not impossible, to understand how discourse cohesion works through such a close lens, they began to take context into consideration in their studies. Of course, once context came into view, it was difficult to say just what should be included and what should not be included. One recent textbook on discourse has said that actually anything that humans communicate has been called discourse and analyzed by discourse analysts now at one time or another.

While we do not take a completely comprehensive view of discourse, which would include all of human communication, we do argue that the Utilitarian discourse system we have described in this chapter plays a major role in our ability to interpret (and fail to interpret) the communications of others. As we have argued in relation to the Utilitarian discourse system, such a system contains within a self-reinforcing circle a complete view of the person as a communicator, the person as a member of society, assumptions about proper socialization and educational practices, and norms governing the ways in which communications should be made. Perhaps we do not need to say that such a self-legitimating circle of discourse, because it constrains the ways in which things can be said, consequently also constrains what can be said.

We have spoken of the historical or philosophical basis of the Utilitarian discourse system as the Utilitarian ideology. The concept of ideology arises when a discourse system, such as the Utilitarian one, comes to assert itself as a complete communicative system. That is, it becomes ideological when it denies or devalues other forms of discourse or communication.

The word "ideology" is a difficult one to use, because it has been used in so many different ways in the two hundred years or so of its existence. We can summarize what we use it to mean as follows: a system of thinking, social practice, and communication (in other words a discourse system), which is used either to bring a particular group to social power or to legitimate their position of social power, especially when the discourse system itself is not the actual source of that group's power. In reference to the Utilitarian discourse system, we would call this discourse system an ideology, because the system takes itself as the cause of its worldwide political, economic, and communicative domination. In other words, within this discourse system it is widely believed that personal economic power can be achieved through direct, deductive expression of information. It is also believed that as a general system of communication, it is this system which has given free market capitalism the worldwide base it now enjoys.

We are neither economists nor political philosophers, and so it would be inappropriate for us to undertake here a discussion of the forces behind the rise of a worldwide market economy and the political structures of law that accompany this system. Any knowledgeable reader knows that this is an extremely complex subject which is, perhaps, not really completely understood by anybody. And that is our point: the actual reality of the international market economy and political structure is far too complex to be attributed to any single cause. One of the causes to which it cannot be attributed is the Utilitarian discourse system. Nevertheless, within that system it is widely believed that this discourse system is the key to success in this international political and economic system. We consider this an ideological position. It is a belief structure which is maintained in the face of a contrary and much more complex reality.

Within the Utilitarian discourse system, it is believed that this discourse system is the reason for its own ascendancy in the world. Nevertheless, within that same system it is widely said that such matters are far too complex to be reduced to such single-factor analyzes. The question then arises, "Why would such a discourse system promote itself so vigorously when it flies in the face of real-world analysis?" To get an answer to this, we need to look at the self-reinforcing aspect of a discourse system. Not only is a discourse system self-evident to its users, it is very difficult to break into from outside. A discourse system rejects communications and participants who do not play the full game.

Let us look at this from the point of view of education, since this book itself is being used in teaching students in programs of professional communication. We can imagine that one major reason someone would be studying in such a field is because he or she plans to work in the field of professional communication upon graduation. The Utilitarian ideology would say to you, "The Utilitarian discourse system is both the means of communication and the source of the success of the worldwide market economy. Learn this system and you will thereby become a member of this political and economic world." What this ideology does not say is that the actual sources of power do not lie within the discourse system as such, but within more traditional concepts of connections among significant players, inherited position, and the exploitation of non-member participants. To put this another way, the C–B–S style of this discourse system appears to favor telling you everything you need to know in a direct, straightforward way. This can easily lead one into thinking that this is actually what a member of this system is doing.

Another aspect of this discourse system is that it tells you that all you have to do to participate in it is to communicate clearly, briefly, and with sincerity; if you quite deductively say what you have to say and quit, you will have done all that is required of you to become a member. It appears to be quite transparently easy to join up. What this ideology does not say is that, in fact, it will be impossible to become a part-time or partial member of this discourse system. It will continue to demand complete allegiance. All other communications and views will be rejected as confused, illogical, or non-self-evident, the worst rejection. In other words, a discourse system such as this tends toward complete and internally consistent fields of discourse in which alien concepts are rejected.

This chapter has considered in some detail the characteristics of systems of discourse, with a focus on the Utilitarian discourse system. We have three reasons why we have gone into this particular discourse system in such detail: it is the system most frequently presented as self-evident to practitioners of professional communication, it is the self-proclaimed "standard" of international discourse, and it can be shown not to be all that it claims to be. The Utilitarian discourse system, in spite of its merits in commerce and in international affairs, represents a particular ideology and as such needs to be carefully analyzed, especially from the point of view of asking what is *not* self-evident within it.

This discussion has brought us to the problem which will be taken up in the following chapters: the problem of communication between different systems of discourse. Of course, there is no telling just how many such systems might be analyzed. As we will see, the Utilitarian discourse system, while it may dominate in business, government, academic, or organizational affairs, does not occupy the entire field of discourse, even within a single culture. One needs to look at different systems and sub-systems of discourse used across ethnic lines, across generational lines, between genders, and even between corporate or professional groups.

We take the position that successful intercultural professional communication depends on learning to move with both pragmatic effectiveness and cultural sensitivity across such lines, which divide discourse systems. At the beginning of this book, we said that successful communication relies on two factors: increasing shared knowledge and dealing with miscommunication. Pragmatic effectiveness in communication means participating as fully as possible in the discourse systems of those with whom one is wishing to communicate, while never taking their requirements as simply self-evident. Cultural sensitivity means being conscious of the ways in which one's own communications may be perceived and also accepting the fact that one is never likely to be considered a full member of most of the discourse systems in which one will participate.

7

What is Culture?
Intercultural Communication and Stereotyping

Two men meet on a plane from Tokyo to Hong Kong. Chu Hon-fai is a Hong Kong exporter who is returning from a business trip to Japan. Andrew Richardson is an American buyer on his first business trip to Hong Kong. It is a convenient meeting for them because Mr Chu's company sells some of the products Mr Richardson has come to Hong Kong to buy. After a bit of conversation they introduce themselves to each other.

Mr Richardson: By the way, I'm Andrew Richardson. My friends call me Andy. This is my business card.

Mr Chu: I'm David Chu. Pleased to meet you, Mr Richardson. This is my card.

Mr Richardson: No, no. Call me Andy. I think we'll be doing a lot of business together.

Mr Chu: Yes, I hope so.

Mr Richardson (reading Mr Chu's card): "Chu, Hon-fai." Hon-fai, I'll give you a call tomorrow as soon as I get settled at my hotel.

Mr Chu (smiling): Yes. I'll expect your call.

When these two men separate, they leave each other with very different impressions of the situation. Mr Richardson is very pleased to have made the acquaintance of Mr Chu and feels they have gotten off to a very good start. They have established their relationship on a first-name basis and Mr Chu's smile seemed to indicate that he will be friendly and easy to do business with. Mr Richardson is particularly pleased that he had treated Mr Chu with respect for his Chinese background by calling him Hon-fai rather than using the western name, David, which seemed to him an unnecessary imposition of western culture.

In contrast, Mr Chu feels quite uncomfortable with Mr Richardson. He feels it will be difficult to work with him, and that Mr Richardson might be rather insensitive to cultural differences. He is particularly bothered that Mr Richardson used his given name, Hon-fai, instead of either David or Mr Chu. It was this embarrassment which caused him to smile.

This short dialogue is, unfortunately, not so unusual in meetings between members of different cultures. There is a tendency in American business circles to prefer close, friendly, egalitarian relationships in business engagements. This system of symmetrical solidarity, which has its source in the Utilitarian discourse system, is often expressed in the use of given (or "first") names in business encounters. Mr Richardson feels most comfortable in being called Andy, and he would like to call Mr Chu by his first name. At the same time, he wishes to show consideration of the cultural differences between them by avoiding Mr Chu's western name, David. His solution to this cultural difference is to address Mr Chu by the given name he sees on the business card, Hon-fai.

Mr Chu, on the other hand, prefers an initial business relationship of symmetrical deference. He would feel more comfortable if they called each other Mr Chu and Mr Richardson. Nevertheless, when he was away at school in North America he learned that Americans feel awkward in a stable relationship of symmetrical deference. In other words, he found that they feel uncomfortable calling people Mr for any extended period of time. His solution was to adopt a western name. He chose David for use in such situations.

When Mr Richardson insists on using Mr Chu's Chinese given name, Hon-fai, Mr Chu feels uncomfortable. That name is rarely used by anyone, in fact. What Mr Richardson does not know is that Chinese have a rather complex structure of names which depends upon situations and relationships, which includes school names, intimate and family baby names, and even western names, each of which is used just by the people with whom a person has a certain relationship. Isolating just the given name, Hon-fai, is relatively unusual and to hear himself called this by a stranger makes Mr Chu feel quite uncomfortable. His reaction, which is also culturally conditioned, is to smile.

In this case there are two issues of intercultural communication we want to use to introduce our discussion of intercultural professional communication: one is the basic question of cultural differences, and the second is the problems which arise when people try to deal with cultural differences, but, like Mr Richardson, actually make matters worse in their attempts at cultural sensitivity.

The first problem is that there is a cultural difference in each of the participants' expectations of what face relationship should be used in such an initial business meeting. Mr Richardson prefers or expects symmetrical solidarity; he expects both of them to use involvement strategies of politeness, such as exchanging given names. The Hong Kong businessman,

Mr Chu, prefers symmetrical deference; he prefers for them both to use independence strategies of politeness, which in this case would mean that they would both call each other by family names and the title, "Mr." This is a cultural difference of considerable significance, because if Mr Richardson persists in using involvement strategies and Mr Chu persists in using independence strategies, a system of asymmetrical relationship will develop, with Mr Richardson in the superior position and Mr Chu in the subordinate position.

The second problem, paradoxically, is that both Mr Chu and Mr Richardson are concerned with being culturally sensitive. Mr Chu's experience in North America has given him the solution of adopting a western first name, David, so that someone such as Mr Richardson will feel more comfortable in addressing him. This also fits within the Chinese pattern of adopting new names as situations change, and so Mr Chu can be comfortable with the use of this western name. On the other hand, Mr Richardson is not familiar with this practice. To him it seems that using Mr Chu's name, David, is forcing a western definition upon Mr Chu, and he wants to acknowledge Mr Chu's Chinese cultural background. He imagines that a Chinese might feel a greater sense of cultural identity with his given name than he would with a name of convenience. He intends to show concern, friendliness, and at the same time respect for Mr Chu's Chinese culture, and so chooses the quite inappropriate first name, Hon-fai, to address Mr Chu.

The result of Mr Richardson's attempt at cultural sensitivity has actually made the situation worse than if he had just used the adopted western name, David. Unfortunately, Mr Richardson also is not aware that one means of expressing acute embarrassment for Mr Chu is to smile. While within North American culture there is consciousness of what might be called "nervous laughter," there is a general expectation that a smile can be taken as a direct expression of pleasure or satisfaction. Mr Richardson misinterprets Mr Chu's embarrassment as agreement or even pleasure at their first encounter, and as a result, he goes away from the encounter with no awareness of the extent to which he has complicated their initial introduction.

In the rest of this book, we will discuss the problems which arise when participants in a discourse are members of different cultures or discourse systems. We will also discuss problems which arise in trying to solve the first type of intercultural communication problem. As we have seen in the example above, it is often the case that one's attempts to be culturally sensitive actually produce a second level of problem, and in those cases it is often even more difficult to realize what sort of problem it is. It becomes hard to accept that one has tried one's best and ended up making things worse, and yet, this is what often happens. This is one of the reasons that very pragmatically oriented professionals sometimes go the mistaken extreme of saying that intercultural communication studies make no real contribution in international negotiations.

How Do We Define "Culture"?

The subject of "intercultural communication" is beset by a major problem, since there is really very little agreement on what people mean by the idea of culture in the first place. The word "culture" often brings up more problems than it solves. On the one hand, we want to talk about large groups of people and what they have in common, from their history and worldview to their language or languages or geographical location. There is some meaning to such constructs as "the Chinese," "the Japanese," "Americans," "British," or "Koreans," which is recognized by most, if not all, members of those groups. This common meaning often emphasizes what members of these groups have in common and at the same time plays down possible differences among members.

On the other hand, when we talk about such large cultural groups we want to avoid the problem of overgeneralization by using the construct "culture" where it does not apply, especially in the discussion of discourse in intercultural communication. From an interactional sociolinguistic perspective, discourse is communication between or among individuals. Cultures, however, are large, superordinate categories; they are not individuals. Cultures are a different level of logical analysis from the individual members of cultures. Cultures do not talk to each other; individuals do. In that sense, all communication is interpersonal communication and can never be intercultural communication. "Chinese culture" cannot talk to "Japanese culture" except through the discourse of individual Chinese and individual Japanese people.

The *Three Character Classic* (*San Zi Jing* – Southern Song Dynasty, AD 1127–1279; Xu Chuiyang, 1990) has been used in Confucian education in China, Japan, Korea, and Vietnam for as long as eight hundred years as a primer for the learning of both classical Chinese writing and Chinese ethical philosophy. It is based on Confucian classics such as *The Analects* of Confucius and *Mencius*, and therefore it embodies the ethical position taken by that school of thought that all humans are born good. It begins with the following words:

> *Ren zhi chu, xing ben shan*
> *Xing xiang jin, xi xiang yuan*

Man, by nature, is good; people's inborn characters are similar, but learning makes them different.

In contrast to this philosophical belief that humans are born with a naturally good character, we could cite a nineteenth-century New Englander who has been quoted by the historian Robert Sunley as saying that all children are born with an evil disposition: "No child has ever been known since the earliest period of the world, destitute of an evil disposition – however sweet it appears" (Sunley, 1955:159).

In a book on professional communication, we are not directly concerned with trying to decide which of these positions on the nature of humankind is the correct one. We will leave that to philosophers and religious writers to discuss. We want to raise a different kind of question, which has two parts: to what extent do individual Chinese or Americans, Koreans or British, Australians or Singaporeans personally represent their culture's beliefs, and do those beliefs make any significant difference in their ability to communicate professionally? For our purposes the main concern is to see how the ideological positions of cultures or of discourse systems become a factor in the interpersonal communication of members of one group with members of other groups.

In other words, for our purposes in this book, we will try to restrict our attention to just those aspects of culture which research has shown to be of direct significance in discourse between groups and which impinge directly upon the four elements of a discourse system – ideology, face systems, forms of discourse, and socialization. This does not mean that other aspects of culture are not interesting or very important. In this presentation we have tried to focus on what we think are the most crucial few dimensions of culture and on aspects of intercultural communication which have proven to be recurring problems in professional communication.

Before moving on, however, we want to mention that there is an intercultural problem in using the word "culture" itself. In English there are two normal uses of this word: high culture, and anthropological culture. The first meaning, high culture, focuses on intellectual and artistic achievements. One might speak of a city as having a great deal of culture because there were many art exhibits, concert performances, and public lectures. Or we might speak of a particular period in history, such as the Elizabethan period (1558–1603) of England, as a high point in English culture because of the great number of musicians and poets of that time whose works we still revere. The Tang period (AD 618–907) in Chinese history is generally regarded as a period of high culture as well.

In studies of intercultural communication, our concern is not with high culture, but with anthropological culture. When we use the word "culture" in its anthropological sense, we mean to say that culture is any of the customs, worldview, language, kinship system, social organization, and other taken-for-granted day-to-day practices of a people which set that group apart as a distinctive group. By using the anthropological sense of the word "culture," we mean to consider any aspect of the ideas, communications, or behaviors of a group of people which gives to them a distinctive identity and which is used to organize their internal sense of cohesion and membership.

Of course, this book is not a work in anthropology as such, and so we will make no attempt to provide a formal definition of the idea of culture or to make complete or rigorous cultural descriptions. As we have said above, our purpose is to single out among all of the many aspects of cultural description just those factors which have been clearly shown to affect intercultural communication. Among that research literature, which is in itself enormous and which continues to grow very rapidly in these days of increasingly frequent internationalization of world business and government, we have chosen to focus most directly on aspects of culture which our research has shown to affect communication between East Asians and westerners.

In the discussion which follows, then, we will be selecting out of the research literature on intercultural communication just those aspects of culture which we feel are most directly significant in order to understand how discourse systems are formed. In chapters 8–11 we will then turn to a discussion of several different discourse systems and the problems which arise in communication between members of those different systems.

Culture and Discourse Systems

The aspects of culture which are most significant for the understanding of systems of discourse and which have been shown to be major factors in intercultural communication are as follows:

1 *Ideology*: history and worldview, which includes:
   (a)   Beliefs, values, and religion
2 *Socialization*:
   (a)   Education, enculturation, acculturation
   (b)   Primary and secondary socialization
   (c)   Theories of the person and of learning
3 *Forms of discourse*:
   (a)   Functions of language:
      – Information and relationship
      – Negotiation and ratification
      – Group harmony and individual welfare
   (b)   Non-verbal communication:
      – Kinesics: the movement of our bodies
      – Proxemics: the use of space
      – Concept of time

4   *Face systems*: social organization, which includes:
    (a) Kinship
    (b) The concept of the self
    (c) Ingroup–outgroup relationships
    (d) *Gemeinschaft* and *Gesellschaft*

Ideology

The first major aspect of culture which we will consider is history and worldview. This is the most familiar way of looking at cultures, by studying their histories and the common worldviews which arise out of these histories. Perhaps the clearest difference between East Asian cultures (China, Korea, and Japan) and so-called western culture is that East Asians have a sense of having a long, continuous, and unified history, whereas westerners tend to emphasize the shorter-term political organizations which have arisen since the Renaissance. An American businessman visiting Korea for the first time, for example, is almost certain to be told that Koreans have a "5000-year history" and to be shown Namdaemun and Tongdaemun, the "new" gates to the city of Seoul, built before the United States was established as a country. The American, on the other hand, is likely to have little consciousness of his own cultural roots in the equally distant past of Mesopotamia. He is more likely to focus on the newness of his culture and the American emphasis on rapid change and the idea of progress.

Hong Kongers are likely to use their position on the boundary between the old culture of China and the newest technological aspects of international business culture as a convenient backdrop in taking pragmatic positions. When it is convenient to take a conservative stance in a business negotiation, for example, a Hong Kong businessman is perhaps more likely to emphasize the Chinese aspects of his cultural heritage. On the other hand, where an impression of quick change and progress is called for, he would rather stress the special status of Hong Kong as a member of the most progressive leading edge of Asian internationalization.

In either case, the consciousness of long, continuous history forms part of the worldview of most Asians. This is sometimes called upon in discourse as explanation or justification for moving more slowly, for not rushing to conclusions, or for taking a longer perspective on future developments. In contrast, the westerner is more likely to de-emphasize his or her own ancient historical heritage dating from Ancient Greece or before. The westerner is more likely to emphasize the need for quickness in concluding negotiations, the need to bring about economic, political, or social change, and the need to "keep up" with world changes.

Beliefs, values, and religion

We want to briefly comment on beliefs, values, and religion, because these aspects of culture have played a very significant role in the communications between Asians and westerners over the past few centuries. At the same time we want to caution against making too direct an application of our ideas about cultural values and, especially, religion in discussions of inter-cultural communication. In such discussions it is common enough to outline the basic principles of, say, Buddhism, Taoism, and Confucianism on the one hand and Christianity on the other, and then to hastily assume that these religious and ethical systems have led to or will lead to major differences in interpretation in intercultural communication.

In many cases, a person's religious beliefs will be quite consonant with those of his or her culture in general. We still need to ask to what extent these beliefs directly affect his or her communication, especially in inter-cultural situations. Unfortunately, it is well known that the trade in drugs which ultimately resulted in present-day Hong Kong was carried out by people who professed the most Christian beliefs. Whether we are speaking of the general belief structure of Christianity, Buddhism, Taoism, or Con-fucianism we have to acknowledge, sadly, that many scoundrels have openly espoused beliefs in these religious systems, supported their churches, temples, or monasteries, and used the cloak of these moral and ethical systems to cover their own illegal or immoral activities.

Face systems

The second aspect of culture we are considering, social organization, is one of the most important in that it refers to the way a cultural group organizes relationships among members of the group. For many scholars the word "culture" is very nearly synonymous with the concept of social organization. We will take up just four aspects of this organization: kinship, the concept of the self, ingroup–outgroup relationships, and what sociologists have sometimes called *Gemeinschaft* and *Gesellschaft*.

Kinship

In Korea, mothers set up temporary shrines outside the university and pray all day while their children inside write their examinations. In the fervor of the Cultural Revolution in China, children were encouraged to criticize their parents. Throughout Asia these and many similar examples indicate that the ancient Confucian kinship relationships are an extremely powerful force in Asian cultural relationships. On the one hand, such relationships may be seen as the major magnetism holding together these ancient cultures. On the other hand, such relationships may be seen as the great barrier to modernization and development. Our point is that either position indicates the centrality of kinship in the thinking of most East Asians.

In contrast to this, a recent United States census accepted fourteen different family types, from the traditional extended family to the single parent with adopted child. Almost any current newspaper from Europe, North America, or Australia will show that for most westerners, kinship is far from being felt as a significant tie among members of society. In many cases, kinship relationships are seen as significant barriers to individual self-realization and progress. The increasingly popular American practice of children calling their parents by first names, for example, would be quite unpleasantly surprising to most Asians.

There are two aspects of kinship which are of direct importance to intercultural discourse: hierarchy and collectivistic relationship. Kinship relationships emphasize that people are connected to each other by having descended from common ancestors. In doing so, kinship relationships emphasize, first of all, that ascending generations are before, prior to, and even superior to descending generations. This hierarchy of relationship is emphasized by Confucius and reiterated in such teaching materials as the *San Zi Jing* (Xu Chuiyang, 1990) or even the public school workbooks used today in Hong Kong, Taiwan, Japan, and Korea, and throughout the rest of East Asia. The primary relationships are not lateral relationships, those between brothers and sisters, for example, but hierarchical, those between fathers and sons, mothers and daughters.

In Asia, as in any other society in which such traditional kinship relationships are emphasized, any individual is acutely aware of his or her obligations and responsibilities to those who have come before as well as to those who come after. From birth one is made conscious of the debt owed to one's own parents, which is largely carried out in the form of duty and obedience. But western readers should also be aware that one is also made acutely conscious of the debt owed to one's own children and other descendants, which is largely carried out through nurture, responsibility, and benevolence.

This emphasis on hierarchical relationship has a twofold consequence for discourse: from very early in life one becomes subtly practiced in the discourse forms of hierarchical relationship. One learns first to show respect to those above, then, in due time, one learns the forms of guidance and leadership of those who come after. The second consequence is that one comes to expect all relationships to be hierarchical to some extent. If hierarchy is not based on kinship relationship, then it is seen to be based on age, experience, education, gender, geographical region, political affiliation, or one of the many other dimensions of social organization within a culture.

The second aspect of kinship which is significant for discourse is that individual members of a culture are not perceived as independently acting individuals but, rather, they are seen as acting within hierarchies of kinship and other such relationships. A son's primary motivation for action is thought to be to bring credit to his parents and to provide security for his own descendants. He is not thought of as acting on his own behalf or for his own purposes. Indeed, such individual action is seen as an aberrant or possibly pathological form.

This emphasis on kinship relationships, which is still characteristic of East Asians to some extent, even in contemporary and "westernized" Asian centers such as Hong Kong, is sharply contrasted with the western emphasis on individualism and egalitarianism. This assertion of individualism and egalitarianism may reach its extreme in North America, but it has been at the center of political values since the eighteenth century in European political philosophy. Contemporary Americans, as we will see in chapter 10 in our discussion of generational systems of discourse, assert an extreme of independence from kinship or other hierarchical relationships.

This difference in egalitarianism and hierarchy will, then, most likely play out in the choice of strategies of interpersonal politeness, with the westerner using strategies of involvement as a way of emphasizing egalitarianism and the Asian using strategies of independence as a way of showing deference. In the short dialogue above between Mr Chu and Mr Richardson, Mr Richardson tried to establish the use of his given name, Andy, and Mr Chu's given name, Hon-fai. Such a difference in approaches and the embarrassment which occurs are a direct result of this difference in emphasis on hierarchy and egalitarianism. The Asian is more likely to be conscious of kinship relationships, which will, in turn, lead to his assumptions of hierarchy. The American on the other hand is likely to have de-emphasized such relationships, and therefore, to assume more egalitarian relationships.

The concept of the self

A second aspect of social organization concerns the concept of the person or of the self as a unit within that group's organization. Individualism, of course, is not something unique to the American continent. It has its roots in the western tradition going back to Socrates or to Jesus. One thing is clear: there is a long tradition of emphasizing the separation of the individual from any other social commitments, especially in the pursuit of social or political goals. The Chinese psychological anthropologist Francis L. K. Hsu believes that the excessive individualism of the western sense of the self has led to a general inability or unwillingness among the psychological sciences to consider the social aspects of the development of human behavior. He goes on to say that even in the anthropological and sociological sciences, culture and society are seen as being built up out of the association of

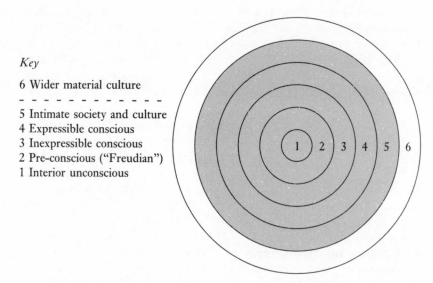

Key

6 Wider material culture

- - - - - - - - - - - -

5 Intimate society and culture
4 Expressible conscious
3 Inexpressible conscious
2 Pre-conscious ("Freudian")
1 Interior unconscious

Figure 7.1   The Chinese concept of the person (based on Hsu, 1985).

individuals, not as primary realities in themselves. In an essay on intercultural understanding in his collection of essays entitled *Rugged Individualism Reconsidered* (Hsu 1983), he says, "The major key (though never the only key) as to why we behave like human beings as well as to why we behave like Americans or Japanese is to be found in our relationships with our fellow human beings" (p. 414). Hsu considers human relationships to be the fundamental unit of analysis, not a secondary, constructed category. He argues that, "the concept of personality is an expression of the western ideal of individualism. It does not correspond even to the reality of how the western man lives in western culture, far less any man in any other culture" (Hsu 1985:24).

    In place of the idea of the individual self, Hsu suggests a concept based on the Chinese concept of person (*ren* or *jen*), which includes in his analysis not only interior unconscious or pre-conscious ("Freudian") levels and inexpressible and expressible conscious levels of the person but also one's intimate society and culture. In this analysis of the self, such relationships as those with one's parents and children are considered inseparable aspects of the self. Where a western conception of the self places the major boundary which defines the self between the biological individual and that individual's intimates, Hsu argues that the Chinese concept of person (*ren* or *jen*) places the major boundary of the person on the outside of those intimate relationships, as we show in figure 7.1, which is based on Hsu's original diagram. The western concept of the biological self can be diagrammed

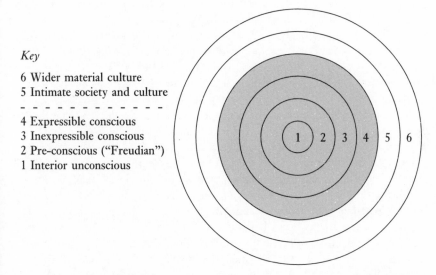

Key

6 Wider material culture
5 Intimate society and culture
- - - - - - - - - - - -
4 Expressible conscious
3 Inexpressible conscious
2 Pre-conscious ("Freudian")
1 Interior unconscious

Figure 7.2   The western concept of the person (based on Hsu, 1985).

using Hsu's categories as indicated in figure 7.2, also based upon Hsu's diagram.

Hsu's point in making this analysis is not just to propose an alternative to the individualistic concept of the self. He argues that the biologically isolated individual is neither culturally nor, in fact, biologically viable. Because intimate human relationships are "literally as important as [a person's] requirement for food, water, and air" (1985:34), it is a dangerous analytical fiction to believe that the individual is the source of all social reality.

We believe that in any society human individuals must have close relationships with other humans as well as the freedom to operate independently. It is hard to imagine a human society in which either one of these extremes was practiced to the exclusion of the other. What is important in studying cultural differences is not whether a society is individualistic or collectivistic in itself, but what that society upholds as its ideal, even when we all recognize that we must all have some independence as well as some place in society.

For professional discourse, the question we want to consider is the relative difference between two people in their concept of the self as an individual or as part of a larger social group. We believe that on this dimension Asians tend to be more aware of the connections they have as members of their social groups, and therefore, they tend to be more conscious of the consequences of their actions on other members of their groups. In contrast to this, westerners, and especially Americans, tend to emphasize their independence. This leads

them to be more concerned about their own freedom of activity than with
their connections to other members of their group.

Each group is also likely to make false assumptions about members of the
other group. Asians will possibly overestimate a westerner's concern about
his group's response to an issue, while a westerner is likely to assume a
greater degree of independence on the part of an Asian with whom he or she
is negotiating.

When we first introduced the concept of face relationships in chapter 2,
we discussed face as having to do with a relationship between or among
two or more participants in a discourse. Now we can see that it is actually
somewhat more complex than this. From an individualistic point of view,
face relationships are very much a matter of individual face. From a
collectivistic point of view, however, one's face is really the face of one's
group, whether that group is thought of as one's family, one's cultural
group, or one's corporation. It is quite likely that in intercultural communication, a person from a highly individualistic culture would pay more
attention to his or her own personal face needs, whereas a person from a
more collectivistic culture would always have the face of others foremost in
his or her mind.

Ingroup—outgroup relationships

The third aspect of social organization we want to consider is the problem
of establishing relationships between members of the group and members of
other groups. One consequence of the cultural difference between individualism and collectivism has to do with the difference between speaking to
members of one's own group and speaking to others. In an individualistic
society, groups do not form with the same degree of permanence as they do
in a collectivist society. As a result, the ways of speaking to others are much
more similar from situation to situation, since in each case the relationships
are being negotiated and developed right within the situation of the discourse.

On the other hand, in a collectivist society, many relationships are established from one's birth into a particular family in a particular segment of
society in a particular place. These memberships in particular groups tend to
take on a permanent, ingroup character along with special forms of discourse
which carefully preserve the boundaries between those who are inside members of the group and all others who are not members of the group.

In the dialogue between Mr Chu and Mr Richardson, Mr Chu was
embarrassed when Mr Richardson called him by his given name, Hon-fai.
Actually a person's Chinese given name alone is rarely used at all, but if
it is used, it is generally only within ingroup communication. When Mr
Richardson calls him Hon-fai, not only has he suggested a relationship of
symmetrical solidarity, but he has also crossed over a line between family

and intimate communications and those used with strangers or others outside of Mr Chu's immediate social group.

Readers should not think that this is entirely a matter of Asian and western cultural differences, however. Many people, east and west, have names or variants of their names which are used only within the intimate circle of their friends or family, and it feels quite embarrassing when someone from outside of that group uses that name.

The cultural difference we are talking about in this case, as in so many others, is one of degree only. What is important in the analysis of discourse is to understand first whether the distinction between ingroup and outgroup communication is significant in any particular case, and then to determine whether a term or a form of speech is used for ingroup or outgroup communication.

In some cases even the language or the register within that language will be associated with the distinction between ingroup and outgroup communication. Recently a study was made of the Japanese used for speaking to Japanese as compared to the Japanese used for speaking to foreigners. Even when speaking to foreigners with a very high level of competence in the Japanese language, Japanese considered it more appropriate to use a simplified "foreigner talk" register when speaking outside of their own group. Those who used a complex register of Japanese when speaking to foreigners were given more negative ratings by other Japanese.

In this case, as in others, members of an ingroup feel that it is a kind of ingroup betrayal to use ingroup forms of language to non-members. In cultures where the distinction between ingroup and outgroup is a significant distinction, this is often paralleled by the use of different forms of discourse such as a special set of personal names or the use of particular registers for ingroup and outgroup communication.

Gemeinschaft *and* Gesellschaft

One of the major and foundational insights of the field of sociology was that there are two very different ways in which society can be organized. In 1887, in a book called *Gemeinschaft und Gesellschaft* (Community and Society) the German Ferdinand Tönnies (1971), argued that the problems of modern society have arisen because of a split with the traditional, community-based social organization of the Middle Ages. He argued that such an organic, community form of social solidarity, which he called *Gemeinschaft*, was based on the fact that individuals shared a common history and common traditions.

In contrast to the *Gemeinschaft* or community organization of social relationships, in modern society relationships are more contractual, rational, or instrumental. This form of society by mutual agreement and to protect mutual interests – one might say corporate society – which developed as part of the industrialization of Europe, Tönnies called *Gesellschaft*. Sociologists such as Emile Durkheim, Max Weber, and Georg Simmel develop this concept in their own foundational works.

In intercultural professional contexts, this distinction has been observed by analysts of the structure of businesses in Asia. In Taiwan and Hong Kong, for example, there is a tendency for businesses to be small, family-owned and controlled structures, which operate very much along traditional lines more closely associated with kinship than more western corporate structures. In such a case we might want to say that such businesses demonstrate a social structure of a *Gemeinschaft* nature. On the other hand, the large, impersonal, utilitarian international corporations show a *Gesellschaft* structure.

There are two major types of discourse system: those into which one becomes a member through the natural processes of birth and growth within a family and a community (one's gender and one's generation, for example), and those into which one chooses to enter for utilitarian purposes such as one's professional specialization or the company for which one works. The social structure of the first kind of discourse system is more like what the sociologists would call *Gemeinschaft*, and the goal-directed discourse systems such as corporations are rather strong examples of the *Gesellschaft* form of social organization.

This distinction between *Gemeinschaft* and *Gesellschaft* is also useful for talking about how people learn to be members of their discourse systems. One learns one's community, one's gender, and one's generational place in life through processes of socialization or enculturation; that is, one learns to be a member largely through naturally occurring, non-institutional forms of learning. On the other hand, membership in goal-directed discourse systems such as the academic discourse system or a corporate structure comes more often through formal education, training, and institutionalized learning.

In intercultural communication many problems arise, particularly in professional contexts, when people make different assumptions about whether *Gemeinschaft* or *Gesellschaft* forms of organization are most appropriate. A western company doing business in an Asian country, for example, might want to set up a subsidiary production facility. From their point of view the most important issue would be to produce the product efficiently, with the lowest possible cost at a predictable flow of production and with a small range of variability in the quality. To do this they would most likely emphasize finding "the right person' for each job. They would be concerned about selecting individual employees on the basis of their training and experience. In other words, they would be most likely to create a social structure along *Gesellschaft* lines of rational, utilitarian purpose.

In contrast to the owners of such a project, the local Asian counterparts might well have in mind major aspects of *Gemeinschaft* or community which they would want to emphasize. It might well be important that the new project would employ certain persons who were well placed in the local community structure, even where they might not have the initial training and experience. From the point of view of *Gemeinschaft*, these would be the best people, because employing them would enhance the community social structure.

No modern culture or discourse system, of course, is purely organized as either *Gemeinschaft* or *Gesellschaft* alone. In any social structure we will see a mixture of elements of both forms of organization. What is important in understanding intercultural communication is to understand in which contexts one of these forms of organization is preferred over the other. It is also important to understand that conflicts and misinterpretations may arise where participants in a discourse do not come to agreement over which mode of organization should predominate.

Forms of discourse

Functions of language

History, worldview, beliefs, values, religions, and social organization may all be reflected through different languages and linguistic varieties in a culture. At the same time, language may be a directly defining aspect of culture, rather than simply a reflection of other, more basic structures. A cultural group may have quite distinctive ways of understanding the basic functions of language, and therefore we will take up the question of the functions of language as the third major aspect of culture which plays a role in intercultural communication.

To give an example of the functional role language itself may play, Chinese in its many forms is a major aspect (but, of course, not the only one) of the definition of Chinese culture. When Chinese are asked to define Chinese culture, they will frequently point to the common use of Chinese writing, both in the present and historically back for several millennia, as the defining core.

Such a definition of culture would be very unlikely in the west. English is the principal language of the United Kingdom, Australia, the United States, and New Zealand, one of the principal languages of Canada and South Africa, and an official or major language in quite a number of other countries. Nevertheless, people who live in those countries may make a strong claim for having a culture quite distinctive from other speakers of English in other English-speaking countries.

It is true that since the Renaissance in Europe, countries have tried to use languages such as German, French, and English as a defining criterion of national and cultural distinctiveness. Nevertheless, Europeans tend to use language more to divide than to unify. One does not often hear of Europeans saying that they share a common culture with everyone who uses the Roman alphabet to write, for example. Nor is there a common sense of culture among the speakers of the Indo-European language family. Not even such relatively close language families as that of Romance languages, which includes French, Spanish, Portuguese, and Italian, are thought to unify a group culturally.

For our purposes, however, the most important aspect of language from a cultural point of view is how a particular culture conceives of the function(s) of language.

Information and relationship   Communication theorists, linguists, psychologists, and anthropologists all agree that language has many functions. In chapter 3 we showed how all language must be used simultaneously in a communicative function as well as in a metacommunicative function. Of course, there is much discussion among researchers about how many functions there are and just which functions take priority in any particular case. One dimension on which there is complete agreement, however, is that virtually any communication will have both an information function and a relationship function. In other words, when we communicate with others we simultaneously communicate some amount of information and indicate our current expectations about the relationship between or among participants.

At the two extremes of information and relationship, there are often cases in which one or the other function appears to be minimized. For example, in those daily greetings such as, "How are you? I'm just fine," there is often a minimum of actual information. After all, we do not really expect the other person in most cases to answer about how they actually are. Nor do we expect them to believe that we are literally "fine." Such exchanges are nearly, but not quite exclusively, relational. The meaning of such exchanges is simply to acknowledge recognition and to affirm that the relationship you have established remains in effect. At the other extreme, such discourses as weather reports may seem almost completely devoid of relationship, focusing only on information about the weather.

What is of concern for us is not to establish whether or not the purpose of language is to convey information or relationship; the use of language always accomplishes both functions to some extent. From an intercultural point of view, we can see that cultures often are different from each other in how much importance they give to one function of language over the other. For example, Japanese culture places a very high value on the communication of subtle aspects of feeling and relationship and a much lower value on the communication of information. International business culture, especially since the introduction of nearly instant global computer communications, places a very high value on the communication of information and very little value on the communication of relationship.

The tradition of communication without language which the Japanese call *isshin denshin* might be translated as "direct transmission" and has been strongly influenced by Zen Buddhism. This influence originated in China in the early Tang Period (AD 618–907) and has had a major impact on Chinese, Korean, and Japanese cultures, even in the modern period. In this tradition of thinking about communication, it is believed that the most important things cannot be communicated in language, that language is only useful for somewhat secondary or trivial messages.

In contrast to this is the tradition of Utilitarian discourse, in which it is assumed that the ideal language use is to purge one's speech and one's writing of everything but the essential information. This very positivist position assumes that what cannot be communicated in this way is hardly worth paying attention to.

We do not suppose that normal international professional communication takes place very often between Japanese-speaking Zen Buddhist priests and English-speaking computer scientists who might hold to the extremes of these two positions on the function of language. Nevertheless, we do know that throughout Asia, members of Chinese, Japanese, and Korean cultures have been strongly influenced in their thinking about language by such traditions. As a result, one might expect the average Asian to be somewhat more skeptical about the value of direct, informational communication, and to place a higher value on thinking deeply about a subject.

An advertisement in a Korean newspaper for a Korean advertising company says,

> DONG BANG THINKS TWICE
> The deeper the thinking, the truer the action.
> Likewise, the deeper the thinking behind advertising,
> the more outstanding are the results.
> Deep thinking and sincere ideas produce advertising
> that is more persuasive than dazzling, more touching, and more exciting.
> By always "thinking twice," the THINKING AGENCY, DONG BANG,
> creates advertising that is believable. DONG BANG's advertising,
> therefore, has the power to persuade consumers
> to buy your products.

In this context, thinking twice implies thinking about the consequences of one's actions on human relationships. It is hard to imagine that this appeal to deep thought would carry much weight in American advertising circles, in spite of the fact that this advertisement was published in English in an English language newspaper, presumably in order to win over potential non-Korean clients.

In regular conditions of intercultural professional communication, this difference between a focus on information and a focus on relationship often leads to a misunderstanding of the purposes of specific communicative events. From the point of view of the functions of language, the westerner may well want to get to the bargaining table as quickly as possible because he or she believes that it is in direct talk that information is exchanged and that any other form of communication is quite beside the point. His or her Asian counterpart, on the other hand, may want to set up a series of social events in which the participants can more indirectly approach each other and begin to feel more subtle aspects of their relationship.

Negotiation and ratification   Having said that there is often a cultural difference in the belief about whether language is primarily used for the purposes of conveying information or expressing relationships, we now need to complicate the picture somewhat further. There is also a difference among cultures in the extent to which relationships are thought to be freely negotiated on the one hand, or given by society in a fixed form on the other. This is the second aspect of the functions of language we will need to consider.

In recent years, for example, there has been a growing cultural reaction in North America and elsewhere to the excessive emphasis on information in human relationships. Psychologists who have specialized in the treatment of stress have pointed out that the American narrow emphasis on information and control in communication is part of what has been called the Type-A Behavior syndrome. This syndrome, which is closely associated with heart disease, has been observed to emphasize an excessive attention to numbers, quantities, and direct communication on the one hand, and to downplay or minimize human relationships on the other.

At the same time, as we will discuss below in chapter 11, scholars such as Deborah Tannen have observed a contrast between women and men in American society in their attention to information over relationship. We will also discuss the major generation gap between the generations born before and after World War II. One of the characteristics of this younger generation is its greater emphasis on human relationships.

Taking these together, we can see that there is a clear movement within contemporary western society toward recognizing that successful (and healthy) communication cannot ignore human relationships. Nevertheless, we believe there remains a major distinction between the way human relationships are understood in Asia (and in other traditional societies) and the way they are understood in contemporary western society. The difference, we believe, lies in whether human relationships are thought of as given by society or, on the other hand, as being spontaneously created between individuals.

As we have said above, kinship is a major source of structure within most cultures, including Asian cultures. In such societies, human relationships are thought of as being largely vertical relationships between preceding and following generations. Whether it is family relationships such as those between parents and their children or relationships outside of the family such as those between a teacher and a student, the significant point is that most of the relationships are understood to be given by the society, not newly negotiated by the participants in the situation. One is born the son or daughter of particular parents, the descendant of particular ancestors, a member of a particular village. These characteristics of one's personal identity are not negotiable; they are given by the situations into which one is born.

In contrast to this, in contemporary western society the word "relationship" has come to mean almost exclusively horizontal or lateral and, in fact, sexual, relationships made between people who freely choose to enter into them. Because of the social and semantic strength of this use of the term, most other uses have been crowded out of the common lexicon. The primary concern in what are called relationships is with the establishment of equality and freedom. In fact, one could safely say that one of the greatest concerns one finds in the popular press about such relationships, as well as any other human relationships, is over how to keep any relationship from taking on hierarchical characteristics.

If we return, then, to the question of intercultural communication, we can see that a major difference between these two points of view lies in the question of negotiation or ratification. Within a traditional concept of vertical and generational relationships, language is thought of as being used for the purposes of ratifying or affirming relationships which have already been given. On the other hand, in the contemporary western concept of relationships, language is seen as a major aspect of the ongoing negotiation of the relationship. Particular care is taken not to ratify existing relationships, but to seek continual change, or as it is more favorably put, growth.

The difference in these two views of language is that in one view the stable condition is seen as the favorable condition and in the other it is the changing condition that is thought of as being favorable. We know of many Asians, for example, who have known each other for many years and who have engaged in mutually profitable business arrangements, but who continue to call each other quite formally by their last names and titles. On the other hand, we know of American business people who have felt that their attempts to develop a better business relationship with Asians have not succeeded because after a long series of encounters with them they have not been able to establish themselves on a first-name "friendly" basis.

Group harmony and individual welfare The third way in which we can see that cultures differ in the focus on information or on relationship in language use is to mention the research of a Japanese psychologist who studied group processes in solving problems. In this research project, subjects were given individual problems to solve in some cases and in other cases they were asked to solve the problems in groups. He found that when there was a conflict within the group about how to solve a problem, group harmony was always the greatest consideration, even if it meant that the group had to select a worse solution. In other words, his conclusion was that members of a group much preferred to say they would go along with the group than to express their own, individual solutions, if those solutions would produce disharmony in the group.

Other scholars have pointed out that one major difference between Ancient Chinese and Ancient Greek rhetoric was on this dimension of group harmony versus individual welfare. Ancient Chinese rhetoric emphasized the means by which one could phrase one's position without causing any feeling of disruption or disharmony. Ancient Greek rhetoric, on the other hand, emphasized the means of winning one's point through skillful argument, short of, Aristotle says, the use of torture.

We do not suppose that contemporary international business circles would approve of the use of torture to achieve a good contract on the western side, and we also do not suppose that Asians would scuttle the possibility of a good contract just for the sake of a harmonious group feeling. Nevertheless, we do believe that this cultural difference in assumptions made about the functions of language will have some effect in intercultural discourse involving Asians and westerners. We know that Asians will tend to state their positions somewhat less extremely if they feel that not to do so would disrupt the harmony of the negotiations. We also know that westerners will tend to assume that each party has only in mind achieving their own best advantage in negotiations, and that they will do so, even if it should cause a feeling of disharmony. This difference in assumptions about what is actually going on can easily lead to more complex misinterpretations in the discourse.

Non-verbal communication

Non-verbal communication might be thought of as any form of communication which is not directly dependent on the use of language. Generally speaking, however, it is very difficult to know where to separate verbal and non-verbal forms of communication. Such non-verbal aspects of communication as nodding the head most often accompany speech and are part and parcel of the verbal system of language use. On the other hand such forms of communication as dance and music often have no verbal component at all. Our interest here is not in providing a theoretically rigorous definition of the difference between verbal and non-verbal communication. Our purpose in using this category is simply to call attention to the fact that many aspects of discourse depend upon forms of communication which cannot be easily transcribed into words and yet are crucial to our understanding of discourse.

Throughout this book we have emphasized communication in speaking and in writing, and yet we realize that much communication also takes place without the use of words. The way a person dresses for a meeting may suggest to other participants how he or she is prepared to participate in it. In fact, we can use virtually any aspect of our behavior or our presentation which others can perceive as a means of communication. This would include our posture, our movements, our attire, our use of space, and our use of time. All of these have been considered by researchers in their studies of non-verbal communication.

While there are many kinds of non-verbal communication, here we will focus on just three aspects of human behavior which are relevant to intercultural communication: the movements of our bodies (called kinesics), our use of space (called proxemics), and our use of time.

Kinesics: the movement of our bodies   At the beginning of this chapter, the incident involving Mr Chu and Mr Richardson ended with Mr Chu smiling, which Mr Richardson interpreted as meaning they had achieved a good interpersonal relationship. One aspect of intercultural communication which is often open to misinterpretation is this one of smiling or laughing. Many researchers have argued that smiles or laughing are universal human characteristics which we all immediately understand. This is, of course, true. There is little doubt that any human being would know when some other human was smiling.

Unfortunately, from one cultural group to another there is a great deal of variability about when one smiles or laughs and what it should be taken to mean. The most obvious and the most often misinterpreted form of this is what in the west might be called "nervous laughter." Perhaps it is only a difference in the amount of smiling or laughter under such conditions, but it has been widely observed that Asians in general tend to smile or laugh more easily than westerners when they feel difficulty or embarrassment in the discourse. This is, then, misinterpreted by westerners as normal pleasure or agreement, and the sources of difficulty are obscured or missed.

We believe that there is a connection between this non-verbal behavior and the tendency for Asians to use communication to promote interpersonal or group harmony. If we think of the smile as a natural means for humans to encourage interpersonal harmony, then we can understand that it is likely to occur when an Asian feels there is some disruption of this harmony. On the other hand, if someone feels that the purpose of speaking is to promote individual welfare or the transfer of information, he or she is likely to assume that a smile means that the individual is pleased and is, therefore, feeling that he or she is succeeding in his or her own personal ends.

From this point of view, we would not want to say that the difference which has caused misinterpretation is attributable to smiles, which are so different from one culture to another. Instead we would want to say that it is the discourse and its purposes which are different. The smile in one case is being used to cover over what is felt as a potential problem; in the other case it is used to directly register satisfaction. If two participants in a discourse have different goals, they are likely to interpret the smile within the purview of their own particular goals and, therefore, miss the fact that the other participant sees that something has gone wrong.

A second aspect of kinesic behavior or body movement that is immediately noticed when one travels between Asia and western countries is bowing. Most of the readers of this book will be quite aware of the fact that shaking hands in the west is the most common form of greeting, especially when being introduced to someone or when seeing someone whom one has not seen for a long time. In Asia there is considerable variability in practices, which include bowing as the main form in Japan and Korea, but also sometimes including shaking hands when westerners are involved. The traditional Chinese practice of clasping one's hands before the chest while making a short bow is now rarely seen outside of movies depicting an earlier time.

There are several problems which arise with these practices. Such greetings are distributed differently in different Asian countries (Japanese and Koreans bow more frequently and more deeply than Chinese), and cultural changes are bringing about changes in these practices. Furthermore, in western countries changes are taking place in handshaking practices. For example, it is now generally assumed that when a woman and a man are introduced they will shake hands in acknowledgement of the introduction, especially, of course, in professional or business circles. It has only been relatively recently, however, that this practice has been widely accepted. Even just a few years ago, it was somewhat unusual for men and women to shake hands. They would generally have nodded to each other.

There are many books on intercultural non-verbal communication which the reader may consult for details of what might be appropriate or inappropriate in any particular social context. Our purpose here is not to go into non-verbal communication in detail. We only want to make the reader aware that we do not intend to ignore the question of it. We are primarily concerned with verbal discourse; as a result, we are only briefly taking up the question of modes of communication which lie outside of this domain of study. Kinesics may not be a major aspect of discourse. Nevertheless, as part of the contextual background within which our discourses take place, it is extremely important to remember that as humans we simply cannot ignore the interpretations and misinterpretations we are making in reading the non-verbal signals of other participants in the discourse.

Proxemics: the use of space The second aspect of non-verbal communication which is important in intercultural communication is in our use of space. Cultural differences in the use of space are a constant source of misunderstanding and confusion in preparing the settings for discourse. In traditional Japanese and Korean rooms, one leaves shoes at the door and sits on the floor at small, low tables. Chinese rooms use chairs and higher tables. Japanese and Korean rooms seem almost empty. This is because objects such as tables, cushions, or bedding not currently in use will be stored behind cupboard doors out of sight. Chinese rooms seem much fuller. In this comparison, Chinese rooms will seem more familiar to westerners, who are also accustomed to sitting in chairs at higher tables.

Differences will, nevertheless, be found between the western placement of furniture such as chairs and tables and the corresponding Chinese placement. A Chinese room will often have two chairs placed side by side with a small table between them. Two people who are to talk to each other will thus sit side by side rather than across from each other, as would be more commonly practiced in a western conversation. It is an interesting twist of contemporary technology and social practice that because of television many westerners are now adopting a pattern which in some ways is similar to the Chinese practice. Because television now often forms a focal point for western casual conversation, conversationalists often sit side by side looking at or toward the television set when they talk.

There are, of course, many other aspects of proxemics which might be considered in intercultural communication. One of these, however, is of recurring importance in preparing settings for intercultural communication, and that is the concept of personal space. It was clearly demonstrated some years ago (Hall 1959) that each person has a "bubble" of space in which he or she moves and in which he or she feels comfortable. Intrusions into that space are acceptable only under circumstances of intimate contact. Outside of that space is a second "bubble" of space in which normal interpersonal contacts take place. Then outside of that is a third "bubble" of public space.

Edward T. Hall, who first described these spaces (1959, 1969), points out that these spheres of space are one aspect of culture which comes into play in intercultural communication. One culture, that of Mexicans for example, will have a slightly smaller sphere of intimate space than another culture, such as that of North Americans. The result of this difference, which can be measured in just a few inches, is that when a North American and a Mexican stand together to converse, the Mexican will nudge slightly closer to the North American in order to get at the right distance for comfortable interpersonal discourse. The North American, who has a slightly larger intimate sphere, will feel that the Mexican is invading his or her intimate space and will, therefore, step back an inch or two. This will make the Mexican feel uncomfortable because he or she will feel too distant and, therefore, he or she will move closer.

The net result of these cultural differences in intimate and personal spaces is that, where norms are different, you will find the person with the smaller sphere constantly moving closer to the other, and that other person constantly moving back a bit to increase the space. These two conversationalists will create a kind of dance in which they will move across a considerable amount of space in the course of a brief conversation. If the space is crowded with other people, they will end up moving around and around in a circle while each person tries to find a comfortable position.

Westerners visiting Asia for the first time often notice this sort of proxemic problem. Generally speaking, Asians have a smaller sphere of personal space than westerners, with Americans at one extreme and Mediterraneans coming much closer to the Asian norm. Asians in North America will experience the opposite feeling, of people being quite distant from them.

This difference leads quite naturally to westerners having a very different experience of Asian city life than Asians themselves have. While such places as central Taipei, the Mongkok district of Hong Kong, or Namdaemun Market in Seoul are among the most densely packed places on earth, the physical crowding is not experienced in the same way by everyone. It depends on the person's expectations of personal space, and those expectations depend, in part, on how space is used in that person's culture.

Concept of time   The authors received a letter recently from a former student in Taiwan who said about Hong Kong, "I presume Hong Kong is a busy area, where people walk fast, talk fast, and overwork to death." One aspect of the concept of time which will be all too obvious to most readers of this text is that there seems to be too little time in which to do too many things. This sense of time might be called time urgency, a term taken from descriptions by researchers into stress and Type-A behavior. As they have described this "hurry sickness," it is a syndrome of behavior in which the person continually tries to accomplish more than can be humanly accomplished. Until very recently, time urgency was thought to be a characteristic of Americans, particularly American males in the generation born in the period from the Great Depression through to the end of World War II (1929–45).

It should be obvious to most of our readers that this sense of time urgency is no longer a cultural characteristic of just this one generation of American males. It is a characteristic of the Asian "salaryman," and is spreading throughout the world rapidly as one aspect of the internationalization of business and government. It does not take much imagination to see that this time urgency fits very nicely within the Utilitarian discourse system which we described in chapter 6. As that discourse system spreads together with international business communications, this sense of time urgency also appears to be spreading.

The most important aspect of this sense of time is that in discourse it will almost always produce a negative evaluation of the slower participants by the faster participants in a communicative situation. Those who share in this concept of time urgency will come to see anyone who moves more slowly than they do as conservative, as uncooperative, as resistant to change, and as opposing progress. Behind the concept of time urgency is the idea that what lies ahead in the future is always better than what lies behind in the past; it is based solidly on the belief in progress.

This belief in progress puts human life and human culture on a Utopian time line from the distant past into the distant future. It is believed that we have yet to reach our greatest accomplishments. It is felt that it is only natural to want to arrive at that future Utopia as soon as possible.

In contrast to this belief in human progress is the concept of the Golden Age. In the China of Confucius, and continuing down to very recently, it was felt that the present time was worse than the times of the past, in which human society was more reasonably ordered, justice and benevolence prevailed, and benevolent rulers concerned themselves with the good of their subjects. Changes in society were justified from the point of view of restoring the better conditions of the past, not with moving toward new conditions in the future.

This same Golden-Age concept of the past was held in Europe up until and through the Renaissance. The thinkers of the Renaissance looked back at their immediate predecessors and considered them to have degenerated from the much higher state of culture of the Roman and Greek ancients, and it was their goal to restore Europe to this former condition.

It is not our purpose to debate the relative merits of these two arrows of time. One arrow, the Utopian arrow of progress, points toward a better and better future; the other arrow, the arrow of the Golden Age, points toward the past and considers the present time to be a degenerate period. From the point of view of intercultural communication, the main point we want to consider is that if two people differ in their concept of time between the Utopian and the Golden Age, they will find it very difficult to come to agreement in many areas of their discourse.

The main point of disagreement, however, will have to do with the concept of time urgency. Those who hold a Utopian concept of time will push for the quicker realization of their goals. Those who hold a Golden-Age concept of time will not be in any hurry to rush forward, because to them most movements forward are actually just getting away from the better conditions of the past. Utopianists will justify taking actions just because they bring about change, and from their point of view change in itself will bring them closer to their goal. In contrast to this, Golden Ageists will resist change on the belief that any change is likely to further deteriorate conditions.

As a result of this difference in point of view, the same facts will be brought into the discussion, these facts may also be widely agreed upon, but then, the conclusions from these agreed upon facts will point toward opposite solutions. At this point participants will become confused, because they believed that all they had to do was to come to agreement on the facts under discussion. What they had never considered was their differences in the concept of time.

In considering these two concepts of time, it should be clear that the Utopian concept of time is most often associated with the Utilitarian discourse system, with modernization, with internationalization, with technologization, and with political change. The Golden-Age concept of time is most often associated with more traditional cultural interests. Throughout Asia, for example, this cultural conflict in the sense of time is being debated not only across cultures (interculturally) but within cultures (intraculturally). In many cases, the Utopian sense of time is thought of as westernization and the Golden-Age sense of time is thought of as traditionally Chinese or Japanese or Korean. We think it is important to realize that this conflict between a progressive and a restorative sense of time is also widely debated within western culture.

Socialization

It is an oversimplification to say that whereas animals have instinct, human beings have culture. Nevertheless, while the exact proportion of inborn, innate behavior to learned, cultural behavior will probably always be debated, most scholars would agree that human beings are born with fewer preset patterns than other animals. What this means is that human beings must begin at birth what is a life-long process of learning how to be human beings. We have used the word "culture" to refer to this complex pattern of knowledge and behavior, and we will use the general term "socialization" to refer to the process of learning culture.

Technical definitions of all of the terms relating to culture learning are difficult to establish, since in different fields, such as psychology, sociology, anthropology, they are used somewhat differently. For our purposes, three terms in addition to "socialization" will be sufficient for a general understanding of how we learn to be members of our cultures and how we learn our systems of discourse: education, enculturation, and acculturation.

Education, enculturation, acculturation

The most important distinction to be made is between what we might call formal and informal means of teaching and learning. While both education and socialization have been used for both forms of learning, we will use the word "education" for formal teaching and learning, and "socialization" (or "enculturation") for informal teaching and learning.

When a person takes up employment in a new company, he or she might be in doubt about the way employees are supposed to dress for work in the office. It is possible that the company would have a handbook in which such things as a code of dress would be specified. In that case we would call that formal education. In the business context it would normally be called training and would probably consist of a formal orientation session, in which the handbook would be introduced, new employees would be guided through the main points, and questions they might have would be answered.

On the other hand, the issue of dress might not be mentioned at all, but when the new employee arrives in the office for the first day of work he or she might notice that there is some difference in the way he or she is dressed and the way others in the office are dressed. It is quite likely that this new employee will take this into consideration and make some changes for the next day at work. Such a process of just looking around to see what others are doing and then trying to match their behavior we would want to call socialization.

It should be obvious that in most cultures the first learning of children is socialization, not education. That is, they are not given explicit training in behavior through rules, guided practice, testing, and other forms of formal assessment. They look around at what others are doing, and others make comments which indicate whether or not they approve.

While in the case of infants there is little to distinguish between the words "socialization" and "enculturation," in most cases the word "enculturation" is restricted just to the early learning of culture. It is what in the next section we will call "primary socialization." When a person learns a new job through observation of the actions of others and through their informal approval or disapproval, it would be best to call that sort of learning socialization rather than enculturation, as it applies largely to adult behavior.

The distinction between education and socialization, then, is based upon whether or not the procedures for teaching and learning are formally worked out by the group or the society and systematically applied to new members (whether those new members are just born into the society or come in as immigrants). The concept of education is most often associated with what sociologists have called *Gesellschaft*, whereas socialization is more often associated with *Gemeinschaft*. This is not a hard and fast distinction; many societies which sociologists consider traditional communities have clearly formal practices of education. Nevertheless, historically from eighteenth-century Europe on there has been a clear association of the rapidly increasing *Gesellschaft* structures of the Utilitarian discourse system and the rapid rise of universal formal public education in those societies which have embraced Utilitarian forms of discourse.

Another aspect of the distinction between education and socialization is that education tends to be periodic or formally structured into units of instruction, whereas socialization tends to be continuous. The units of instruction in education tend to have entrance or admission procedures and requirements as well as exit requirements and ceremonies, along with completion credentials. On the other hand, it would be difficult to say in the process of socialization just when one is actually engaged in learning. As a result, there is often a corresponding devaluation of the learning one acquires through socialization and an exaggerated valuation of learning acquired through formal education.

A third point is that education and socialization are often, perhaps nearly always, mixed. For example, in entering a new position, a person might receive specific training as we have mentioned above through handbooks and manuals of company procedures, while at the same time being expected to observe the general practices of older and more experienced employees and to follow their behavior.

Finally, to close out these first definitions, we want to briefly comment on the term "acculturation." Anthropologists and sociologists have used this term to talk about situations in which two different cultural or social groups come into contact. When one group is more powerful than the other and therefore produces a strong influence on that second group to forget or put aside its own culture and to adopt that of the more powerful group, that process of enforced culture learning is called acculturation. Generally speaking, acculturation is used as a negative term, since the process of cultural loss is considered by analysts to be an unfortunate one.

Primary and secondary socialization

We have one further terminological complication to add to this picture. Social psychologists have widely used the term "primary socialization" to refer to what anthropologists would be more likely to call "enculturation"; that is, primary socialization consists of the processes through which a child goes in the earliest stages of becoming a member of his or her culture or society. Generally speaking, this learning takes place within the family and among close intimates. In this same framework, then, secondary socialization refers to those processes of socialization which take place when the child begins to move outside the family, such as when the child first goes to school and begins to interact with other, non-familial children.

One might think it pointless to talk about secondary socialization instead of just calling it education when a child goes to school, but the point being made with these terms is that there are really quite complex processes of learning taking place. Education remains the best term for the formal processes of school learning – the curriculum, if you like; secondary socialization refers to those informal processes of learning which take place in and around or even during the other, more formal processes.

While it goes beyond the purposes of this book to go into primary socialization in detail, it is important to bear in mind what sorts of thing a child learns as part of this process. For our purposes, language and social behaviors are the most important. Linguists are in agreement that the great majority of the basic syntactic and phonological structures of one's language are learned (or acquired) as part of one's primary socialization (or during the period of one's primary socialization). For many, probably most humans, the ways one learns to speak during this period of early learning among the family and close intimate relatives places an indelible stamp on one's discourse for the rest of life. This is when one picks up the "accent" one will carry, with relatively few modifications, throughout life. This is when one becomes handy at using the basic syntactic structures and functions commonly used in one's community. Whatever other forms of discourse one might learn later on, for most of us they are largely learned against the background of the language acquired during this period of primary socialization.

Patterns of social behavior are also given a firm cast during the period of primary socialization. The child learns and develops patterns for relating to those of higher and lower status, older and younger and same age, boys and girls, and he or she learns how to be a boy or girl as well. Beyond these general forms of learning, the child also receives toilet training, and learns how to dress, how to eat, and how to play with others. All of these very fundamental aspects of human behavior are first learned during this period, and while they may undergo changes later in life, those changes are set up against this early learning as modifications and revisions more than simply taking on entirely different behavior patterns. Whatever discourse systems we may become members of later in life, the discourse systems which we enter through primary socialization have a weighted advantage over any we enter into later on.

Figure 7.3 summarizes our usage of these various terms. Socialization is being used *both* as the term covering all forms of cultural learning *and* as the more specific term to cover informal aspects of cultural learning. In the text which follows, we will try to make it clear in the context which meaning is to be understood.

Theories of the person and of learning

It is comfortable to think that all humans are alike in basic human processes, and that is certainly true to a considerable extent. Unfortunately, every culture has quite specific ideas about the nature of the human person and of human society, which it simply takes for granted as the obvious truth and yet which another cultural group would find quite surprising or with which

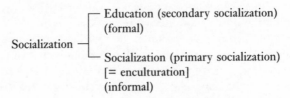

Figure 7.3 Terms for socialization.

they would strongly disagree. We will only consider three of the ways in which cultural groups may differ in their understanding of the nature of humans: their assumptions about whether humans are good or evil, their views about whether the group or the individual is the basic unit, and their understanding of the human life cycle.

We have quoted the *San Zi Jing* (Xu Chuiyang, 1990) as saying that we are all born good. This view that human nature is basically good has been held in Confucian ideology from at least the time of *Mencius* to the present. In contrast to this, in Christian ideology it has been believed that humans are basically evil or sinful. Of course within Chinese history there have been many arguments put forward for why it would be better to consider humans not to be basically good, and in western history many arguments have been put forward that humans are really good.

The important issue for us is not to try to decide whether or not humans are good or bad; we are more interested in what this issue means for socialization into a culture or a discourse system. If you assume humans are basically good, in trying to teach them you will assume that they are trying to do what is right and that what is needed is to show them the right thing to do. Motivation will be based on the learner's own intrinsic desire to do what is right.

On the other hand, if you assume humans are basically evil, in trying to teach them you will assume that they will do everything they can to distort your teaching, to turn it to their own mischievous purposes, or to refuse to cooperate. Motivation of such learners is more likely to be based on punishment and threats than rewards and promises. In other words, the theory of education and socialization which is held by a society or within a discourse system will be based on the more general concept of the good or evil nature of its members.

A second factor which will be important is whether the group believes that individuals or collectivities are the basic units of society. As we have discussed above, the anthropologist Francis Hsu and many others have argued that Asian society is primarily founded upon a "self" which is larger in scope than the "self" predicated in western society. This Asian self includes intimates of the immediate family, whereas the western self does not include such intimates.

A society which emphasizes the individual as its basic unit will adopt forms of education and socialization which focus on individual learning and individual success, even where those individuals become competitive with each other and destroy group harmony. On the other hand a society which emphasizes a broader concept of the person that includes familial intimates, such as traditional Confucian Asian society, will focus education and socialization on the development of that broader unit. The activities and the successes at learning of the individual unit will be seen as part of the activities of the larger units of society, and their successes will be gauged against their contribution to those larger units.

It is now well known that the children of Asian immigrants to the United Kingdom and to North America tend to do very well in schools, sometimes even against the odds of having to learn the new language, English, into the bargain. While this mystifies some educational observers, who focus on the individual students, it is clear that the social practices of the group are strongly supporting this learning. One sees even in very crowded living conditions that after dinner the table is cleared and the children settle down to doing homework, with each child helping the other so that all of them succeed in completing their tasks. This social behavior forms a strong contrast with the more typical American pattern, for example; of each child going to separate rooms to listen to music or to watch television while making half-hearted attempts at getting the homework finished.

Finally, a third factor in understanding the concept of the person and of learning for a particular group is that group's conception of the human life cycle. In western popular thought the terms and concepts of the social psychology of the past century have become well established. It is taken as common knowledge that the human life cycle can be divided into such phases as infancy, childhood, adolescence, early adulthood, the midlife transition, and so forth. Such terms are so widely used that they are taken as the only imaginable division of the human life span into developmental periods. Nevertheless, many cultures make rather different divisions of the human life cycle.

If we take only Europe in contrast, we can see that in earlier historical periods there was little recognition of the major divisions between childhood and adulthood we now consider to be so important. Furthermore, we tend to forget in these days of longer life expectancies that for many people now on earth as well as for much of our own earlier history, when an expected life span was closer to fifty years, an "old" person might well have been a person in his or her late forties or early fifties. When child bearing is expected to begin shortly after puberty, a person of the generation of mothers might be in her teens, a grandmother in her thirties. If we compare

this to the rather late child bearing of some contemporary mothers who are
having their first children even in their forties, we can see that it becomes
very difficult to make direct translations of the experience of motherhood
and the practices of primary socialization between mothers in such different
periods in their lives. A contemporary mother who is a professional woman
in her forties approaches the problems of primary socialization very differently from a mother who is in her early teens, whatever else these two
women might have in common.

Seen from the point of view of the individual, differences in the society's
conception of the life cycle include major differences in the importance
ascribed to various periods as well. The prolonged adolescent period which
contemporary westerners experience – we do not necessarily want to say
enjoy – is in sharp contrast to the plunge into a short lifetime of hard work
experienced by the children of the early Industrial Revolution. As lifetimes
have increased under industrial development and as the overall complexity
of society and its technologies have increased, more and more of the person's total lifespan is given over to educational preparation. In some societies, direct socialization through apprenticeship into the adulthood tasks is
sufficient for most members of the society. In modernized contemporary
society or in what some have called post-modern society, much of one's life
is spent in preparation for fully legitimate "adult" activity.

A childhood friend of one of the authors is now a brain surgeon. In a real
sense his period of education and training lasted nearly forty years; he was
in his forties before he was sufficiently well prepared to stand on his own
feet as a fully legitimated practicing brain surgeon. His life experience may
be compared to an Athabaskan hunter also known by the authors who
entered into his full adulthood occupation when he was fifteen years old.
While there is much to separate the experiences of these two men, the point
we wish to make here is that if we want to understand their membership
within their cultures and within their discourse systems, it will be important
to see that the processes of socialization for each of them are strikingly
different.

Cultural Ideology and Stereotyping

Now that we have introduced a number of dimensions which should be considered in analyzing intercultural discourse between Asians and westerners,
we think it is important to take up the question of cultural ideology and
stereotyping. We have said above that a balanced cultural description must
take into consideration the full complexity of cultural themes. When one of
those themes is singled out for emphasis and given a positive or negative

value or is treated as the full description, then we would want to call that ideology rather than cultural description. A much more common term for such cultural ideological statements is "stereotyping."

Ideological statement or stereotyping often arises when someone comes to believe that any two cultures or social groups, or, as we prefer to call them, two discourse systems, can be treated as if they were polar opposites. For example, in chapter 5 we introduced the concept of two different rhetorical strategies, the inductive and the deductive strategies, for the introduction of main topics in a discourse. There is a danger in such a concept when someone comes to consider Asians to be inductive and westerners to be deductive. That would constitute an ideological statement, by trying to make a clear division between Asians and westerners on the dimension of rhetorical strategies. As we argued in chapter 5, both strategies are used in all cultures that we know of. What might be different is the way communicative situations are established in different cultures, and especially the relationships among participants.

In the preceding section on cultural differences in time, we argued that the Utopian sense of time urgency is often thought of as western, and opposed to the Asian Golden-Age concept of time. This binary contrast is obviously too simplistic, since we see so many cases of the Utopian sense of time in Asia as well as cases of the Golden-Age sense of time in the west. Cultural ideologies in intercultural comparison are the fallacy of opposing two large cultural groups upon the basis of some single dimension, such as the introduction of topics in discourse or the sense of time.

Such general cultural ideological statements, then, focus on simplistic contrasts between cultural groups. Stereotyping arises from such ideologies by focusing upon individual members of cultural groups. It is the process by which all members of a group are asserted to have the characteristics attributed to the whole group.

Stereotyping is simply another word for overgeneralization. The difference, however, is that stereotyping carries with it an ideological position. Characteristics of the group are not only overgeneralized to apply to each member of the group, but they are also taken to have some exaggerated negative or positive value. These values are then taken as arguments to support social or political relationships in regard to members of those groups.

For example, it is clear that the sense of time urgency is characteristic of many of the residents of Asia's urban capitals, such as Tokyo, Taipei, Hong Kong, Seoul, or Singapore. It would become an overgeneralization to simply assume that, because someone was a resident of one of these cities, he or she would show a constant sense of time urgency. It becomes stereotyping to assume that this is a particularly good or bad quality of that person upon the basis of his or her membership in the group of residents of that city.

Stereotyping is a way of thinking that does not acknowledge internal differences within a group, and does not acknowledge exceptions to its general rules or principles. Ideologies are largely based on stereotypical thinking, or, to put it the other way around, stereotypes are largely ideological. There is usually a good bit of accurate cultural observation which underlies stereotypes; it is not the truth of those observations which is the problem. The problem is that stereotypes blind us to other, equally important aspects of a person's character or behavior. Stereotypes limit our understanding of human behavior and of intercultural discourse because they limit our view of human activity to just one or two salient dimensions and consider those to be the whole picture. Furthermore, they go on ideologically to use that limited view of individuals and of groups to justify preferential or discriminatory treatment by others who hold greater political power.

Researchers and consultants who are concerned with the analysis of intercultural communication range from anthropologists and sociolinguists to speech communication analysts and teachers of English. While their theoretical interests are often quite different, these researchers share a basic set of common assumptions in their work. Among these are four:

1   Humans are not all the same.
2   At least some of the differences among them show culturally or socially predictable patterns.
3   At least some of those patterns are reflected in patterns of discourse.
4   Some of those differences in discourse patterns lead directly to unwanted social problems such as intergroup hostility, stereotyping, preferential treatment, and discrimination.

We want to focus now on the problem of oversimplification of intercultural (or intergroup) analyses, which arises when people accept an ideological conceptual division of humanity. This is, of course, a very common situation. We will give one quite innocuous example.

Recently one of us was lecturing in America to a group of teachers from Taiwan who were in America on a cultural exchange program. The purpose of the lecture was to discuss some of the aspects of intercultural communication between Chinese and Americans. When we took a break for lunch, one of the American women present said that she was struck by how much the differences between Chinese and Americans were "just like the differences between women and men as Tannen had outlined in her book." She was referring to the book *You Just Don't Understand: women and men in conversation* by Deborah Tannen (1990a).

Even though we were carefully trying to avoid the fallacies of ideological and stereotyping statements – in fact, that was the point of the whole lecture – the form of analysis, contrastive analysis, provided the basis for one of the people there to make such an intuitive leap. This woman went on further to ask if it was not the case that the "American" in our analysis was not really better described as "an American man," since she felt the characteristics we had described for the "American" really did not seem to apply to American women, while at the same time the characteristics given for the Chinese did seem to fit better.

In a sense this is correct. As we will describe in chapter 11, there was actually a legitimate basis in the research literature for this woman's insight. At the same time, it is patently absurd to suggest that all Chinese, men and women, are "just like" American women. The problem we had run into was that of ideological oversimplification, or what we might call "binarism." The lecture had presented binary contrasts as the most graphic way of showing areas where miscommunication might arise. The woman, who was one of the teachers of this group of Chinese, was rather concerned to develop common grounds of solidarity with her Taiwanese students.

In discussing the differences between Chinese and Americans in that particular situation, there was little direct cause to wander further afield into other intercultural and intergroup comparisons. The audience consisted of Chinese English teachers who were in the United States for the purposes of learning more about English and about American culture. Their primary concern was not with gender differences as such, nor was it with other such differences as communication between Athabaskans and Anglo-Americans, or Chinese and Japanese. As a result, the framework which had been set around this presentation was that of a binary comparison.

At the same time, the American woman had just recently read Tannen's book. The framework set on that analysis by the subtitle on the cover is "women and men in conversation." As a perfect case in point, Tannen is very careful throughout her text to include many other intercultural comparisons, and yet Tannen's scrupulous presentation of her gender analysis within the context of much broader sociolinguistic comparative work was swept aside by her reader, whose own interpretive framework had settled into the ideological binarism of a polarized difference between American men and American women.

The solution to the problem of oversimplification or binarism and stereotyping is twofold: comparisons between groups should always consider both likenesses and differences, that is, they should be based upon more than a single dimension of contrast, and it must be remembered that no individual member of a group embodies all of his or her group's characteristics. As we will discuss in detail in chapters 8–11, we all are simultaneously members of multiple groups, or, as we call them, "discourse systems." None of us is fully defined by our membership in any single group. One is simultaneously a son or a daughter, a father or a mother, a member of a particular company, a member of a particular generation, and so forth in an indefinite number of discourse systems. One's sense of identity and group membership is a composite of all of these identities and a complex and sometimes difficult interaction among them.

Negative Stereotypes

Any form of stereotyping is potentially an obstruction to successful intercultural communication, because it will blind us to real differences that exist between the participants in a discourse. The most obstructive form of stereotyping, however, is also sometimes called negative stereotyping. In such a case, the first step is to contrast two cultures or two groups on the basis of some single dimension. For example, someone might say that all Asians are inductive and all westerners are deductive in their introduction of topics. Such a statement may have some basis in observation, but it ignores the fact that in many cases Asians also use deductive strategies on the one hand, and on the other inductive strategies are frequently used by westerners.

The second step in negative stereotyping is to focus on this artificial and ideological difference as a problem for communication. Unfortunately, this step is essential for any analysis of intercultural discourse, and as a result, it requires a great deal of care in such analysis to forestall stereotyping. We might say, for example, that because Asians are inductive and westerners are deductive, it is difficult for them to communicate with each other easily or successfully.

If we have already forgotten that our first premise was somewhat oversimplified, that is, if we have already forgotten that both inductive strategies and deductive strategies are used in both cultures, and if we have forgotten that we can never classify all Asians together and all westerners together, it becomes natural at this step to jump to the conclusion that Asians and westerners can never successfully communicate with each other. This is false, of course, but at this step in the process it can easily be forgotten.

The third step, then, is to assign a positive value to one strategy or one group and a negative value to the other strategy or group. At this step, for example, a westerner might say the problem with intercultural communication between Asians and westerners is that *they* refuse to introduce their topics so that *we* can understand them. The simple descriptive difference leads to the idea that somehow members of the other group are actively trying to make it difficult to understand them.

The fourth and final step is to regeneralize this process to the entire group. One reasserts the original binaristic contrast as a negative group contrast. One might say, for example, that *all* Asians or *all* westerners are like this; they always try to obstruct communication. Often one final step is taken; these characteristics are assumed to be genetic or racial characteristics.

Negative stereotyping is a perennial problem in intercultural communication. This is because these stereotypes are usually based on some accurate observation. It is accurate to say that in many instances there will be some difference in topic introduction between an Asian and a westerner. As we have argued above, in chapter 5, this difference does not result from Asians trying to be indirect or westerners trying to be direct. This is based on deeper assumptions being made about the face relationships one can adopt in certain communicative situations. It would be quite correct to say that in a communication between strangers, most Asians would be careful to use strategies of independence out of deference and respect for the other person. One of those strategies would be the rhetorical strategy of inductively introducing one's own topics.

It would also be correct to say that in communication between strangers, most westerners would try to bring the situation around to one of symmetrical solidarity. This would be because of the value placed in most western societies on egalitarianism and individualism. One strategy which would be used to do this would be to use a deductive rhetorical pattern for the introduction of topics.

If we forget the deeper reasons why these rhetorical strategies are used, we can easily move into negatively stereotyping members of other groups who are working from different basic assumptions about the most respectful way to treat strangers. The result is an overall negative impression of members of the other group.

Positive Stereotypes, the Lumping Fallacy, and the Solidarity Fallacy

We have mentioned above the woman who thought that our description of "Chinese" characteristics was just the same as Deborah Tannen's description of those for American women. Now we can go back and look at just what led this woman to this conclusion. The point we were discussing which led her to it had to do with the function of language. As we have said above, language has both the function of conveying information and the function of maintaining relationships among participants in speech events. We said that generally speaking, if we contrasted Chinese and Americans, we would see that Chinese would be on the relationship end of this continuum and Americans would be on the information end of the same continuum. In other words, Chinese tend to be concerned that good relationships are maintained, even if this means that less information may be exchanged, while Americans and Europeans in general will tend to emphasize the exchange of information, even if relationships cannot be easily maintained.

Tannen has observed that in communication between American men and American women, there is a tendency for men to emphasize information over relationship and for women to emphasize relationship over information. She characterizes this difference as that between report and rapport, with men emphasizing report and women emphasizing rapport.

Both of these characterizations, that of American women in comparison to American men and that of Americans to Chinese in general, have a basis in actual observations. The solidarity fallacy comes into play here when this woman tries to group together American women and all Chinese on this single dimension of information and relationship. There is no reason to deny that on this single dimension one would expect to find better understanding between American women and Chinese in general. The mistake – the solidarity fallacy – is to proceed from there and conclude that because there is common ground on this single dimension, there will be commonality across all of the cultural characteristics of these two groups.

If we look at just one other dimension, that of egalitarian and hierarchical relationships, it will become clear that while all Chinese, both men and women, and American women may have some common ground on the question of their perceptions of the function of language, when it comes to the question of relative status, there is little or no agreement at all. Particularly in contemporary times, American women tend to emphasize egalitarian relationships throughout society. In contrast to this, throughout the history of China up to the present day, Chinese in general have always emphasized clear hierarchical relationships. Ideologically, of course, this has been somewhat more to the advantage of Asian men then Asian women. To bring this statement up to date it should be noted that throughout Asia many women are now urging or hoping for greater equality in their relationships with Asian men.

The solidarity fallacy of putting American women together in a single conceptual group with Chinese is shown to be impossibly wrong when the question of hierarchy comes up. On that dimension one might see them as polar opposites. Of course, no two groups are either polar opposites or exactly identical. The problem of negative stereotyping is one of seeing members of different groups as being polar opposites. The problem of positive stereotyping is one of seeing members of different groups as being identical. In either case, it is a problem of stereotyping which arises from making a comparison on the basis of a single, binary dimension of analysis.

When the grouping is based on falsely combining one's own group and some other group, we would call it the solidarity fallacy. In the case we have just described, the American woman falsely included her group, American women, with Chinese on the belief that they had the emphasis on relationship in common, while ignoring the major differences between their groups. When the person making the false grouping is doing so in reference to two other groups, we would call that the lumping fallacy. For example, when westerners consider all Asians to be members of the same group without taking into consideration the major differences among these groups, this would be called the lumping fallacy. In the same way, grouping together all westerners would also be the lumping fallacy. In both cases, positive stereotyping occurs when the person making the categorization takes the characteristics he or she used to make the stereotyping as positive, while negative stereotyping results when the basis of comparison was considered to be negative.

Whether the stereotyping is positive or negative in intent, it should be clear that it stands in the way of successful communication because it blinds the analyst to major areas of difference. As we have said at the very beginning of this book, communication is inherently ambiguous. Effective communication depends on finding and clarifying sources of ambiguity as well as learning to deal with places where miscommunication occurs. Such clarification is impossible when the analyst does not recognize areas of difference among participants, because he or she will assume common ground and mutual understanding. The perennial paradoxical situation of the analyst of intercultural communication is that he or she must constantly look for areas of difference between people which will potentially lead to miscommunication, but at the same time he or she must constantly guard against both positive and negative stereotyping.

Differences Which Make a Difference: Discourse Systems

In this chapter, we have reviewed several areas in which researchers have demonstrated that cultures may differ significantly from each other. While we have only touched upon each of these areas with a few examples, we hope it is clear that the potential for intercultural misunderstanding is great. At the same time, now that we have reviewed these many areas of potential difference, we want to point out that not all cultural differences are equally problematical in intercultural communication. In fact, some cultural differences do not make any major difference from the point of view of discourse analysis. The reason for this is that cultures tend to be very large groupings with many internal sub-groupings. There is hardly any dimension on which you could compare cultures and with which one culture could be clearly and unambiguously distinguished from another.

To give just a few examples, we have observed earlier that the inductive and the deductive rhetorical strategies are not sufficient to distinguish between cultures because both strategies may be used in virtually any culture.

If one tries to distinguish between cultures on the basis of egalitarianism or hierarchy, one will always find contexts in any culture in which one or the other structure will predominate. If we classify on the basis of the functions of language, again, one will find that while Americans and Chinese are different on the dimension overall, with Americans tending toward the function of information and Chinese tending toward the function of relationship, yet American women will tend to be more like the so-called "Chinese" value. And, of course, one will find within Chinese culture many areas in which the emphasis is, in fact, on information, not relationship.

One strategy which has been used, of course, is to use multiple dimensions to contrast cultures. While it is more accurate, still it is difficult to draw very direct connections between aspects of culture and actual situations of discourse.

In chapter 6, we described the nature of discourse systems. Such systems are smaller than whole cultures and tend to take on somewhat more homogeneous characteristics, if not ideological unity. For example, it would be impossible to talk about western culture in any clear and unambiguous way. On the other hand, it is possible to describe quite clearly the Utilitarian discourse system, its practices of socialization, its assumptions about face politeness, and the forms of discourse that are used as a result of this face politeness system of symmetrical solidarity. This is because, on the whole, the Utilitarian discourse system is an ideological system which quite self-consciously seeks ideological unity.

As we have shown in this chapter, there are many characteristics of culture which may influence discourse as long as it is possible to clearly show that the participants in a particular discourse are different from each other on that dimension or factor. For example, if two participants in a discourse are different from each other in their choice of deductive or inductive strategies for the introduction of topics, whether or not they are from different cultures, they will find themselves confused as to how to interpret what is being said by the other person. What is significant is not the difference in culture; it is the difference in that particular rhetorical strategy.

The same argument can be made for differences between any two participants in a discourse on the basis of any of the factors we have just discussed. They could find difficulties in communicating based upon their belief about whether humans were essentially good or evil, their religion, their kinship relationships, their sense of ingroup loyalty, their understanding of egalitarianism and hierarchy, their emphasis on individualism or collectivism, whether they conceive of language as being used primarily for information or relationship, whether negotiation or ratification of those relationships is thought to be primary, or the assumptions they make about the most effective ways of socializing either their children or new members to the group.

Their emphasis on group harmony or individual welfare could lead to a different interpretation of such non-verbal aspects of communication as smiles or their use of space. Even a difference in such an abstract factor as their concept of Utopian or Golden-Age directions in the "arrow of time" could lead to major problems of interpretation in discourse.

We would be very unlikely to find any two cultures or members of any cultural groups who would differ completely from each other on all of these dimensions. As a result, we believe that in discussions of intercultural communication, we will be more effective by narrowing our focus to discourse systems, which are sub-cultural systems where contrasts between one system and another are somewhat more strongly made. In chapters 8–11 we will focus on communication which takes place across boundaries between groups which are defined as discourse systems. From this point of view, intercultural communication might better be analysed as interdiscourse system communication.

8

Corporate Discourse

Discourse Systems

We have introduced the idea of the discourse system in chapter 6 to capture this regularity in our day-to-day experience and use of language. In chapter 7 we discussed a number of ways in which a culture influences the discourse systems found within it as well as the problem of stereotyping. Now our goal is to elaborate on the concept of the discourse system by drawing somewhat detailed portraits of four of the more common systems of which most of us are members. We will focus especially on the two main types of discourse systems: goal-directed or voluntary systems (such as corporate cultures and function-oriented discourse communities, for example, those of professional groups like foreign exchange officers, importers and exporters, teachers, or people who work in travel industry management), and involuntary discourse systems (such as generations and gender).

The basic concept of the discourse system which we introduced in chapter 6 and elaborated in chapter 7 involved four elements: a group of ideological norms, distinct socialization practices, a regular set of discourse forms, and a set of assumptions about face relationships within the discourse system. We took as our example the Utilitarian discourse system which first began to develop in the seventeenth century as part of the Utilitarian economic and political philosophy of the Enlightenment. It continues down to the present day to be the primary discourse system identified with business, both within European-derived cultures and increasingly throughout international business and governmental circles. This is a cross-cutting discourse system which is found widely across cultural boundaries, while at the same time it does not represent more than a portion of the discourse within any particular cultural group.

With the example of the Utilitarian discourse system in mind, we can recall that a discourse system can be defined with four characteristics:

1 Members will hold a common ideological position and recognize a set of extra-discourse features which define them as a group.

These extra-discourse factors which define members of a discourse system may be common experiences (such as those shared by members of the same generation), a common historical background (such as immigration from the same country of origin), a common race or gender, a common language or linguistic variety, or even common treatment by outgroup members. Their ideology will guide their attitudes toward outgroup members.

2 Socialization is accomplished primarily through these preferred forms of discourse.

A somewhat circular, self-reinforcing system is set for potential members of discourse systems in that one learns how to be a member through learning how to use the preferred forms of discourse, and then one shows one's membership through competent use of these forms of discourse. In the case of a voluntary discourse system such as a corporation, one "learns the ropes" by a form of on-the-job training. One learns to do a business letter in the corporate style by following the formats used by one's predecessors in the corporation. As a special precaution, in many cases voluntary, goal-oriented discourse systems will set up training programs or even credentialling courses. Such courses will often focus on the forms of discourse required for successful participation.

Involuntary discourse systems such as those of generation or gender do not normally have formal systems for teaching the preferred forms of discourse. One becomes a member through socialization or enculturation. One is simply told, "Don't talk like a girl," "Don't talk to your mother like that," "Good girls don't say such things," or "We don't say such things." One is left to work out the system as one progresses toward membership and identity over a period of apprenticeship.

3 A set of preferred forms of discourse serves as banners or symbols of membership and identity.

These preferred forms of discourse may include the use of involvement or independence face strategies, certain genres (such as letters of credit, invoices, and purchase orders in business), certain specialized forms of address, a highly specialized lexicon (such as is used in law, linguistics, or the travel industry), or, in fact, any other aspect of the grammar of context which we have outlined in chapter 2 or any of the cultural aspects which we outlined in chapter 7. The crucial point is that these preferred forms of discourse serve to symbolize identity and membership for members of the discourse system.

One consequence of the fact that preferred forms of discourse function as banners of identity and membership is that a person will be reluctant to shift patterns of discourse, because this will be experienced as a change in identity. In the same way, members will use these forms as a guide to test others for membership in their discourse system. As codes or badges of membership, these preferred discourse forms will come to dominate discourse within these systems.

4   Face relationships are prescribed for discourse among members or between members and outsiders.

A discourse system can be identified in part by having regular expectations for how members will speak to each other as well as for how members will speak to non-members. The Utilitarian discourse system, for example, prescribes a face politeness system of symmetrical solidarity for public discourse among members. The Confucian discourse system described in the *Li Ji*, as we mentioned in chapter 5, prescribes a system of hierarchy between ruler and ruled, father and son, and elder and younger brothers. It prescribes a system of "difference" (perhaps symmetrical deference) for husband and wife, and a system of symmetrical solidarity between friends. As we will discuss below in looking at other discourse systems, there are also significant expectations for discourse among men, among women, between men and women, and among people born into different generations.

Voluntary and involuntary discourse systems

It is useful to distinguish between two types of discourse commonality which, in turn, form two types of discourse systems: voluntary and involuntary. Voluntary discourse systems are goal-oriented discourse systems such as corporations or governmental and other institutional structures which have been formed for specific purposes. These purposes might be to gain a profit for the owners in the case of a corporation or to educate children in the case of schools. In the case of professional groups or organizations, the goals will be to provide support to other colleagues and to enforce professional practices and codes of conduct.

Involuntary discourse systems are those formed by gender, race, generation, ethnicity or other such characteristics, in which individual members have relatively little choice about whether or not they share in the characteristics. This does not mean, however, that they have no choice about membership and identity. It is not uncommon for individuals who share in the characteristics of a particular discourse system to reject identity and membership, as when a member of some ethnic group chooses not to identify himself or herself as a member. In such cases there is often a conflict created between membership and identity, since members of the group are likely to treat this person as a member in spite of his or her attempts to reject identity with the group.

Identity in a discourse system is often displayed through attention to the goals or the extra-discourse features of the group and by expressing its ideology. In a corporation, a member might be criticized for paying too little attention to the goal of gaining a profit. A man might be criticized for betraying the common experience of men on behalf of equality for women. A member of an ethnic group might be criticized for ignoring the oppression his or her group has felt historically in an attempt to achieve better communication with someone from outside the group. In each case, the criticism is based upon some defining characteristic which is recognized by the group.

Finally, before going further we need to comment on our use of the word "ideology" in our discussion of involuntary discourse systems. The defining aspect of a voluntary discourse system is that it is goal-directed. This might be considered another way of saying that it has a self-conscious ideology; such a system is created specifically to put forward a point of view or to accomplish a task. This implies that some set of values underlies the discourse system, which overtly or covertly guides its operations and its processes of making decisions.

Involuntary discourse systems, on the other hand, are not created by conscious choice. One is born into a time and a place which are not of one's choosing and thus one becomes a member of a generation. The generation itself has little to say about the historical and cultural circumstances which surround it. In the same way, humans are born into two relatively bifurcated sexes, the biological grounding of gender distinctions. Furthermore, most cultural groups practice some degree of gender specialization and polarization. A person is born with genetically determined sexual characteristics and with culturally given gender expectations over which he or she has relatively little choice.

The discourse systems which arise around these involuntary groupings of humans show, as we will discuss below, rather distinctive characteristics not unlike those of voluntary discourse systems. That is why we feel we can describe both types of discourse system with the same vocabulary of description.

Nevertheless, we need to sound a note of caution in using the term "ideology." The word suggests, as we have said, that we are going beyond simple objective description and saying or implying that the characteristics we are describing are, in fact, consciously controlled, purposive, and value-laden. When we say that members of the Depression/War generation of Americans are obsessed with punctuality and scheduling, that might be a

simple objective description. On the other hand, if members of that generation come to think that these are good qualities, ones which should be
fostered in schools, rewarded in business activities, and prescribed in bringing up children, they have moved over into ideology. Characteristics which
might well have been unwittingly adopted through the circumstances of
place, of culture, and of history have become consciously promoted as ideal
human behavior.

In our discussions of the involuntary discourse systems which follow,
we will continue to use the word "ideology" to cover our description of the
general historical and social characteristics of these groups, but it should be
remembered that members of these groups will vary in the extent to which
they actively promote these characteristics as a self-conscious ideology.

Five Characteristic Discourse Systems

We have said above that the concept of culture is too broad a social organization to be very useful in the analysis of discourse. We do not think that
it is useful to describe a culture as a discourse system at all. In the contemporary world, virtually every culture can be shown to consist of a number
of internal, cross-cutting, and overlapping discourse systems, such as those
of generation, ethnicity, and gender. In addition to these discourse systems,
virtually all cultures participate in the worldwide economic system of the
extraction of resources and the production and distribution of goods, as well
as having some contact with the worldwide system of exchange of news
and entertainment, though, of course, the amount of this exchange varies
considerably from place to place.

In a book such as this one it would be impossible to give a comprehensive
description of even a single discourse system, let alone adequate descriptions of even the most basic overlapping discourse systems within which we
all communicate. On the other hand, we feel it is important to sketch in at
least the outlines of a few main discourse systems, while pointing out the
major issues which need to be analyzed in order to understand how individual members take on their identity within those systems, and to understand how communication between members of those systems works.

Mr Kim, a mechanical engineer for Kolon company in Seoul, works for
one of the major South Korean corporations, which has branches not only
throughout South Korea, but also throughout Southeast Asia, North America,
and Europe. He is married and has two young children. His own mother
has passed away, but his father lives with him.

Mr Kim is simultaneously a member of quite an array of discourse
systems. As an employee of one of South Korea's largest corporations,
he enjoys the prestige of being identified with their corporate culture. As

an engineer, Mr Kim is a member of the discourse system of mechanical engineers; he belongs to their professional association, receives their journal, and has attended training sessions in order to keep up with his specialization. As a member of such a corporation doing international business – Mr Kim has worked on a joint venture team in Frankfurt – he is a member of the Utilitarian discourse system which predominates in such international business and professional exchanges. At the same time Mr Kim, as a Korean, participates in the widely shared Confucian discourse system, which is reflected in his attitudes toward education, toward his position in society, and toward his family. Mr Kim is in his late thirties and this means he is a member of the generation of Koreans who were born just after the Korean War. This separates him from his father and mother, who were born during the period of Japanese occupation before World War II, and it also separates him from his own children, who have been born in a period of great affluence and economic development. Mr Kim, as a man, finds himself too a member in the discourse system of Korean men, which means from time to time going for drinks after work with fellow employees and generally finding that most of his social relaxation is in the company of other men and not with his wife or family.

Most professional discourse takes place within these five major types of discourse system:

1   the corporate culture;
2   the professional group;
3   the Utilitarian discourse system;
4   the generational discourse system;
5   the gender discourse system.

The first two of these are, on the whole, voluntary or goal-directed discourse systems. That is, the corporate culture and the professional group are motivated by a goal-directed ideology. As we have argued in chapter 6, the Utilitarian discourse system is a broad, overarching ideological system widely spread through international business and governmental organizations. As a kind of background to corporate culture, on the one hand, it could be considered to be a goal-directed discourse system. On the other hand, most of its members begin their socialization into this system at a very early age with little recognition of its ideological status. It might therefore better be considered an involuntary discourse system for many members.

Finally, the generational discourse system of which one is a member as well as one's gender group are involuntary discourse systems in that one is born into them, though, as we will argue in chapter 10, even these so-called involuntary discourse systems will often take on goal-directed characteristics.

In the chapters which follow, we will give descriptions of these separate discourse systems. In doing so, we will bring out crucial points which such discourse systems raise for our overall understanding of interdiscourse system communication. We hope that this strategy will accomplish two purposes. The first of these is simply to illustrate the complexity of these multiple discourse systems as they operate in our day-to-day lives. Our second purpose is to encourage the reader to undertake his or her own analysis of the discourse systems of which he or she is a member.

In the outline sketches or profiles which follow, we will emphasize the discourse systems for which significant research has been undertaken. For example, most of the research on generational discourse systems has been carried out in North America. As a result, most of our examples will consider contrasts between generations of largely urban, largely middle-class North Americans of European origin. We do not mean to suggest, however, that readers should expect to be able to transfer this profile directly to generational discourse in other parts of the world or to other populations even in North America. We hope that our reader will be encouraged to analyze his or her own generational discourse system, whether that be European, Australian, or East Asian.

Gender discourse has become a very active field of research among researchers in North America, in the United Kingdom, and in Australia, as well as in other, non-English-speaking European countries. There is, to date, very little research available concerning gender discourse among Asians and so we also wish to encourage the reader to begin the analysis of gender discourse in these other as yet not well-known areas. Our purpose is to encourage further research and analysis, not to present finished findings for the reader to simply study and digest.

An Outline Guide to the Study of Discourse Systems

The outline guide for the study of discourse systems which follows is the basic format around which we have organized our comparative studies of discourse systems. There are four key questions, based upon the four main elements of a discourse system, as well as a number of secondary questions which have been raised in earlier chapters of this book:

1   *Ideology*: what are the historical/social/ideological characteristics of the group?
    (a)   Natural or purposive (that is, involuntary or voluntary)
    (b)   History
    (c)   Worldview
    (d)   Beliefs, values, religion
    (e)   Place in culture, stance regarding other group

2 *Socialization*: how does one learn membership/identity?
   (a) Education, enculturation, acculturation
   (b) Primary and secondary socialization
   (c) Theories of the person and of learning
      – Good and evil
      – Individual and collective
      – Life cycle
3 *Forms of discourse*: what are the preferred forms of communication?
   (a) Grammar of context (chapter 1) especially:
      – Situations and events
      – Genres
      – Media
   (b) Face strategies (chapter 3)
   (c) Patterns/types of cohesion (chapter 4)
   (d) Rhetorical (face) strategies (chapter 5)
   (e) Functions of language (chapter 7)
      – Information and relationship
      – Negotiation and ratification
      – Group harmony and individual welfare
   (f) Non-verbal communication (chapter 7)
      – Kinesics
      – Proxemics
      – Concept of time
4 *Face systems* (social organization): what are the preferred or assumed human relationships?
   (a) Kinship
   (b) The concept of the self
   (c) Ingroup–outgroup relationships

In this chapter and in the three chapters to follow we will vary the format of our presentation to highlight several analytical issues. Here we will use the analysis of corporate discourse as a way of introducing the outline guide we have just presented above. Our goal will be to show how these questions might provide a fruitful analytical guide to begin the analysis of corporate discourse. In doing this analysis we will not focus on any particular corporate group, but rather consider a wide range of such groups from manufacturing and sales corporations or service corporations to governmental and other institutional organizations.

In chapter 9 we will discuss professional discourse systems. In this case our goal will be to illustrate how the concerns of professional membership, identity, and development form a discourse system which cuts across corporate or institutional membership. As our example we will take the worldwide professional group of teachers of English as a second language

(ESL teachers). Our reasons for this choice are that this book is being written to be used within ESL (or ESP – English for special purposes – or EPC – English for professional communication) classrooms at the tertiary level. We assume that most of the teachers who use this book will themselves be members of this professional group to some extent. Furthermore, English teachers themselves are members of a group of professional communicators who are involved largely in intercultural and interdiscourse communication. We have chosen this particular professional group to encourage our readers to examine more closely the discourse structures within which they are using this book itself.

In chapter 10 we will turn to the analysis of an involuntary discourse system, the generational discourse system. Our purpose will be to demonstrate two major issues: the functioning of involuntary discourse systems, and the complexity which arises when there are systems within systems, or sub-systems. Our analysis will be based on the four currently most salient American generations, focusing particularly on the major division between pre-war and post-war generations.

Finally, chapter 11 will turn to discourse between men and women, or the gender discourse system. Our analysis will be quite directly contrastive between the complementary systems of men and women, highlighting first the differences which arise and secondly the misunderstandings which are the result of these differences.

The Corporate Discourse System (Corporate Culture)

When we use the term "corporate" discourse we have in mind the overriding discourse system practiced in the sorts of multinational corporation in which we presume many, if not most, of our readers will ultimately be employed. Nevertheless, we do not mean to exclude more locally owned businesses or the very wide range of governmental and other institutional organizations in which our readers may be employed. From the point of view of the analysis of discourse systems, there may actually be little difference between the functioning of a hospital and an airline company. A local arts council founded for the purposes of arranging art exhibits and concerts will, in fact, demonstrate many of the same principles of corporate discourse structures as a corporation listed on stock exchanges throughout the world. We are not concerned with examining what is usually known as organizational communication – that would differ considerably from structure to structure. We want to focus on the most significant ways in which institutional discourse systems come to be the overriding factors in understanding ordinary discourse among members.

Ideology

The corporation, also known as a limited liability company in contrast to sole proprietorships and partnerships, is without question the dominant form of business organization in the modern world. The roots of corporate law extend back to the time of Rome, but it was not until the nineteenth century that the form of the corporation as we know it now really came to be established. By the turn of the century, the limited liability company or corporation had come to dominate.

As the reader will be aware, this period in which the modern corporation evolved into its present form is the period of the rise of the Utilitarian ideology. It is not an exaggeration to say that the limited liability corporation is the organizational and legal expression in business affairs of the Utilitarian ideology. One of the key concepts is that of the juridical personality, which means that the corporation is taken as a legal person or individual. To put this another way, under corporate law, the corporation is the one person who can best exemplify the Utilitarian ideology, because this person is entirely fictive and can be logically defined as nothing more than or other than an economic entity.

Because we have already presented the Utilitarian ideology in chapter 6, here we will only need to say that the dominant ideology in corporate discourse systems is normally Utilitarian ideology. This matching of ideology and organizational structure is the goal which was pursued by the first generations of Utilitarians, and finally accomplished by the monopolistic American corporations of Rockefeller, J. P. Morgan, and the rest.

Natural or purposive?

The first consideration is that corporate discourse systems are goal-oriented. That is, they are brought into being to achieve certain purposes and, at least in the beginning, those purposes will dominate the ideology of the discourse system. In most cases the founding purposes will be stated in such documents as articles of incorporation and charters. They will sometimes be restated as "mission statements," which are used internally to produce cohesion in staff ideology and externally for marketing or public relations purposes.

There are two broad classes of purposes for which corporate structures come into existence: (1) to make a profit for the owners, and (2) to provide some service to some constituency. A manufacturing company is most likely to be governed by the purpose of making a profit. A school, on the other hand, is more likely to be governed by the second type of purpose, that of providing a service.

One should be alert to the possibility that these two broad motives may well be combined in the basic ideology of the organization. A private school may, indeed, be founded for the purpose of providing an education, but it may also be required to do so, if not at a profit, at least not at a loss. In other words, such private educational institutions as Stanford University are well known for the fact that along with providing their foundational educational services, they also manage to make profitable returns on their many investments, which constitute a form of ongoing financial support for the educational goal.

A secondary purpose of most corporate discourse systems is to provide employment. Sociologists have often pointed out that while institutions come into existence with certain external goals in mind, it is not long before internal and quite secondary goals come to dominate. American automobile manufacturers, for example, had as their original purpose the production of cars and other motor vehicles in order to earn money for their owners. Nevertheless, after a period of time the employees, through the medium of their organized labor unions, voiced the view that the purpose was to provide them with employment.

This is not the place to engage in an analysis of the past thirty years of international automobile production and of the labor market. The point we are making is that a corporation or other organization may begin with one set of stated goals or purposes, but those goals and purposes may change significantly over time and, in fact, come to dominate the operation of the organization. Often that shift in goals is described by sociologists as a change from external motivation to internal motivation. The main purpose of the organization comes to be maintaining the existence of the organization, whether or not the organization serves any external purpose.

The ideology of most corporate discourse systems, then, is likely to consist of two major elements: the stated, foundational purpose and an implicit, evolved, internal purpose. In making an analysis of corporate ideology, one should remain alert to the likelihood that the purposes which appear in corporate handbooks, in founding documents, and in corporate training activities may well be only the original, externally motivated purposes of the organization. They are quite likely not to be the more tacit, unstated, or even largely unrecognized internal purposes. Nevertheless, discourse within such a discourse system is likely to be measured against the standard of the more internal goals.

History

At the time Ron Scollon worked for Ford Motor Company, many of the employees of the company who were retiring were the original employees of the company. Like many other of the major automobile corporations and their feeder companies in Detroit, these companies, which were just then being established, had hired new immigrants to America in the 1920s. These new Americans, like the elder Mr Scollon, went to work for these new companies, often within days of arriving in the new country, and then worked for the same company until the day they retired some forty years later. As a result, in the 1960s, the history of these companies was virtually inseparable from the history of American industry in the interwar period (between World War I and World War II) and from the history of European immigration to the Midwest.

This can be starkly contrasted with those same companies in the decades which have passed since. Two major historical developments had the effect of major restructuring of these corporations. On the one hand, the companies have developed into multinational corporations which can no longer be identified with the regional history of any particular country, and on the other, employees of these companies no longer have the long personal parallel attachments to these companies. In the 1960s, the history of the Ford company could largely be told in the histories of the individual employees who had lived out their employment lives in the company. By the 1990s, such companies have come to take on much more consciously developed and abstract characteristics. The corporate culture of the Ford company was once very much the same as the cultural history of downriver Detroit. Now the corporate culture is carefully crafted by specialists in personnel.

This, then, is the major question to be considered in analyzing a corporate discourse system from the point of view of its history: to what extent is its history grounded in the history of a particular place and time? Generally speaking, the smaller and more local a corporate discourse system, the more it will share in the characteristics of its time and place. Large, multinational systems will often take on rather artificial, consciously designed characteristics, which have as their purpose to provide some sense of history and of corporate culture in the absence of more naturally occurring local or regional history and culture.

Worldview

Of course history and culture are closely tied to worldview. As we have argued starting in chapter 6, most international corporations and governmental organizations have taken on as their organizational worldview the ideology of the Utilitarian discourse system. This is so much the case that in recent years it has become a struggle among management analysts to see if such organizations can be restructured along lines that would modify some of the less productive aspects of this dominant discourse system.

As Japanese manufacturers began to dominate American and then world markets, many western corporations began to look at Japanese management for clues to their success. Starting perhaps with Ouchi's *Theory Z*, attention began to be focused on aspects of Japanese management which emphasized consensus rather than individual competition. The individualism of the Utilitarian discourse system, at least to some management specialists, was becoming unproductive at the level of day-to-day management of work or task groups.

We do not need to go into further details concerning the most current views of management culture other than to say that there is an ongoing debate in management circles about what is the right combination of individual competitive motivation on the one hand and group or task motivation on the other. Most such discussions, however, come up against the fact that underlying most thinking in management circles is the Utilitarian ideology, which continues to foster concepts of the creative, innovative individual.

Beliefs, values, religion

Corporations established for the purposes of doing business generally adopt the Utilitarian ideology. As we have said in chapter 6, one major historical aspect of this ideology is that the authority of the rational, logical, human individual came to replace the authority of the church or of formal religious belief. This economic and rational concept of humans tends to take a strongly secularist position in modern corporate discourse systems. In most cases there is a formal policy, or at least an informal understanding, that employees will leave their beliefs, whether political or religious, at home when they report to work. Discourse is organized around the idea that objective facts and logical processes should be sufficient to determine courses of action.

This same ideology of objectivism and rationalism dominates even in organizational structures which are not strictly organized for economic purposes. Schools throughout the western world, for example, typically eschew the explicit treatment of beliefs and values by taking a rationalistic and relativistic stance. In both cases, it should be observed that the ideals of "freedom of belief" and "freedom of expression" are generally proscribed. One is free only to express the Utilitarian ideological position of empiricism and rationalism.

Nevertheless, in some cases there are corporate structures which are organized specifically for the purpose of advancing beliefs, values, or religious principles. Most churches are now organized as not-for-profit corporate structures and have their fundamental beliefs encoded in their articles of incorporation or charters. In these cases as well there is no espousal of freedoms of belief or expression. Membership in such discourse systems is tied to the expression and support of the foundational beliefs. In other words, the Utilitarian ideal of freedom of individual expression is rarely to be found within corporate discourse systems, whether they are of the economically motivated type or of the not-for-profit type.

Place in culture

The final aspect of the ideology of corporate discourse systems to be considered is the question of how that discourse system sees itself as part of the larger culture within which it functions. Chief executive officers of large corporations have traditionally viewed themselves as major contributors to the welfare and stability of their cultural environments. In more recent years, multinational corporations have grown to be larger institutional structures with greater resources than all but the largest of the world's nations. In a real sense, some of the world's largest corporations are the defining entities and the world's nations the smaller units which feed into those structures. This constitutes a significant reorganization of the world political structure within the past several decades.

From the point of view of discourse systems, the crucial question is how a particular corporate discourse system views itself in this worldwide complex structure of nations, cultures, and corporations. A meat buyer working for McDonald's will approach a potential supplier knowing that he or she has the structure of one of the world's largest and most popularly known corporations to rely upon. On the other hand, a buyer for a small jewelry shop in Tokyo will have no such internationally known back-up support. While this difference in size or in degree of internationality may not make a direct difference in ideology, it will make a difference in how strongly the employee can put forward the company ideology in his or her dealings with others outside of the company. For a member of one of the world's large multinationals there will be some expectations that part of his or her agenda will, in fact, be to put forward the company ideology. For a member of a small, family-held business, in contrast, the governing ideology is likely to be put into the background or even set aside where necessary.

The point we want to make in taking up this question of the place a corporate discourse system has in the broader picture is that the corporate ideology itself may be a more or less central aspect depending on the relative strength of the corporation. The stronger the position of the corporate discourse system, the more its employees are likely to think that strength derives from corporate ideology and therefore the more likely they are to self-consciously take on that ideology and to bring it to the attention of others.

There are, of course, many other aspects of the ideology of corporate discourse systems which we might have considered. Our goal here is simply to introduce the reader to the kinds of issue which must be analyzed if we are to develop an adequate understanding of such discourse systems.

Socialization

Education, enculturation, acculturation

As goal-oriented discourse systems, corporate cultures have a large component of formal institutional learning as part of the means by which members become socialized. As we have said in chapter 6, public schooling in European countries developed right along with industrialization as an inseparable aspect of the Industrial Revolution, and most corporate discourse systems assume that entrance will be limited to appropriately schooled candidates.

Of course, a major distinction is usually made in the qualifications for "white-collar" (or "salaried") and "blue-collar" (or "hourly") employees, with higher levels of formal education required for higher levels of status and pay. As anyone who has worked in such corporations certainly knows, such a distinction bears little comparison with actual distinctions in knowledge, work responsibility, or importance to the company of the work accomplished. In virtually all organizations one can find relatively low-paid hourly workers with little official educational background carrying rather significant loads of decision-making work. One finds, for example, secretaries who have worked for years in an office who, through experience and informal socialization into the job, know a good bit more about how to accomplish the work of the office than their newly hired, highly credentialed, and much better-paid supervisors.

In the preceding paragraph we wrote "little official educational background" because we wanted to signal that it is not the actual educational background which matters in most cases, but rather the officially sanctioned educational background. It often happens that a person with rather extensive formal educational credentials ends up working in a job which requires only the minimal educational qualifications. Within corporate or institutional discourse this virtually always means that he or she will be treated according to his or her official status – an "hourly" worker – not his or her actual competence. This experience is, unfortunately, widely shared among women, immigrants, members of ethnic minority groups, and even majority populations under colonial rule.

In other words, the amount and kinds of formal, schooled education and training are a significant measure used in setting job requirements and in screening potential members of these corporate discourse systems, whether or not those qualifications are actually significant in carrying out the functions for which new members are hired. These formal credentials remain a significant aspect of members' participation in and advancement through such systems of discourse.

Once a person has passed through the "gates" of a corporate discourse system, that is, once a person has been hired, both education and enculturation are major aspects of that person's learning how to become a full member. As we have said in chapter 6, most corporations, businesses, government offices, or other goal-directed discourse systems have prepared materials for the education of new members. There are employee handbooks, policy statements, newsletters, bulletins, and standard operating procedures (SOPs) as well as orientation and training sessions to introduce the new member into the ideology and daily procedures of the company and the job.

There is a longstanding recognition that, even though most organizations require formal educational credentials for most positions, nevertheless new employees will require training for the specific tasks they are expected to do. Such on-the-job training programs recognize that the formal educational credentials are serving some purpose other than directly training future employees for such corporate structures.

At the same time, it is widely recognized that a great deal of the learning that new members need to do will be done quite informally, by observation and imitation. In other words, there is a widespread recognition that success in taking on corporate identity and in being accepted as a member depends upon successful enculturation. This enculturation, oddly enough, is often carried out across the lines of institutional status. Much in the way that enculturation of the infants of members of the world's upper classes is often actually carried out on a day-to-day basis by servants of a different class, and often of a different ethnic or cultural group, frequently a new "lieutenant" is broken in and shown the corporate ropes by a well-seasoned "first sergeant." Often enough one finds a secretary with meager academic or formal educational background enculturating a highly credentialed supervisor who is struggling through the first stages of becoming a member of a new corporate culture.

Finally, while the terms "enculturation" and especially "acculturation" are normally used in anthropology to refer to cultural processes, there is an important way in which acculturation is significant in studies of professional discourse. As we said in chapter 6, acculturation refers to the process by which a dominant culture comes to supplant the culture of people over which it has come to exercise its power. In recent years throughout the world there has been a marked increase in the consolidation of smaller companies into larger, multinational conglomerate structures. Many employees of the smaller companies which have been involved in these mergers and take-overs have experienced acculturation when the parent company comes to enforce its own corporate culture throughout its merged system. As a problem of learning membership and identity, acculturation shifts the focus from learning a new membership to accepting a membership which is being forced upon one. It is not unusual for continued employment to ride at least partly upon how quickly and how well a member is willing to put aside the former sense of membership and its ideology and to take on the identity of the new corporate discourse system.

Primary and secondary socialization

Since primary socialization as well as secondary socialization normally refer to processes which are well developed before people come to the age of taking up jobs within corporate cultures, they might seem to be of no particular relevance to the analysis of corporate discourse systems. Nevertheless, in intercultural professional communication there are many ways in which membership in a corporate discourse system comes into serious conflict with membership in the discourse systems of one's primary socialization.

For example, remember that the majority of the world's international corporations have adopted the basic ideology of the Utilitarian discourse system, which places a high value on progress, on the creative, free and equal individual who functions as a rational economic entity, and who seeks first of all his or her own advantage. In most of the western world these are also the basic values into which children receive their primary socialization. From the earliest days of their lives they are enculturated into this Utilitarian individualistic ideology.

One can see, then, that there is a quite natural match between the children who have grown up within this ideology and the corporate ideologies in which they will seek employment as adults. On the other hand, as these corporations extend their operations throughout the world, they seek employees from the countries in which they are operating. In many cases those potential employees have not received their primary socialization into the Utilitarian discourse system. At most these potential employees have only come into contact with this ideology through their secondary socialization; that is, these potential employees have run across the Utilitarian ideology only in the schools they have attended. Outside of these schools they have been enculturated, for example, to an ideology such as the Confucian one, which places a strong emphasis on interpersonal and familial relationships and which puts the success of the group ahead of the success of the individual. For them this individualistic ideology is something foreign, something taken on only for instrumental purposes. It is not something deeply felt as part of their very definition as human beings. It may even feel deeply inhuman and mechanical.

As international corporations which espouse the individualistic Utilitarian ideology take on employees who have been primarily socialized to a very different ideology, conflicts begin to arise between these two ideologies. There are no particular problems if employees can maintain clear separations between their purely instrumental corporate identities and their more fundamental, non-corporate identities. In fact, our observations throughout

Asia lead us to believe that this is just how most Asians cope with this potential for conflict between these two ideological systems.

Problems arise, however, when employees are expected to break down the separations between these two discourse systems. This difference in primary socialization and the ideological systems of corporate discourse systems is one of the factors which contribute to the development of separate and quite isolated communities of expatriates, non-Asian in Asia and Asian in western countries. Even where people from these different cultural groups are able to maintain very successful and cordial relationships under working conditions, that is, within the corporate discourse system, these relationships do not carry over into discourses outside of the corporate system.

Theories of the person and of learning

In chapter 6 we pointed out that in socialization, whether by that one meant education or enculturation, motivation depends upon whether or not the person was thought of as being, first, basically good or bad and, second, self-oriented as in individualistic ideologies or other-motivated as in collectivistic ideologies. In fact, there seems to be a good bit of ambivalence within corporate discourses on the first of these conceptions of the person. Most frequently the problem is resolved by employing both incentive and coercive motivations for the learning of the new members of the discourse system. On the one hand there are various incentives for becoming a successful member, such as advances in pay, special privileges, and preferential work assignments. On the other hand there are forms of coercion, such as company policies, disciplinary committees, or the threat of contract terminations. The position taken by most corporate discourse systems is that while one cannot be sure whether people are basically good or bad or whether they are most likely to be motivated by incentives or by punishment, they will leave nothing to chance and use push–pull strategies of socialization into corporate ideology.

The second point, however, is often quite significant. Most institutional rewards or punishments take the basic position that the person functions as an isolated unit of the sort put forward in Utilitarian ideology. This frequently goes against the actual needs of corporate task organization. A basic conflict is created when motivation for becoming a member of a corporate discourse system is based upon individual performance and yet the accomplishment of corporate tasks depends on successful cooperation among small or large groups of corporate members.

In the past two decades, especially with the development of newer international corporations, there has been much discussion of this sort of paradox in corporate learning. While the issue is far from settled, there now seems to be a recognition that the motivation for performance within a corporate discourse system needs to be brought in line with the assumptions made about how corporate tasks are best accomplished. As an issue of socialization for the new member of a corporate discourse system, there is often a personal conflict over whether he or she should pay most attention to the successful accomplishment of corporate tasks or to individual performance. It still remains the case that integrating oneself into the corporate structure may appear to be what the discourse system is asking of one, while those who do not fit in receive the greatest rewards because they display the individualistic characteristics of the Utilitarian discourse ideology.

Life cycle   From the point of view of corporate discourse, the most important issue regarding socialization and the life cycle within recent years has been the male mid-life transition on the one hand and the entry of more women into corporate careers on the other. Up until the mid-1970s, at least within European- and North American-based corporations, management levels of corporations were populated almost entirely by men. Women, when they worked within the corporate structure, tended to hold lower positions if they were in salaried ranks, or worked in secretarial or clerical positions.

What this has meant for education as well as for socialization, as we will discuss in more detail below under our analysis of gender discourse systems, is that men were educated to take these higher-level and higher-status positions and women were educated for the lower-level and lower-status positions or, in most cases, not to enter corporate discourse systems at all. This polarization of the workforce into two discrete classes along gender lines has produced frustrations for both men and women, though these frustrations have had somewhat different manifestations.

In recent years it has become more common for corporations to recognize that the levels of stress which have built up both within their structures and within their employees lead to problems with health and with overall loss of productivity. At the same time, there has been a great increase in career changes as men have entered into the mid-life transition (a period somewhere around forty to fifty years of age). As men begin to see that they have reached the top of their potential for advancement, they also tend to shift away from their interest in advancing corporate goals in favor of emphasizing more personal goals.

The result of these trends has been that corporations have seen many more men reaching mid-life and, instead of staying on until retirement, moving out of the corporate life into some other, often quite unrelated activity. The further result of this is that corporations lose the experience and continuity these members of the discourse system had formerly provided them.

The second trend is that more women are seeking professional careers within corporations. At least in the first waves of this development, many of these women are somewhat older than their male peers. They often follow a pattern quite complementary to these males in the same age cohort. Whereas the men have moved directly through secondary and tertiary education straight into employment and then in mid-life turned to look for other avenues of self-development, the women have interrupted their educational and professional careers to raise their families. In some cases they have not returned for further education or training until their children have become teenagers.

The result of this is that corporations have had two types of employee, who may have quite similar formal educational backgrounds and credentials, but among whom the men tend to be much younger and without subsidiary experience, while the women are somewhat older and have considerable world experience. As we have said above, corporations often officially recognize only the formal credentials achieved through education and devalue the experience one gets outside of schools. This pattern of placing a higher value upon formal, schooled credentials and a lower value upon experience has made it difficult both for men and for women. For men it has been difficult to move outside of the formal structures of corporate discourse systems when at mid-life they have sought other avenues of experience. For women it has been correspondingly difficult to enter into the formal structures of corporate discourse, even though they bring with them considerable experience.

There is a large research literature on corporate training, on organizational and management structure, and on organizational communication. We have not, of course, been able to do more than to raise a few of what we think are the more important issues regarding socialization into membership in corporate discourse systems. If there is one point we might make in summary, it is that there is much more to socialization into such discourse systems than at first meets the eye. Most of the large literature on these subjects treats the problem as one largely of skill development. As important as professional communication skills are, in themselves we believe they are hardly sufficient to allow the student of professional communication to "read between the lines" of corporate discourse systems. Our purpose in this section has been to highlight a few of the areas in which socialization into corporate discourse systems goes beyond the simple approach of learning the job.

Forms of discourse

Corporate discourse systems are goal-oriented. Furthermore, as we have said above, the corporation itself is the outcome of the rise of the Utilitarian ideology. It should not be surprising to find, then, that the preferred forms of communication within corporate discourse systems are the most focused, goal-oriented forms of discourse, as they were within the Utilitarian discourse system. To put it quite generally, goal-oriented discourse systems tend toward the use of anti-rhetorical, positivist empirical, deductive, individualistic, egalitarian, and publicly or institutionly sanctioned forms of discourse.

This close paralleling of the Utilitarian discourse system and corporate discourse systems raises the question of whether or not it is worth making a distinction between them as two different types of discourse system at all. We believe it is worth making this distinction. The Utilitarian discourse system is a very widespread ideological system which is favored in many contexts which go considerably beyond corporate discourse. What sets corporate discourse apart to be treated separately is that it is an almost perfect embodiment of this discourse ideology. Corporate discourse is in some ways the model Utilitarian discourse system. In the discussion of the forms of discourse of the corporate discourse system which follows, then, we will not recapitulate our discussion of chapter 6, but simply bring up a few points which we believe are useful for further analysis.

Grammar of context

The idea of focused interaction dominates the grammar of context. The corporate ideology is that in discourse nothing should be left to chance. Speech situations and events are carefully orchestrated and controlled. For example, a business meeting may have an agenda which will include open discussion. Within corporate ideology it is necessary to keep open discussion from springing any surprises for the controllers of the agenda. Often such points will be anticipated and then discussed in advance of the meeting, with responses even rehearsed so that what appears to be "open" is, in fact, equally focused.

A second aspect of this control of speech situations and events is that in corporate discourse, outside contextual factors are expected to be eliminated. Often staff members will be assigned to prepare business meetings, for example, just to ensure perfect uniformity of the setting. Each position will have a chair, a note pad, relevant papers tabled, a glass or cup of refreshment, and so forth. Uniformity and regularity are corporate ideals so that participants can produce a highly regular, scripted, and mechanized performance.

Genres, of course, vary considerably in corporate discourse systems. In chapter 5 we gave a partial list of situations, events, and genres commonly found in corporate discourse. To extend this list the reader could consult any textbook on professional or business communication. Having such a long list, however, may mislead the reader into thinking that the genres of corporate discourse are extremely varied. While there are many of them, they all share to greater or lesser extent the basic features of the forms of Utilitarian discourse.

What we need to ask is: what is missing? One does not find in corporate discourse the use of lyric poetry, novels, songs (rock, popular, classical, or traditional), folk tales and myths, religious texts, prayers, ritual discourses (weddings, funerals), literary criticism, ethnography, or any of the many, many other genres of discourse used so commonly in other discourse systems. These other forms of discourse are proscribed because they do not fit the ideological characteristics of the five Ws and the one H; they do not carry forward the goal orientation of the corporate ideology.

One caution must be considered here. In the first place, one may find these genres within the discourse of corporate members within the walls of the corporation. Employees may engage in quite a variety of unofficial or non-legitimated behavior while otherwise operating within the corporate discourse system. The crucial point is that these genres and this behavior are considered unofficial and it is legitimate for corporate members to ask that they be stopped.

Thus within corporations all kinds of underground communications may develop, from e-mail gossip to photocopying and faxing of jokes and cartoons. Most companies tolerate a fairly large amount of these communications on the principle of allowing their employees to work in a relaxed, more "humanized" environment. Nevertheless, it is understood by all that these non-legitimated forms of discourse are inappropriate in official contexts – they should not show up at business meetings, for example – and that there is some unstated limit on just how much the company will tolerate.

One further consideration is that we would want to distinguish between corporate forms of discourse and corporate products. We have said that songs are not used in corporate discourse. Nevertheless, many very large media corporations exist for the purpose of producing songs and other forms of music. While these corporations produce music, it would certainly be taken as odd for such a corporation to produce its annual report to stockholders in the form of a rock concert with annual production figures set to music.

Finally, concerning the question of genre and of media, advertising raises considerable problems for our analysis. Corporate communications with the world of clients and customers is carried on largely through advertising. We have said that corporate discourse is anti-rhetorical, for example, and yet advertising freely employs virtually any and all rhetorical strategies to accomplish its purposes. We have said that songs are not used in corporate discourse, and yet they are widely used in corporate advertising campaigns.

While we have a partial answer to these questions, we believe that it is really beyond the scope of this book to fully analyze this apparent contradiction. We might, for example, argue that advertising is not, in fact, communication within the corporate discourse system, but a product of the corporation. We might argue that the corporate discourse system applies the corporate ideology rigorously only within the boundaries of the discourse system. That seems to be stretching a point to us.

If we look at the history of advertising, as has the sociologist Ruth Cowan in her book *More Work for Mother* (1983), we see that in the first period of advertising, around the turn of the century, it followed rather closely the principles of Utilitarian and corporate discourse. Advertisements at that time concentrated on two basic themes, descriptions of the product and its manufacture on the one hand, and instructions for the use of the product on the other. In this we could see that advertising at first followed the principles of the five Ws and the one H.

It was in the 1920s and the 1930s that advertising became "psychologized" and advertisers began using themes of guilt and other psychological needs to spur potential consumers into making purchases. Advertisers began to introduce more and more classical rhetorical strategies, until today advertising may well be the best example of the use of Aristotelian rhetorical strategies for the purposes of convincing an audience.

We cannot say whether or not advertising represents an exception to our otherwise quite consistent patterns of corporate discourse. It could well be that advertising, along with the rise of electronic entertainment media in the past two or three decades, represents an ideological or paradigmatic shift to the dominance of a quite different ideological system. From that point of view, historians of the future might well look back upon this period as the end of the two- or three-hundred-year-old Utilitarian discourse system and say that it was ultimately advertising and electronic entertainment media which brought about the change.

Face strategies

Because corporate discourse systems epitomize the Utilitarian discourse system, the face strategies one finds in corporate discourse are those we have described in chapter 6. Communications within a corporation are generally hierarchical, public communications are characterized by symmetrical solidarity, and communications with other corporate discourse systems are determined by the relationships between them. Communications from parent company to subsidiary will show predominantly strategies of involvement as from higher to lower in an asymmetrical hierarchical face system.

Patterns/ types of cohesion

There are many forms of cohesion, as we have said in chapter 4. Two aspects of cohesion are relevant to corporate discourse systems: logical relationships and schemata.

There is in corporate discourse an emphasis on the positivist empirical characteristic of the Utilitarian ideology. As a result, there is a corresponding emphasis in corporate discourse on the presentation of "objective facts" and the use of logic for analysis. One finds in corporate discourse a strong preference for clear logical lines of analysis and presentation, which steer away from rhetorical appeals to emotion. Conjunctions which are associated with logical structuring (causal "because," "so"; adversative "but") can be expected to occur more frequently than conjunctions which are associated with narrative (temporal "and then"; additive "and"). This preference is not for the conjunctions themselves, of course, but for the overt statement of logical chains of cause and effect.

Rhetorical (face) strategies

We have said above in many places that in corporate discourse there is a preference for deductive strategies for the introduction of topics. Now we need to clarify that this does not mean that one will never find inductive rhetorical strategies employed by members of corporate discourse systems.

One of the authors has undertaken a study of business telephone calls (Scollon 1993b) which shows that the use of these strategies depends on the actual relationships between the people who are communicating with each other. Where the participants are in a client relationship, that is, where their primary purpose is economic exchange, telephone calls take on a deductive structure. In contrast, however, where the relationships is that of colleagues, that is, when information is exchanged without an accompanying economic transaction, a more inductive strategy is used.

The point we want to make is that the choice of inductive and deductive strategies is not simply a matter of the overall discourse system. In chapter 5 we argued that one could not say that the deductive or inductive strategies were either "western" or "Asian," since both strategies are used within both cultures. Now we want to say that while there is a clear preference for the deductive strategy for introducing topics in corporate discourse, that does not mean that one will not find the inductive pattern. In corporate discourse, one crucial contextual distinction is the type of relationship between or among the participants. The normal or most characteristic pattern in corporate discourse is the client relationship. This relationship may well be dominated by the deductive pattern. On the other hand, in collegial relationships within which there is the exchange of free information, our study leads us to believe the inductive pattern will be the normal pattern.

Our point is that in the analysis of discourse systems, one needs to be watchful against rigid application of general statements. While deductive strategies may be preferred, they will not be used exclusively. It becomes an important analytical point to ask why other strategies are used and when.

Such questions will usually highlight features of the discourse system which might otherwise be missed.

Functions of language

Corporate discourse, because it is goal oriented, tends to emphasize information over relationship, negotiation over ratification, and individual creativity over group harmony. Having said that, we should be careful to notice that, in the first place, in the preceding section we have pointed out that in collegial relationships, the information function of language is buffered by careful attention to the collegial relationship.

In the same way, there is a stated ideology within corporate discourse of the value of negotiation. From external marketing and sales negotiations to internal brainstorming activities, corporations tend to express a high value for the negotiation of relative positions of power and status. "Anyone can succeed" is the underlying motto within most corporate discourse systems. At the same time, however, it is well known that those who get the institutional rewards of promotion and privileged work assignments are often the "yes men," the ones who clearly, often loudly, ratify the existing structure of power and status.

One major point of contemporary discussion in management circles has to do with the question of group harmony over individual success within corporations. There is a feeling that Asian corporations have succeeded to a great extent because they quite naturally or culturally adopt patterns of communication which strengthen the group and the ability of the group to work in concert. It is also felt that at least some part of the divisiveness of western corporate discourse can be traced to excessive individualism on the part of members of the discourse system.

While such questions are open for managerial discussion, underlying these discussions are deep cultural beliefs. There seems little question that within western corporate discourse, the individual remains the fundamental unit of organization and, therefore, the most basic assumption is that the function of language is to communicate the ideas of individuals to each other. Within Asian corporate discourse, there is an underlying cultural sense that one of the major functions of language is to promote group harmony, whether or not that harmony works to the advantage of individuals in the group. Such a deep cultural division is a point that must be watched for in the analysis of corporate discourse systems if our concern is with intercultural professional communication.

Non-verbal communication

In chapter 7 we outlined three of the major elements of non-verbal communication which we believe it is important to consider: kinesics (the movement of our bodies), proxemics (the use of space), and the concept of time. Each of these is a very broad topic and we can do no more than to mention here some of the aspects of non-verbal communication which are of relevance to the corporate discourse system.

It is no accident that corporate life is often called "the rat race." Life within corporations has come to be dominated by a fast pace in which more and more is done in less and less time. If there is one defining kinesic characteristic of corporate life it is this ever increasing rapid pace. Erickson and Shultz (1982), for example, analyzed criticisms of African-American employees in American companies. Even though their production schedules met or exceeded those of employees from European-based ethnic groups, their employers described them as "lazy" workers. Erickson and Shultz established that this judgement was based upon the very subjective impression their employers had formed upon the basis of their posture. These African-American employees who were working on a production line used a relaxed stance and moved with casual, swinging motions as compared with members of ethnic groups who stood with a more rigid posture between actions and then when they moved did so with highly focused, direct, and energetic movements.

Our point is that as a form of discourse, such aspects of kinesics as the movements of our bodies and our postures communicate to others how well we are fitting into the corporate discourse system. In the example above, the posture and movements of the African-Americans was taken by their employers to be communicating an attitude of less than enthusiastic membership. It was this aspect of discourse, not their actual production of work, which was being evaluated.

Edward T. Hall, who has led the field in observations of the role of non-verbal communication in intercultural communication, has pointed out that in corporate discourse the use of space is a major aspect of how we communicate power and status as well as our availability for communication with others (Hall 1969; Hall and Hall 1987). As he notes, in American corporations, large corner offices are awarded to members of high status while, in contrast, though Japanese corporate officials may have similar offices, they rarely use them for day-to-day operations. Japanese high-ranking officers prefer to work within an open area of many other employees so that they will be part of the give and take of operational discourse.

Where separate offices are used, there is a considerable amount of variation in who chooses to have doors closed or open and under what circumstances. This topic has hardly been studied and so we can do no more than indicate the main dimensions. Generally speaking, American corporate officers prefer to have the doors to their offices left open (though, for very important people, with a secretary or administrative assistant stationed at a desk just outside to monitor or intercept the flow of visitors). British and other European corporate officers tend to prefer having the door closed but to be available to anyone who knocks first. In this, Chinese in Taiwan and Hong Kong seem to fit the European pattern of closed office doors for major figures and open communal offices for members of lesser importance. Korean offices follow the Japanese pattern of open spaces with the more important figures placed in the center and toward the back of the space.

The intercultural consequences of these differences have only been explored in a few studies, but the implications should be obvious to the reader. An American who is visiting a Japanese business is likely to underestimate the importance of a Japanese corporate officer because he finds him seated at a desk in the middle of a busy room like he was a secretary. On the other hand, a Japanese businessman consulting in an American company may well feel he has been shunted off the main flow of the discourse when he is taken to the corner office of one of the key corporate figures.

Where members of different cultural groups work within the same corporate discourse system, as happens throughout the world now, they are likely to unknowingly adopt different practices of signaling to others whether they wish to be left alone to concentrate on their work or, on the other hand, they are open to being visited. Where the American leaves the door open, he or she may still feel interrupted by a visitor who has assumed the open door signaled that he or she was not otherwise occupied. While the research does not give us major findings in this area, we feel such issues are well worth further analysis, especially in situations of intercultural membership of a corporate discourse system.

Finally, the concept of time is a major aspect of intercultural miscommunication within international corporate discourse systems. Analysts such as Edward T. Hall (1969) have argued that there are two basic dimensions of time, monochromatic and polychromatic. Erickson and Shultz (1982) have argued that we might also distinguish between what he called (borrowing Greek terms) *kairos* and *chronos* concepts of time.

A monochromatic sense of time simply means that one feels that things should be done one at a time. A person with a polychromatic sense of time prefers to maintain multiple threads of different activities. Because of the goal-driven nature of Utilitarian ideology, there is a strong tendency for corporate discourse systems to adopt a monochromatic sense of time. There is a tendency to parcel out tasks so that individuals or task groups can concentrate their thoughts and energies on accomplishing a single goal without distractions.

While this Utilitarian ideal is the underlying ideology of corporate discourse systems, there is much cultural variation in its application, which raises problems for intercultural professional communication. As Hall (1969) and others have pointed out, Asian corporate structures, while internally utilizing a monochromatic sense of time, are surrounded in non-corporate life by a polychromatic sense of time, and therefore interactions between corporate life and non-corporate Asian life must negotiate between these two time senses. This is not so much the case in European and American corporations, where the corporate sense of monochromatic time is widely shared throughout non-corporate events and activities.

The distinction between *kairos* time and *chronos* is not quite the same as that between monochromatic and polychromatic senses of time. If we think of *chronos* time being "clock" time, then we can see that it contrasts with *kairos* or "appropriate" time. Corporations tend to do things by clock time. They set production and sales goals to be met and time lines for sub-stages of projects. Hours are kept on employees and, with the rise of computers, even the efficiency of the number of keystrokes per minute of clerical personnel is now tabulated.

In contrast to this, appropriate or *kairos* time paces events according to when it is appropriate for them to occur. It should be clear that traditional farming, for example, is a perfect example of appropriate time. Everything depends on the weather, over which no farmer has control. One plants when the frosts are over and reaps before the frosts begin, or planting and harvesting must be timed to the coming of seasonal rains and droughts.

As an issue of intercultural professional communication, as in the case of kinesics and proxemics, the Utilitarian emphasis on clock time runs parallel with that same sense through most European-based cultures, though certainly most cultural analysts would associate clock time more with Northern Europeans than with Mediterraneans. In contrast to this, throughout Asia, appropriate time dominates in all cultural spheres outside of corporate life. Consequently, there is a constant tension and negotiation between these two senses of time both within and outside of the corporate discourse systems which operate in Asia.

Face systems

In the preceding section, under the topic of face strategies, and in chapter 6 we discussed the face systems which predominate in corporate discourse systems, and so we will not take up that issue again here. Here we want to bring up three quite closely related issues which are likely to be important, especially in intercultural communication within corporate discourse systems: kinship, the concept of the self, and ingroup–outgroup relationships. The question of their importance arises because within the Utilitarian discourse system there is a strong ideological position that individuals are isolated, autonomous, rational entities. As members of corporate discourse systems, it is felt that they should behave as such, even if that means downplaying relationships with their families or spouses, other groups to which they belong, or members of other discourse systems. The general terms which cover this problem are "nepotism" and "conflict of interest."

A person the authors know is a Native American. Within her cultural group, kinship ties are very strong and lines of authority are drawn along lines of kinship. In other words, in such a system if I want to have somebody employed under me in an institution over whom I want to be sure I can exercise my authority and who I can expect to respect that authority, I will employ a niece or a nephew. By doing so I can bring both institutional authority and kinship authority to bear upon this employee.

This person was the head of a department in a governmental office and, using the cultural practices of her group, hired her nephew for a job. She did this in the interest of advancing the work of her department, knowing that this person was both competent to do the work and quite constrained by her authority to do it as well. Unfortunately, governmental regulations quite specifically proscribed such hiring, on the grounds that she would be likely to show favoritism to her nephew and be unable to expect a normal work performance from him.

This case illustrates a conflict which runs throughout corporate discourse systems from France and Italy to Hong Kong and Singapore. The ideology of the Utilitarian discourse system has it that individuals should set aside personal, cultural, and other group-derived relationships and enter into purely logical relationships in corporate discourse. On the other hand, many, perhaps most, cultures emphasize that human beings are deeply connected to each other through their kinship ties. It is a rare culture, actually, which asserts the Utilitarian ideology of the isolated, autonomous individual.

As a problem for corporate discourse systems, most members of these systems find themselves in constant conflict between the goals of the corporate system and their own personal goals, which are often group-derived. It is common enough in western corporate discourse, for example, to honor the "woman behind the man"; it is another question whether or not western corporations are ready to have the spouses of corporate members hold positions within the same corporations.

What holds true within corporations is even more strongly felt in relationships with people outside of corporate discourse. Should an officer of a corporation take into consideration the opinions of the community in which he or she lives when he or she implements corporate decisions? In most cases, such exercises in community opinion are not for the purposes of making more informed decisions; they are largely marketing and public relations activities designed to get the community to more easily accept decisions already taken internally by the corporation.

The size and scope of corporate discourse systems

Now that we have completed our outline guide for the analysis of discourse systems with this section on corporate discourse systems, there remains one consideration: the size and scope of such a system. On the one hand we would argue that the very broad, overarching discourse system which we have called the Utilitarian discourse system is too broad, too vague, and not sufficiently institutionally grounded to really do more than provide broad historical and ideological outlines.

If the Utilitarian discourse system is too broad, what is too narrow? Would we want to consider a multinational corporation such as McDonald's or Sony Corporation a single corporate discourse system? Or, on the other hand, might it be better to consider a regional office of such a corporation to be a single corporate discourse system operating as a subsidiary of another, larger system?

Ultimately, while there might be much interesting discussion in trying to resolve such questions, we do not believe that any clear resolution would ever be achieved. Any discourse system is constantly in the process of evolution and change, and the point is not to try to fix the description of any one system permanently in place. The point, we think, is to open up the questions for analysis, which will allow professional communicators to analyze the dimensions which will be of the greatest use in coming to understand intercultural discourse. Our purpose here has been more to raise questions than to provide final answers.

9

Professional Discourse

The Professional Discourse System (ESL Teachers)

The authors have often enough been in conversations which begin as follows:

Q: What do you do?
A: I teach at City Poly.
Q: Oh, what do you teach?
A: I teach English.

Sometimes, however, this same question-and-answer sequence goes somewhat differently:

Q: What do you do?
A: I teach English.
Q: Oh, where do you teach?
A: At City Poly.

These two sequences show the underlying problem of membership and identity faced by members of voluntary discourse systems; in most cases one is simultaneously a member of a corporate discourse system and a professional or occupational discourse system. In the first sequence, we interpreted the question, "What do you do?," as a question about corporate or institutional membership. Then we have treated our membership in the worldwide professional discourse system of teachers of English as a second language (ESL) as a secondary membership.

The second sequence goes the other way around. We have first interpreted our primary membership as membership in the professional discourse system. We are first identifying ourselves as English teachers. Secondarily we are presenting ourselves as employees of a particular institution.

Although in this case we are focusing directly on the professional group of ESL teachers, the same would apply in many occupations. One might say that he was an electrician (occupational identity) and then later point out that he worked for Kolon Corporation. On the other hand, someone might point out that she works for Singapore Airlines and later clarify that she is an accountant.

Our purpose here is to introduce the concept of cross-cutting voluntary discourse systems such as those of corporation and professional group, and to discuss how identity in those two cross-cutting discourse systems may produce conflicts of identity for members of those systems. These conflicts of identity, in turn, lead to confusion or misunderstanding in discourse among people who sense such cross-cutting identities. The important point is that such conflicts and multiple identities are not problems which can be solved; they are characteristic of virtually all situations of professional communication. What is important is to recognize that such cross-cutting identities exist and will be operating in most communications which take place either among professional colleagues or among members of the same corporate structure.

Ideology

English is now used as the major language of international business and governmental communication. One consequence of this widespread use of English is that more than half of the speakers of English speak it as a second, learned (schooled) language. That, in turn, means that the professional discourse system of ESL teachers is a discourse system spread throughout most of the world. The history of the development of language teaching, especially of English-language teaching, is not our main concern here and, as that history has been given full treatment in the scholarly literature, we are only concerned with the broadest outlines of the profession in the contemporary world.

ESL teachers may be found in a bewildering array of organizations throughout the world. ESL teachers work primarily in schools, of course, but those schools range from elementary to graduate schools, from small private schools to huge state or national universities with specialized ESL departments or institutes, and from fly-by-night night-study "institutes" to fully developed doctoral research programs. Outside of those schools, ESL teachers also work for corporations in corporate training programs and centers, they work for governmental development agencies, and they work as private consultants.

There is little formal organization within such a widely dispersed group of professionals. Nevertheless, there are a number of professional organizations which provide the means of communication and overall cohesion to this professional discourse system. TESOL (Teachers of English to Speakers of Other Languages) is the largest and most centrally significant of these professional organizations. TESOL organizes annual professional conferences and summer institutes for members, it publishes a number of special-interest group newsletters in addition to its more general journal *TESOL Quarterly*, and it provides a number of other services such as access to group insurance and employment services.

There are two broad classes of ESL professionals: those who are native speakers of English from the English-speaking countries of North America, the United Kingdom, Australia and New Zealand or, perhaps, South Africa, and those who are bilingual in English and some other language and who have learned English as a second or formal or schooled language within a largely non-English speaking culture. The experiences as well as the ideologies of these two groups are rather different and we will treat them separately, beginning with native speakers of English.

Although the career paths of native-speaking ESL professionals are extremely varied, perhaps the most common experience of an ESL teacher begins with a college degree in English, language or linguistics, or one of the social sciences. Many ESL professionals enter the field after a period of international travel which includes taking occasional impromptu English teaching jobs to finance their travels. They later return to college to develop further training and credentials. In any case, the majority of ESL teachers have some form of travel and cross-cultural experience as a significant aspect of their résumés. Furthermore, teaching ESL is often a means of support for such teachers who find themselves living in a largely non-English speaking environment for a variety of reasons. These reasons range from missionary work to accompanying a spouse who has been relocated for business or governmental reasons.

For bilingual or non-native-speaking ESL teachers, the most common experience is that they have studied English in schools as a second or a foreign language. Whether they have developed an ability with English or they have become attracted to cultural aspects of English-speaking countries, these non-native-speaking ESL teachers often see themselves as non-traditional or even anti-cultural members of their own home societies. In some cases their concentration on English studies has meant the inevitable neglect of linguistic and cultural studies of their mother tongue or culture. In any case, they often are among the most outward-oriented and multi-cultural members of their cultural group. In many, perhaps most, cases, these teachers have traveled outside of their home countries to gain fuller experience in English-speaking cultural contexts. In this they often have greater cross-cultural experience than their non-English-teaching colleagues.

Unlike their native-speaking colleagues in the ESL profession, non-native-speaking ESL professionals tend to be rather well educated. Where the native-speaking ESL teacher may have only an undergraduate degree, often not in English, the bilingual or non-native-speaking ESL teacher often has a graduate degree and, furthermore, has given many years of study to the language itself. The virtue of native ESL teachers is that they carry deep intuitions about the use of English, but they often carry about precious little formal or structural knowledge of the language. Non-native ESL teachers, on the other hand, cannot claim native speaker intuitions, but they normally have spent many long years in formal study of the language.

What gives ESL teachers a sense of being members of the same discourse system is this common experience of travel and English teaching, membership in a common professional association such as TESOL or one of the more regional foreign language associations such as JALT (Japan Association of Language Teachers), reading professional journals such as are published by these associations, and attendance at professional meetings where they meet others of the same profession. Needless to say, members of this professional discourse system vary in the degree to which they will claim identity, from those who may teach English but who do not belong to any of these associations, and who do not read the journals or have much association with other English teachers, to those who seek office on the boards of such associations or who take up academic positions teaching or researching in the field of ESL.

With this brief profile of ESL teachers as background, we now want to turn to the discussion of two of the ways in which the professional discourse of ESL teachers cuts across the ideological lines of institutions or corporate discourse systems: it strongly emphasizes individual success over organizational goals, and it is highly relativistic.

The professional discourse system of ESL teachers is a voluntary discourse system, and as a goal-oriented discourse system it shares many of the properties of corporate discourse systems. What is different, however, is that the overriding goal of this discourse system is to provide support, contacts and connections, and resources to its members in the pursuit of their own individual career development. As we have said above, ESL teachers typically enjoy world travel and living in intercultural environments. The professional discourse system provides ESL teachers with information about jobs in other places, comparisons of pay and benefits, and overall security in their professional identity.

This professional identity often works at cross-purposes with identity in the corporate discourse system in which the ESL teacher finds himself or herself employed. He or she is more likely to draw a comparison with another English teacher who is in a country across the world than with a history teacher who is teaching down the hall. The ESL teacher is more likely to engage in correspondence with, to join in research projects with, and to read of the research of another ESL teacher in some other country than to be aware of the work of colleagues in the same institution who teach in other fields. Because of this outside primary reference group, the ESL teacher is likely to be somewhat resistant to internal pressures to conform to the corporate culture of his or her own employing institution.

The second point of ideological conflict or possible conflict with most corporate discourse systems derives from the fact that ESL teachers tend to place a high value on travel and on job mobility. In most cases they have worked for a variety of different institutions operating within different cultural contexts. As a result they tend to develop a highly relativistic and anti-ideological stance. From a pedagogical point of view this means that ESL teachers tend to believe that what they are teaching is a neutral and even culture-free tool which students may use for their own ideological purposes. This point is currently under considerable debate within the profession, with many people arguing against this position.

The consequence of this anti-ideological or relativistic ideology is that ESL teachers do not easily become supportive of the corporate ideological position, whatever it may be. Even working within well-established schools and universities, members of the ESL discourse system tend to be rather skeptical of the corporate culture of the university's discourse system and go about their own business with the minimum of commitment to corporate ideology.

Since our concern is not with a detailed description of a professional discourse system, but rather with showing ways in which membership in such a system may cut across membership in a corporate discourse system, we will not go further into the ideology of ESL teachers. What is important to remember is that in virtually all goal-directed discourse systems there will be such cross-cutting professional or occupational discourse systems. Individuals will simultaneously be members of both systems, and in some cases membership in one system will tend to undercut or call into question full membership in the other system. In the career of a single person there are often periods of greater or lesser identification with professional goals, and of corresponding complementary identification with corporate goals. Of course, individuals also take different positions in respect to these two systems: some will see themselves primarily as English teachers and pay little attention to the goals of the school in which they are currently employed; others will come to work primarily on behalf of the school with relatively little concern for their sense of professional membership.

Socialization

For many years, the answer to the question for native English speakers of how one became a member of the ESL professional discourse system was that one happened to need a job somewhere in a foreign country, one could speak English, and so one was hired to teach. After a period of such teaching, one's inadequacies became apparent and one returned to school for advanced training specifically in teaching ESL. Perhaps because of this rather haphazard pathway toward professionalization, many colleges and universities began to offer short courses and then full degree programs in ESL for the purposes of training such teachers.

As socialization into the occupation began to give over to formal education into the profession, schools, corporations, and other potential employers began to upgrade their requirements. Whereas twenty years ago a native speaker of English might easily get a first job teaching ESL with little more than a few years of college by way of training, now it is more likely that an undergraduate degree or a higher diploma in ESL or, of course, EFL (English as a foreign language), ESP (English for special purposes), EPC (English for professional communication), or any of the other specialized subsidiary fields is required for regular institutional employment.

For non-native-speaking ESL teachers there has also been a corresponding upgrading of the formal educational requirements. New training programs and degree courses have been developed both within their home countries and in English-speaking countries, in which these ESL teachers can receive more advanced formal credentialization.

What this means is that the professional discourse system of ESL teachers is now just coming into full professional status in most places around the world. This shift from a more occupational status, with its informal processes of socialization through experience, to professional status has brought with it a shift in the relationships among ESL teachers and their other colleagues in corporate discourse systems. Whereas two decades ago ESL teachers, at least at the tertiary level, rarely were taken to have equal status with colleagues in other departments, now with the development of full degree programs, research agendas, and an active set of professional organizations, ESL teachers have come to find that even within the professional discourse systems, education has come to predominate over socialization in membership and identity.

This shift from an emphasis on socialization, that is, learning through teaching experience in the classroom, toward education, that is, formal learning through coursework and research, has benefited ESL teachers as members of corporate discourse systems. They are more likely to be accepted as full members because their qualifications and credentials are more like those of other members of these institutional discourse systems. On the other hand, there remains a strong feeling within the ESL discourse system that no amount of research and analysis can replace classroom experience. That is, there remains a strong ideological commitment to practice in the field, to actual teaching over research, to action over theory, which continues

to set them apart from other full members of the institutional discourse
systems in which they are employed.

Forms of discourse

The forms of discourse practiced by ESL teachers include many or most
of the forms of discourse used in the English language. English language
teachers teach everything from simple conversational openings – "Hi, how
are you?," "Fine, and you?" – through literature, folk tales, drama, and
poetry, to business correspondence, résumés, and meeting agenda writing.
Since ESL teachers often teach even slang and other culturally proscribed
forms of discourse as well, one wonders what form of English discourse
might not be taught somewhere by an ESL teacher.

For our purposes we will consider only two aspects of the forms of
discourse in the discourse system of ESL teachers, which are of direct
relevance to the question of how this discourse system cuts across or inter-
acts with institutional discourse. The first of these is what we might call the
metalinguistic interest of ESL teachers in discourse, and the second is the
commercial form of discourse, the ESL textbook.

While it is true that ESL teachers may teach virtually any of the forms of
discourse used by any discourse system which functions in English, classroom use of these forms of discourse is always set into the "as if" framework.
In the first chapter we illustrated what we called teacher talk with the
question, "What time is it?" In the elementary classroom as well as in night
classes for adult business people across the world, we can hear English
teachers rehearsing this formula. The point is that while ESL teachers may
teach any and all forms of discourse, they rarely actually use most of the
forms they teach.

An ESL teacher of business communication may daily teach his or her
students how to write business letters, but he or she might only rarely have
any need to write a business letter. The discourse of ESL teachers is a kind
of metadiscourse. By that we mean that it is a discourse about discourse. As
a result, ESL teachers frequently come to pay more attention to form than
to function, and for them the primary function is not normal use, but use
as an example in their classes. The contemporary concern with what is
called "communicative" language teaching is an attempt to overcome this
tendency to focus on form at the expense of function, but many analysts
have argued that because of the fact that classrooms are removed socially
and structurally from the situations of actual use, there is little which can
actually be done to make ESL classroom discourse really functional.

ESL teachers tend to form a habit of metalinguistic or metadiscourse consciousness which makes them nerve-wracking colleagues for others who are more focused on the actual functions of language in use. At a meeting of a faculty research committee, it is likely to be the ESL teacher who will wonder about the quality of the proposed research on the basis of several spelling errors in the text. In a staff development group where other colleagues are concentrating on the problem of organizing the contents of their lectures, the ESL teacher will be raising questions about the overall effectiveness of the lecture genre as compared to the study and small group discussion format. In other words, because they specialize in teaching language and discourse, ESL teachers are likely to raise issues having to do with correct or effective language use even among colleagues who consider themselves quite competent in these areas.

One other aspect of the metadiscourse consciousness of ESL teachers is that they may be easily distracted from the actual functions of the discourse in real situations. While others in a staff meeting are looking to the next item on the printed agenda, the ESL teacher is thinking, "I should make a copy of this agenda for my lecture next week on the discourse of professional meetings." In a sense the entire world of discourse, from word usage to the structure of speech situations, is the professional domain of the ESL teacher, and he or she is likely to think of this whole world of discourse as teaching materials or as research data and forget that it is also the reality within which other participants are functioning normally.

Finally, some mention should be made of the fact that, throughout the world, books on English are a very successful commercial activity. In Vancouver, Tokyo, Sydney, Hong Kong, London, or San Francisco, bookstores have sections of books on ESL and other related specializations. In Asia, the size of these sections in bookstores is hard to comprehend. If English could really be taught successfully with books, why are there so many of them sold and yet so few people with comfortable competence in English? Of course, these books are all written by members of the ESL professional discourse system. Many of these people are very successful authors.

This commercial activity points out the tension ESL professionals often experience between their professional membership and their institutional or corporate membership. As teachers, ESL professionals are widely agreed that the most effective materials are the ones which are most closely adapted to the specific students who will use them. As writers of books who are seeking an international market, these same ESL professionals know that wider sales come by being less specific to the students in any one place. This is just one aspect of the dilemma of membership in both corporate and professional discourse systems. Our purpose is to argue that, in general, these two types of membership are not easily reconciled because they are often opposed to each other. If one strengthens one form of membership, one weakens the other.

Face systems

Although ESL teachers generally take a strong anti-ideological stance, behind this expressed position can be observed strong support for the individualism and egalitarianism of the Utilitarian ideology. This is expressed for both native and non-native ESL teachers in their willingness or even enthusiasm for going against traditional and cultural expectations and for asserting their right as individuals to develop their own independent careers.

There are many historical and cultural reasons for the development of the so-called communicative language teaching methods and approaches of the recent two decades, but it is safe to say that in contemporary English teaching the most central ideological position is that the purpose of teaching and learning English as well as the most effective methods are "communicative." It would go considerably beyond the purposes of this book to cover communicative language teaching in any depth. For our purposes, the most important aspect of this array of methods and approaches is the emphasis on individual communication. This pedagogical emphasis directly reflects the underlying ideology of individualism and egalitarianism of the people who are ESL professionals.

As a teaching methodology, communicative language teaching tends to emphasize one-to-one or small group interactions in which individuals express their own original thinking. Of course, in practice these discourses are guided by the teacher – often to the extent that they are not very communicative after all. Nevertheless, the consequence for the classroom face system is that teachers who espouse communicative language teaching tend to try to foster a face system of symmetrical solidarity, both among students and between teachers and students. As we have said in chapter 3 and again in chapter 5, a system of symmetrical solidarity is the face system in which both (or all) participants use predominantly face strategies of involvement. This face system is consonant with the deductive strategy of introducing topics, such as introducing one's own thought on a particular subject.

This is not the most appropriate place to take up the question of the cultural conflicts this methodology sets up when students in ESL classrooms are oriented toward a hierarchical face system, especially in relationship to their teachers. We have found, for example, that Chinese students in Taiwan, Korean students in Korea, as well as Chinese students in Hong Kong who are placed in such communicative classrooms find it difficult, at least at first, to deal with the inherent difference between their cultural expectations of a hierarchical system and the communicative classroom expectations of symmetrical solidarity.

The point we are considering here is that contemporary ESL teachers tend to assume a system of symmetrical solidarity in their ESL classrooms. To add to this emphasis along with the habitual use of face strategies of involvement, professional discourse among ESL teachers is also predominantly a system of symmetrical solidarity. Even complete strangers come to speak to each other on a given-name basis within minutes at professional meetings. In correspondence with strangers one often finds the opening formula, "Dear Ron (if I may)," in which the writer begins the correspondence by using the given name followed by a parenthetical apology.

As we have argued above in our discussion both of the Utilitarian discourse system (chapter 6) and the corporate discourse system (chapter 8), the face system which is normally practiced within institutions is a hierarchical, asymmetrical system in which involvement strategies are used downward and independence strategies are used upward. This poses a potential problem for ESL teachers, in that within both professional circles and their primary working environment, the classroom, they customarily use and expect to receive face strategies of involvement. Such teachers come to habitually express themselves as members of systems of symmetrical solidarity. This produces a conflict in corporate discourse where asymmetrical face strategies are the norm.

For a member of the ESL professional discourse system to work effectively within a corporate discourse system requires him or her to become highly self-conscious in employing the appropriate face strategies without excessive carry-over either from the classroom or from outside professional discourse. In at least some cases, their inability or their unwillingness to fine tune their use of face strategies of politeness in corporate discourse further confirms for members of that discourse the marginality of ESL teachers in that discourse system. Such language use is in some cases taken as a lack of successful socialization into the corporate discourse system.

Other professional discourse systems

We have used the professional discourse system of ESL teachers to illustrate how conflicts may arise between membership in one's professional discourse system and membership in the corporate discourse system of one's employment. We might well have focused on any other professional or occupational discourse system, such as that of electrical engineers, travel industry managers, bus drivers, traders in foreign exchange, sports journalists, advertising photographers, electricians or carpenters, or symphony orchestra musicians. In each case there is a comparable problem: one is simultaneously a member of the discourse system of one's professional or occupational group and of one's institutional, organizational, or corporate discourse system.

These two forms of membership are in conflict because they are goal-directed systems which often have competing goals. The corporate discourse system normally has some primary goal, such as earning a profit, and the secondary goal of self-preservation of the system. The professional discourse system has the goal of supporting its members in the realization of their own career interests. Those individual career interests may well be in competition with the corporate goals.

We can summarize the problems which arise from multiple membership in discourse systems as follows:

1 *Conflicting ideologies*: the purposes of the two (or more) systems pull the person toward different goals, and as he or she places a value on both sets of goals, it becomes a recurring problem to decide in any particular case which set of goals to emphasize.
2 *Fragmentation of socialization and experience*: often the education or experience which is valued in one system is devalued in one or more of the other systems to which a person belongs. A person must select from among his or her total experience as a human just those aspects each discourse system values, and this produces a feeling of fragmentation.
3 *Dilemmas in choosing the most appropriate forms of discourse*: each of the multiple systems favors different forms of discourse, and difficult selections must sometimes be made. The engineering report which would be most useful within the corporation might be considered oversimplified or naive to professional colleagues or, vice versa, the most professional engineering report might seem loaded with jargon or excessively academic for corporate planning purposes.
4 *Multiple faces*: the separate system may require the presentation of a different set of face relationships, and the person may come to feel quite "two-faced" in maintaining both corporate and professional relationships.

As simultaneous members of two types of cross-cutting discourse systems, a successful professional communicator must constantly tune and adjust his or her sense of identity and membership so that the goals of both systems of membership are at least minimally satisfied. For most professionals this is an interesting and rewarding, if at times stressful, experience.

10

Generational Discourse

Involuntary Discourse Systems

A person is simultaneously a member of many discourse systems. This is, perhaps, the most important aspect of the concept of discourse systems. In chapters 8 and 9 we discussed two voluntary discourse systems: the corporate discourse system and a professional discourse system. As we have said, a member of a corporate discourse system is normally at the same time a member of a professional or occupational discourse system. The tension between his or her identity as a member of these two discourse systems is a perennial discourse problem to be solved.

In a parallel way, cutting across membership in these voluntary discourse systems are two other involuntary discourse systems in which all of us participate: those of generation and gender. These add two more dimensions of simultaneous membership and therefore of potential conflict among ideologies and identity. These involuntary systems also provide what in the long run are probably even more complex problems of interpretation in communication with members of other discourse systems.

This increased problem of communication arises from the fact that involuntary discourse systems such as those of generation and gender are normally invisible to us. After all, we make certain conscious choices in becoming employees of our institutions and in choosing our professions or occupations (though it would be a mistake to exaggerate the extent to which we actually choose our membership in these voluntary discourse systems). Furthermore, most voluntary discourse systems are based upon quite conscious and explicit forms of socialization through formal education and credentialization. In contrast, we do not go to school to study how to become a member of our generation or of our gender group, we begin learning the ropes of these identities from our earliest days of life, and, as we will argue below, that early life experience remains the strongest influence toward the maintenance of our sense of membership in these groups.

Since the 1960s it has been part of the common vocabulary, at least of Americans, to speak of a generation gap. This gap is most clearly perceived to have opened up between those Americans born after World War II, the Baby Boom generation, and those born before that time.

As an example of the relevance of this perception of a generation gap, people writing in management and marketing analysis emphasize the need to recognize this generation gap both for successful management of one's own company and for the successful marketing of products. Because this generation gap is so widely discussed, we will base our discussion of generational discourse systems on the generations of Americans which have been described in this research and popular literature.

In a recent discussion between Neil Postman and Camille Paglia on literacy and the newer electronic media, the generational difference between these two critics rises to the surface.

Postman: Now I won't ask you how old you are.
Paglia: I'm forty-three. I was born in 1947. And you graduated from college in 1953. I checked! I wanted to know, because I think this information is absolutely critical to how one views the mass media. I graduated from college in 1968. There are only fifteen years between us, but it's a critical fifteen years, an unbridgeable chasm in American culture (Postman and Paglia, 1991:47).

This bit of dialogue emphasizes several points. One is that the generation gap is taken as a real and obvious cultural phenomenon by Americans. Another is that this difference in generations is taken to be of considerable explanatory power. The reader is expected to accept that one can account for Postman's strong defense of literacy not on the internal grounds of his argument but on the grounds of his historical placement among the generations of Americans. A third point, which perhaps in the long run is the most significant, is that this view of the generations is advanced by the younger member of the polarity. One might almost say that the belief of the Baby Boom generation that there is a clear generation gap becomes self-fulfilling. At least in this case, Postman, the member of the older generation, chose not to accept this generational explanation as sufficient.

In other words, among contemporary Americans there is a strong belief that the experience of having been born into American culture at a particular time and in a particular place is taken as giving one membership in a particular discourse system. It is widely felt that communication between people born after World War II and those born before that time is a form of intercultural communication. In our terms we would call this communication between systems of discourse or interdiscourse communication.

The ideologies of American individualism

Some one hundred fifty years ago, the French observer Alexis de Tocqueville described Americans as highly individualistic. He believed that this American individualism was inseparable from the new American concept of egalitarian democracy. In the 1830s he wrote: "Not only does democracy make men forget their ancestors, but also clouds their view of their descendants and isolates them from their contemporaries. Each man is forever thrown back on himself alone, and there is danger that he may be shut up in the solitude of his own heart" (Tocqueville, 1969:508). From the point of view of the European Tocqueville, this American democratic individualism was, indeed, extreme. That is to say, Tocqueville if he were writing today would call this ideological individualism. It should be remembered in reading Tocqueville, of course, that the background against which his observations were made, and against which Americans exercised their individualism, the mid-nineteenth century, was still very traditional in many ways. He was, in fact, observing American individualism just at the point where it was beginning to take on the ideological position of Utilitarianism. "Individualism is a calm and considered feeling which disposes each citizen to isolate himself from the mass of his fellows and withdraw into circle of family and friends; with this little society formed to his taste, he gladly leaves the greater society to look after itself " (Tocqueville, 1969:506). At that time of the nineteenth century, the family was still firmly in place as a grounding social structure. Individuals accepted their places within their families, however democratic and egalitarian they might otherwise have been. The assumption that it was the place of parents or the older generation to lead and of children or the younger generation to follow was unquestioned.

In their re-study of American culture some one hundred fifty years after Tocqueville, Robert Bellah and his colleagues (Bellah, et al. 1985) have found that what was a new term at the time of Tocqueville, "individualism," has become an entire language of individualism, which now dominates American self-analysis. While there are a number of forms in which American individualism is manifested, the most significant of them is what Bellah and his associates call ontological individualism, that is, the belief that "the individual has a primary reality whereas society is a second-order, derived or artificial construct" (1985:334). This form of individualism is very much what Jeremy Bentham was putting forward when he wrote, "The community is a fictitious *body*" (Bentham, 1962:35), as we quoted in chapter 6.

Ontological individualism is the point of view that all psychological and sociological analysis is based on the primary reality of the individual. Tocqueville argued that historically American individualism developed out of the anti-aristocratic democracy of the United States of America. In other

words, in his view American democracy as well as the American individual
were defined negatively; they were revolutionary in character. American
individualism is based more on what it is not than on any direct expression
of what it is. Thus, American individualism emphasizes that the individual
is *not* subject to arbitrary laws without representation, and the individual is
not subject to domination by historical precedent and preference. The political and social individual in America is defined negatively by his or her
escape from the control of historical and social forces.

The fundamental American ideology of individualism can be summar-
ized in two statements:

1 The individual is the basis of all reality and all society.
2 The individual is defined by what he or she is not.

In a recent study of the discourse of Americans on the popular television
talk show *Donahue*, Donal Carbaugh (1989) showed how this discourse of
negative (or as he calls it "polemical") individualism has become embedded
in the day-to-day language of Americans. The *Donahue* show is a daily television show which is watched by millions of Americans, and hosted by Phil
Donahue. While the topics of discussion cover an extremely wide range of
subjects, they tend to be topics which are currently high in popularity. The
format consists of leading questions by Donahue, responses by panel members, and then responses and discussion by Donahue, audience members,
and panel members in a free-flowing set of conversational exchanges.

Carbaugh's analysis of this language of *Donahue* is that the person is
first symbolized as an individual, that is, ontological individualism lies at
the center of the definition of the person. This individual, in turn, has or
contains a self. This metaphor of containment is expressed in such phrases
as, "I am relatively self-contained," "I have got my self together," "I am
trying to put the pieces back together again," "reveal a piece of yourself,"
"the person inside me," or "There is nothing wrong with getting angry.
It's just how you handle it . . . keeping it inside is no good" (Carbaugh,
1989:78–9).

Most significantly, this self is understood as being opposed to what are
referred to as "traditional social roles." As Carbaugh puts it, "Society and
social roles are semantic loci of oppressive historical forces that constrain
self " (1989:92). This polemical code of negative, ontological individualism is
expressed in statements such as the quotation below from the *Donahue* show.

> While we're talking about men and women, if people would just concentrate
> on themselves, and their goals, and being individuals. Society says that you
> have to earn money [or wash dishes, raise children, be pretty, etc., etc.] to be
> of any value. I feel that that's very ingrained in men right now. That is what

women are fighting. I feel that I am fighting that right now, myself (quoted in Carbaugh, 1989:100).

This ideological discourse of negative or polemical ontological individualism is not, of course, something created just in or for the television program *Donahue*. As Bellah and his group have argued, it is the first language of contemporary American discourse.

While there is a deeply held belief among Americans that the Americans before and after the generation gap are participants in completely contrasted discourse systems, what remains constant is the American ideology of individualism. The individual is assumed to be the central organizing reality for human experience. This concept of the individual is also negative or polemical; that is, the individual is primarily defined by the categories of definition which he or she rejects; the individual is defined by what he or she is not. What has changed across the American generations, from the Americans observed by Tocqueville to those we see on *Donahue*, is the nature of the oppositions against which the individual is observed and expressed.

Four generations of Americans

As early as two decades ago, the behavioral psychologist Layne Longfellow (1978) in his corporate management seminars was using generational differences as a framework in which to analyse productivity in the American workforce. He associated three major lines of psycho-sociological research, which to some extent parallel the elements of a discourse system as we have analysed them: studies of changes in child-care practices as well as studies of developmental stages in the human life cycle (*socialization*), and studies of the modal behavioral syndrome known as Type-A behavior (*ideology*).

The four living generations of Americans analyzed by Longfellow are as follows:

Authoritarians	1914–28	66–80 years of age in 1994
Depression/War	1929–45	49–65 years of age in 1994
Baby Boom	1946–64	30–48 years of age in 1994
Infochild	1965–80	Under 30 in 1994

These divisions are based on practices of enculturation, that is, they are based upon child-rearing and parenting practices in early childhood and upon the impact of significant world and national events at transitional points in the life cycle (secondary socialization). While we will base our analysis on

Longfellow's original categories, we will also include a discussion of the forms of discourse, primarily the preferred media, and face systems.

The clearest division is that between the Depression/War generation and the Baby Boom generation. Because the youngest generation is now just reaching maturity, it is not of major concern for us here. The somewhat lesser division between the two earliest generations, however, is of considerable interest for the study of American individualism as well as for the study of systems of discourse in America.

The Authoritarians, born between 1914 and 1928

Ideology   The Authoritarian generation's view of the world was dominated by war. The first of this generation's members were born during World War I and the bulk of them reached their early adult transition (around eighteen to twenty-one years of age) during World War II.

For the development of American individualism, World War II was significant in several ways. In the first place, as Tocqueville saw so clearly, individualism is greatly strengthened by the breaking of social ties. World War II broke ties for many Americans simply because, as immigrants and children of immigrants, they found themselves at war with their own countries of origin. The German, Italian, French, and other immigrant Americans who returned to Europe to fight against their own cousins severed forever a tie of loyalty to Europe which, though it had been weakened by immigration, had never before been so severely tested.

For Asian-Americans the break was similar, though in most cases Asian-Americans were not put directly into battle with their own cousins. Most Asian-Americans felt that they were under direct pressure to renounce any suggestion of loyalty to their countries of origin. This cultural separation remains a source of pain for Asian-Americans to this day.

The American separation from Europe was also completed by World War II in the sense that the United States emerged from that war in a position of economic and political dominance over Europe. By the end of the war there was little sense left of the US being the poor cousin of the stronger British Empire.

By the time the Authoritarian generation had moved out of World War II into the positions they took in American government, business, and education, there was little left to maintain the lingering ties to Europe which had persisted in America until then. War continued to be the theme for this generation of Americans. Just as they came into their mid-life transition period (the early forties or so), the war in Vietnam broke out. As children born into war and as adults who matured as individuals in war, this third war seemed to them to be part of the nature of human society. They did not question it at all. It was their children, the Boom Babies, who questioned the war. At this time of life, when it is common to review the course of one's life and to settle into the enjoyment of the benefits of one's work, not only did this generation of Authoritarians find their authority being questioned, but their belief in the past as a major influence on the present was no longer accepted by the younger generation. Although the Authoritarians began the transition from the nineteenth-century individualism described by Tocqueville to the *Donahue*, self-expressive, polemic individualism of the end of the twentieth century, the complete devaluing of trust in authority was more than they have been able to accept.

Socialization, enculturation   The psychological anthropologist Martha Wolfenstein studied the sequence of changes in parenting styles as reflected in the extremely popular and widely distributed US government publication *Infant Care* (West 1914; Wolfenstein 1953; Goodrich 1968). In the first period (beginning in 1914) she observed a very strict emphasis on limiting the child's self-exploration. This concern is at direct odds with the sorts of expression found verbalized on *Donahue* in present-day America. The very conservative style of parenting of the earlier period is part of a general picture of the nature of infancy which had continued undiminished from the nineteenth century.

In chapter 7 we quoted the New Englander who said that no child has ever been known who did not possess an evil disposition – however sweet it might appear. It is clear enough that the ideological individualism of this oldest generation of Americans was strongly affected by this assumption that human nature was basically evil. The advice given by the US government to new parents is clearly based on this assumption. They were to exercise their parental authority in the strongest way to limit the activities of the child.

Forms of discourse   The world into which the Authoritarians were born had just begun to feel the effects of the first of the electronic media, the telegraph. Radio and movies broke into their consciousness in the 1920s, when they were teenagers. Television did not become the major feature of American communication until they were close to mid-life. For the Authoritarians, literacy and oratory were the principal means of communication in public life. These media carry with them a deeply historical sense of time, the Golden-Age sense we discussed in chapter 6. This historical sense of time ties these Authoritarians both to the past and to the future. They have been avid newspaper readers and have had a high sense of being in the eye of history in their public acts. They have also had a sense of seeing the world degenerate into worse and worse conditions.

One further aspect of the Authoritarian experience which has had an impact on their lives as well as on the rest of the world is the rise of monolingualism during their early lives. This was the period in which the longstanding multilingualism of the American population began to be challenged. Language schools were closed; laws were passed asserting that English was to be the only language allowed in various states. The Authoritarians were the first Americans to see loyalty to their country as symbolized by the exclusive use of English.

Face systems   It is not, perhaps, surprising that the Authoritarian generation developed a very high sense of authority coupled with a very low need for the expression of their own desires. There was a high consciousness of the dangers of both physical and moral dirtiness. The relationship between adults and children was understood as strongly dominated by the adult. From this we can see that, even though there was an emphasis on political egalitarianism, the hierarchical differences between adults and children were to be preserved.

Summary   This generation of Americans is very much like the Americans observed by Tocqueville. Individualism was best expressed within the narrow confines of family, friends, and business associates. As a polemical form of individualism, they found their identity in being American, not European or Asian. They further found themselves in opposition to such controlling forces as the government and government regulation. There was as yet no opposition to the control and authority of the ascending generation. The authoritarians accepted the domination of their parents and assumed that their descendants would accept their authority. While they had become highly individualistic, they had not yet become egalitarian.

The Depression/War generation, born between 1929 and 1945

Ideology   The most important life event for the Depression/War generation is, of course, the Great Depression, beginning in 1929 and running through the end of World War II. This is the world into which they were born. As we will see when we look at the primary socialization of this generation, doubt had been expressed by the parents of these children as to whether or not the adult would win out in the battle for dominance. It is significant to see that the parents of these children were actually living under very precarious social and economic conditions. First the Depression had crushed their expectations by eliminating their savings if they had any, their jobs, and their faith in the American political process. The great entrepreneurs had lost fortunes; workers were coming close to starvation. The labor unions rose throughout the country to call into question what had seemed obvious – that democratically organized free enterprise was the most productive political and economic system.

At the same time the chaos and terror of World War II, while it did not devastate the continent of America the way it did that of Europe, left these babies in many cases without fathers. Many of this generation remember the sad, long evenings waiting for news of beloved fathers and brothers and sons. It was a time in which it was hard to maintain that one's success in life would come as an inheritance from the older generation. It is not surprising, then, to see in this generation the development of the belief that if one was going to succeed, one was going to have to go it alone.

In many ways this Depression/War generation is the transitional one in America. The authority of the older generation was no longer simply assumed, and yet there is nothing in this generation of the open self-expression of the Baby Boom generation. Depression/War generation individualism is very much the go–it–alone independence of the self-made man who does not identify with either those who went before or those who came after.

Socialization, enculturation   The preceding generation, the Authoritarians, were brought up in a world which assumed that the little infant was basically depraved and needed to be kept from any form of self-pleasure or self-expression at all costs. For babies of the Depression/War generation, the emphasis changed from self-denial to self-regulation and excessive scheduling of behavior. This was most strongly manifested in the emphasis on very early control of the bowels. Infants of this generation were expected, according to government advice, to be bowel trained by six months of age.

In the edition of *Infant Care* which was revised for this generation, there are three aspects of this emphasis on bowel training which should be noted. The first is that, at least in contemporary pediatric opinion, six to eight months of age is far too early to expect a normal child to complete bowel training. In other words, this is a wholly unreal expectation placed upon the infant. The second thing to notice is the battle for dominance between the adult and the child. With the Authoritarians it was taken for granted that the adult was in the position of authority. This was unquestioned. Thirdly, the emphasis on absolute regularity in bowel movements, not varying by more than five minutes from day to day, manifests a society-wide, new emphasis on time-scheduled regularity.

This new emphasis on regularity of timing and control was not by any means limited to child care. One sees it, for example, in Frederick Taylor's *Scientific Management* (1911), with the newly popular time and motion studies in American industry. Such studies had led to Henry Ford's production line assembly of cars in Detroit in the 1920s. Cowan (1983) has argued that during the interwar period there was a steady and systematized process which she calls the "industrialization of the home." This widespread mode of thinking penetrated down into such intimate details as the bowel training of American infants.

The characteristics of this generation are based on the three characteristics of the child care of the Depression/War generation: (1) the emphasis on the struggle between the child and the adult, (2) the expectation of absolutely regular behavior (along with the impossibility of achieving it), and (3) the very early time set on this child's achievement of bowel training. These characteristics are strikingly similar to those described by Friedman and his associates for the adult Type-A behavior pattern (Friedman and Rosenman, 1974; Friedman and Ulmer, 1984).

Major components of the Type-A personality include insecurity of status, the need to control, and a sense of time urgency. Once the connection is made between this behavior pattern and cardiac and other stress-related disorders, it is not difficult to see how the Depression/War baby has been primed from the earliest days for this behavioral syndrome. This person's insecurity of status was first reflected in the doubt shown by the writers of *Infant Care* that the adult could win in the battle for this baby's control. The insecurity was further established in the economic losses and failures of the Depression and the war. To that was added in many cases the absence of many significant men in this child's life. Often those absences were permanent, when fathers and uncles died at war.

The need to control was both modeled by this child's parents in their concern to dominate him or her and emphasized in this child's own need to master bowel control at an age when it was virtually impossible. And, of course, not only was this need to control emphasized, it was timed to within five minutes on a daily basis.

This behavioral syndrome, which Friedman has called "hurry sickness," is so widespread now in American society as to hardly need further comment. It is also widely recognized as problematical, which is shown in the abundance of self-help books on stress and time management and in the training sessions offered so widely by government and business managements. This is the primary group which participates in the Utilitarian discourse system which we introduced in chapter 6.

Forms of discourse   This might be called the news generation. Perhaps it was because of the strong influence of World War II, but this generation was the first to grow up with the constant sound of radio news in its ears. One of the manifestations of the Type-A syndrome is an obsession with information and with numbers. This obsession is constantly being fed by both news and sports broadcasts.

At first, of course, these broadcasts were radio broadcasts. This generation was well into its early adult transition period before television became a major factor, and so for them television is not yet the major medium. What is important, however, is the time sense projected by both news and sports broadcasts. This is a much shorter time sense than that of earlier, literate media. Reality comes to be seen as operating in shorter bursts of hours or minutes. As a simultaneous reflection of both the time and motion studies of "scientific management" and of the new electronic media, this generation tends toward a much more compressed sense of time than any preceding generation of Americans.

Face systems The preceding generation, although it expressed an egalitarian ideology, was still basically hierarchical in relationships within the family. This generation, the Depression/War generation, was the one in which the struggle for domination between adults and children in the family is the main theme. As a transitional generation, many of the forms of address of the preceding hierarchical generation remained in place. Children called their parents "mother" and "father" (or "mom" and "dad"), but never would use their parents' given names. Nevertheless, underlying these surface forms of respect was an attitude that the younger generation really was more deserving of respect and authority than the older generation. The net result was that for this generation there are frequently mixed signals and less than clear agreement on the appropriate relationships between members of the same or older and younger generations.

Summary For this generation, the primary opposition by which individualism was maintained was that to the way of life into which they had been born. They were strongly motivated by a vow never to suffer another depression or the poverty of those times. The vow of Scarlet O'Hara never to be poor again in the movie *Gone With the Wind*, while it was staged as the voice of an earlier period, was certainly calculated to strike a resonant note with the first viewers of this film in 1939, as they themselves were taking the same vow.

Perhaps because of the fear of poverty and struggle, this generation is above all characterized by its insecurity of status. For the Depression/War generation, the breakdown of the authoritarian system made it less clear just what the basis for their individuality was, and at the same time the very clear post-war individualism of the Baby Boom generation had not yet emerged. It might well be said that as a transitional generation, this one has never achieved any clear identity. Being neither Authoritarian nor Baby Boom, they were largely pushed aside by the open conflict between the two generations before and after them.

Cultural observers have noted that in the succession of American presidents, H. Ross Perot was the only candidate from this generation to stage a real presidential campaign. It is characteristic of this generation that Ross Perot's presidential campaign was backed by no existing politically established party or group; he was very much a loner in his quest for the American presidency. Significantly, he lost, and the succession skipped from the Authoritarian generation (Presidents Kennedy through Bush) to the Baby Boom generation (President Clinton). Radical ideological individualists, this generation has worked assiduously to spread the Utilitarian discourse system about the world through the medium of international business structures.

The Baby Boom generation, born between 1946 and 1964

Ideology　The post-war boom babies were born into a world of abundance. They were, in fact, part of that abundance. Paradoxically, because of the rapid post-war economic expansion they were born into an increasingly rich country, yet at the same time, because there are so many of them, their share of that richness has never been guaranteed. From shortages of diapers in their infancy and a shortage of schools in their childhood they have gone on to experience shortages in the job market and to fear shortages of social security benefits when they reach old age.

It is probably more significant for the Boom Babies, however, that they were born into a period in which the historical sense of time had been fractured. The understanding of the past was blocked by an older generation who wanted to put the period of the Depression and World War II quickly behind them. At the same time, this generation was born under the shadow of the Cold War and the potential of total world destruction. They are really the first generation of Americans to be born into a world in which humankind had finally reached the possibility of complete technological destruction of the earth. As a result, many who belong to this generation invested even less thought in the future than in the past.

If asked to name the most important world event in their lives, most members of this generation would name the war in Vietnam. This war came along just as this generation began to reach the early adult transition. This is the period in life, remember, when the individual is expected to firmly begin to establish a life independent of that of his or her parents. This generation, being the first to have been raised in radical, egalitarian, onto-logical individualism, assumed that it was their right to decide whether or not they would do things, and their decisions were largely based on the extent to which the things they did would bring them enjoyment or at least encourage self-expression.

The war in Vietnam allowed for them neither enjoyment nor self-expression. In their view, that war was the product of a generation with which they had nothing in common, and it quickly became the strongest symbol of the oppression of culture, history, and social institutions. It quickly became the central symbolic threat to their radical individualism, and they quite naturally opposed it fervently.

Here it is useful to remember that ontological individualism, at least in America, is negative or polemical – the self is defined by what it is not and by what it resists. At this crucial time in the life cycle of the Baby Boom generation, the central definition of the self for this generation was anti-war or anti-establishment. In this resistance to the war of the Authoritarian generation establishment, the Baby Boom generation completed the definition of the American individualistic self.

Socialization, enculturation While the US government's *Infant Care* has continued to be published to this day, the book for the parents of the Boom Babies was *Baby and Child Care* by Benjamin Spock (1976), the second bestselling book after the Bible in American history. From its opening words it is clear that a generational, even a historical watershed has been crossed. Indeed, Spock's opening words signal the final, complete victory of negative ontological individualism in America. Those words are,

TRUST YOURSELF.
You know more than you think you do (Spock 1976:1).

This opening paragraph goes on polemically to say that perhaps you have had advice from friends and relatives, from experts in magazines and newspapers, and even from doctors and nurses. His advice is to always trust your own judgement first. This individualism is clearly phrased negatively: "Don't take too seriously all that the neighbors say. Don't be overawed by what the experts say. Don't be afraid to trust your own common sense" (p. 1).

The babies of the baby boom from 1946 to 1964 were brought up in a social environment which was radically different from that of the preceding Depression/War and Authoritarian generations. On the crucial issue of bowel control, Spock says almost nothing. No longer is the parent in control. It is the child who decides, while the parent waits patiently for this decision to be made. The emphasis in Spock's book is on the child's "own free will." The mandate to extend equality to all has now been extended to infancy. From Dr Spock on, no American will be assumed to have the right to make judgements about what is right for another, not even the parents of a child. The right of complete self-determination is asserted by Dr Spock to come into play from birth. The Baby Boom generation is the first completely egalitarian American generation.

The self-exploration which the Authoritarians saw as such a danger for the child is recast by Dr Spock as wholesome curiosity. There is no hint of the "infant depravity" assumed for the Authoritarian generation, though Spock himself was a product of that generation. This Spock Boom Baby is on the path to radical self-discovery and self-expression, so consonant with ontological individualism and so strongly manifested later in such discourses as those seen on *Donahue*.

Finally, it is important to see the relationship of the adult and the child. In Spock's comments on bowel training, it is clear that the role of the adult is to wait and observe while the child decides. In a section in which Spock treats the question of security, he suggests the great value in providing "comforters." He writes, "The little girl (or boy) recreates certain comforting aspects of her parents out of the cuddly toy and her thumb for example; *but* it's not a parent who can envelop her or control her; it's a parent *she* can control" (p. 236). What Spock emphasizes here is the great comfort and security the child receives from role-playing her control of the parent. Again, in this detail Spock emphasizes the value of the individual child, which arises directly from that child's control of the world.

Forms of discourse   Could there have been an anti-war movement in the United States without recorded music and without television? Could there have been a civil rights movement without them? Perhaps, but it is very difficult to imagine "the sixties" without either of these media. Much has been written, including the comment quoted above from Camille Paglia, about the nearly complete interpenetration of the idea of a Baby Boom generation and the electronic media, especially recorded music and television. There is little to be added to that discussion here. The one crucial factor from the point of view of the development of American individualism is the flattening of the time perspective that comes with these media.

A lead-in to the dialogue between Postman and Paglia describes the latter as follows: "Paglia was born after World War II, an accident to which she ascribes great significance. To hear her talk is to confirm her theory about the influence of the modern media: She speaks in a rush of images, juxtapositions, and verbal jump cuts . . . Television, Paglia says, *is* the culture" (Postman and Paglia, 1991:44). For our purpose it is not necessary to prove that the development of the electronic media in the period following World War II was the cause of the communicative style of the Baby Boom generation. One would wonder how that might be done in the first place. What is important to observe is that it is widely believed among that generation that they are the products of music and television. Their discourse system is the system of electronic communications. The strongest aspect of this belief is the distrust of linear argumentation and historical or traditional precedent. Ideas for this generation have a very short shelf-life. What is crucial to this generation is to keep moving, to continue to exercise new options, to avoid any form of even apparent permanence or stagnation. Television, of course, may not be the cause of this phenomenon, but it is an appropriate medium for its expression.

Face systems   One final but important point to be considered about the Baby Boom generation is the rise of the concept of "relationships." One aspect of the Baby Boom lifestyle has been the rise of such loosely knit organizations as relationships, networks, and support groups. These social groups are quite unlike either the traditional relationships of family, community, or business found among the Authoritarian generation or the more limited and highly utilitarian business contacts of the Depression/War generation. The groups and networks of the Baby Boom generation form and disperse along the lines of common interests, needs, and issues.

If we could call the most traditional of relationships, those of the family, hierarchical and vertical (lasting through time across generations), those of the Baby Boom generation might be called egalitarian and horizontal and of insignificant temporal existence. One might almost say that they must of necessity be limited in time so that these network and support group relationships do not come to be perceived as oppressive to the individual. This generation has completed the transition from the hierarchical structures of relationship of traditional European society to the egalitarian and lateral relationships of contemporary America. As a paradoxical result, one finds simultaneously among this generation a much higher concern for relationships than in any preceding American generation, and a high degree of skepticism about the endurance of any relationship.

Summary The polemic which motivates the Baby Boom generation individual the most is what is usually referred to as "traditional social roles." This is the language of *Donahue*. This opposition began as these Spock babies were brought up in an atmosphere of full and spontaneous self-expression. From the start, anything which might limit or narrow the scope of this self-expression and self-realization was seen as the problem to be challenged and opposed. In the 1960s, the strongest expression of polemical individualism was expressed in opposition to the war in Vietnam, or more generally to "the establishment." It is significant that often "the establishment" is not more clearly defined, because for this generation, the point is *any* establishment, any a priori assumptions about what one ought to do or what one ought to be, are a danger to the full development of the self. As this generation of Americans has reached full maturity, this opposition to tradition has become fully developed in a language where even the choices one makes for oneself are problematical because of the limits they place on one's future. For the fullest self-expression of one's individuality, *all* conceptual limits must be questioned. In a real sense, this Baby Boom generation has completed the revolution of American ontological polemical individualism which Tocqueville observed in its first stages.

The Infochild generation, born between 1964 and 1980

Ideology The first Infochildren were born into the time of the Vietnam War, but at least in this very short time perspective they seem to be less affected by world events than any preceding generation of Americans. One author has suggested that the most characteristic aspect of this generation of Americans is their apparent lack of interest in entering on the normal path of life's stages (Littwin 1986). She has referred to this generation as "the postponed generation," a generation of Americans which is basically putting off getting out of school, getting into the workforce, and establishing families.

Socialization, enculturation   This is still a young generation of Americans, with the oldest in their late twenties. This is the age of our own children and the majority of our students. As a result this generation is of a great deal of interest to us and, we presume, to our readers. Unfortunately, there is very little research to make reference to in discussing its characteristics. We will have to make do with only a few comments which will outline the gist of the changes involving this generation. While Dr Spock's *Baby and Child Care* continued to remain very popular, *Infant Care* was revised. By the time these children were born there were two important shifts in such forms of advice to parents. The first shift was in the authorship of *Infant Care*. In the past it had first been written by Mrs Max West (1914 edition), and then later it was revised by individual medical doctors as editors (Wolfenstein 1953). By the time Infochild was born, however, *Infant Care* was written by a committee of over one hundred medical, psychological, and child-care experts (Goodrich 1968). What was once a booklet of housewifely suggestions had become a full-length book of "expert" advice.

This emphasis on expertise was not only seen in the preparation of the book, but was also urged as the path to successful child rearing. The book begins by lamenting that women are not taught child care in public schooling. It goes on to say that one does not need to despair, however, because the ultimate authority, the doctor, is always available.

The theme of professional expertise is reiterated throughout this generation's early life. The mother is told that there is nothing much she can do. Not only is Infochild expected, like the Baby Boom child, to develop on his or her own, now the parent is expected to step aside and refer all questions and serious care to hired professional experts. It is emphasized that there is too much information for the ordinary person as a parent to be expected to understand and digest. Infochild was born into a world which was assumed to be complex and quite beyond the scope of any single person's understanding. It is worth remembering that the panel of experts who prepared *Infant Care*, as well as Infochild's parents and doctors, were, on the whole, members of the Depression/War generation. This advice to leave the care of Infochild up to someone else was entirely welcomed by them. They were already hurrying themselves into their own world of Type-A-driven success.

Forms of discourse   If there is still some question about which life events will prove to be most significant in the life cycles of Infochild, there is little question that this is the computer generation. In a period in which the highest value is placed on professional expertise, the computer as a medium has in many ways come to be the driving metaphor of such objective competence. These Infochildren have had computers as a basic aspect of their lives from earliest childhood and, more than any other Americans, take them for granted.

Face systems　The Baby Boom generation before this one was the first generation to begin to call their parents by their given names. Two factors have brought about the almost complete elimination of any indications of generational hierarchy. In the first place, members of the Infochild generation have clear cultural and technological dominance in the spheres which are so widely valued in the society, the uses of computer and electronic technology. As a result of their competence in these areas and of the dependence of modern society on their competence, they feel themselves the equals of members of any other generation in most contexts highly valued by the society.

The second factor is that throughout the period beginning after World War II, there has been a major demographic change in the structure of the American family. The most recent census counted some fourteen different "family" types. That is to say, the majority of the members of this generation have grown up in families not of either the traditional extended family type or the nuclear family type. Their parents are more typically divorced and remarried. There is a strong resistance to naming the second spouse of their own mothers and fathers with kin terms such as "father" and "mother." It seems inappropriate for a child to call his own father or mother's spouse "Mr" or "Mrs." The solution which has been taken is to call all adults by given names, which dodges the issue of the exact relationships in a world in which such relationships are taken to be in constant flux.

Summary　Most likely it is too early to say anything much about Infochild. We are tempted to suggest that Infochild is taking the Baby Boom generation's alienation from social roles to the extreme of alienation from the human reality altogether. In their love of both computer and video technology, there is certainly a sense of disappointment in the dullness, slowness, and weakness of the human individual. Many of these young people are starting to show the stress which comes with excessive use of high-speed computer technologies.

The shifting ground of American individualism

The four generations of Americans which we have described here are those which have preceded and followed the radical post-war break in American individualism. The Authoritarians were in a sense the last of the old Americans, the ones described by Tocqueville. There is much in their lives which shows an awareness that change is overtaking them and their world. The generation of the Baby Boom, on the other hand, see themselves proudly as being firmly on this side of a radical discontinuity. For this generation there is a clear rejection of tradition and of history in a way that Tocqueville is unlikely to have imagined possible or desirable. The Depression/War generation in this analysis is the transitional generation. They were the generation to suffer the disillusionment of both the Depression and World War II. While they saw little which attracted them in the past and in tradition, they also see little to attract them in the spontaneous, interest-group relationships of the Baby Boom generation. Without a deep sense of time and tradition, they also do not have a strong sense of contemporary lateral relationships.

The individualism of the Authoritarian generation is the polemical ontological individualism which Tocqueville describes, but it is tempered by the assumption of at least a certain fundamental human grounding in family and tradition. The individualism of the Depression/War generation is, perhaps, the most negative in its strongly go–it–alone nature, in which individual success is upheld as the highest value. The individualism of the Baby Boom generation is the assertive, self-expressive, *Donahue* individualism.

While most analysts focus on the discontinuities between these generations as a problem in communication, we prefer to focus on the continuing development of individualism as the common theme within a broader American version of the Utilitarian discourse system. What all of these Americans have in common is the assumption that the person as an individual lies at the center of any meaningful social analysis. What has changed is the "other" against which each generation has established its individualism. The egalitarianism on which this individualism is based has been with us since the time of Bentham and Tocqueville in the middle of the last century. Down to the time of World War II, however, Americans still developed their sense of individuality within a context of a close network of family and friends. As the authority of the older generation was first questioned in the child rearing of the Depression/War generation and then overturned with the Boom Babies, American individualism has moved from defining itself polemically in a world and national political context to defining itself polemically in the day-to-day network of social relationships.

From this review of the four generations of Americans, we can draw several conclusions about discourse systems operating within American culture. In the first place, it should be clear that it would be impossible to consider American culture to be either entirely hierarchical or egalitarian in regard to its assumptions about human relationships. The Authoritarian generation was quite strongly hierarchical in its assumptions, and the Baby Boom generation is quite strongly egalitarian. As a result of this difference, communication between members of these two generations is very much like communication between "Americans" and "Asians." We put these in quotations to signal that neither of these terms is really at all acceptable;

both are stereotypical. In fact, the stereotypical "American" egalitarian behavior is not at all typical of the oldest generation of Americans.

If we were to look at another dimension of interdiscourse analysis, the dimension concerning the assumptions made about the functions of language, we would see that the oldest generation, the Authoritarians, would probably take a fairly balanced position and assume that language has both informational and relational functions. The Depression/War generation, however, has a tendency to place a greater emphasis on the informational aspects of language use. The Baby Boom generation, in contrast to these, tends to place a very high emphasis on relationships, as we have said above.

We believe that these intergenerational differences are sufficiently marked that it is fair to describe each generation as having a unique discourse system. In each case the discourse system will share some features with other American discourse systems, but it will also contrast with the other systems in other features. All of them will share, as we have argued above, an emphasis on individualism, but this individualism will be expressed in different ways. For the Authoritarian the emphasis will be on the independence of Americans from outside, particularly European, influence. For the Baby Boom generation American, the emphasis will be on independence from tradition, the past, and the excessive influence of given human relationships such as those of the family or the community.

By developing this generational analysis of the four American generations, we hope to have demonstrated clearly why it is impossible to make such a simple categorization as "the American discourse system"; there is really no such analytical unit. We must also make one final qualification before going on to consider other involuntary discourse systems. The generational discourse systems we have just described are based on a research literature which says little or nothing about different ethnic or regional groups in American culture. What we have described above would apply most clearly in major East Coast cities among the Northern European-based English-speaking populations of those cities. In other geographical regions, among other ethnic groups, or in rural regions of the country there may be many exceptions. Nevertheless, because this population of Americans has had such a dominating role in the development of American culture, especially in international environments, we have gone ahead with this description, even though we know we must be very careful in making applications directly from it.

Asian Generational Discourse Systems

This review of the different American generations leaves us wishing that we could now present a similar review of generational differences among significant Asian cultural groups. Unfortunately, there is no comparable study of any such group that we know of. Recently Hong Kong's *South China Morning Post* carried a feature in which it described the lives of several significant Hong Kong Baby Boomers. That study, however, simply took the dates and generations which have been analysed for North Americans and applied them to Hong Kong. We believe that this sort of comparison is doomed to gross misunderstanding and misrepresentation, because there is very little in common between the generational experiences, child-rearing practices, and other life experiences of Hong Kong people and those of North America.

When we were teaching at a corporate training center in Korea, we had the opportunity of presenting this generational analysis to groups of Korean business people and engineers. Their responses have led us to believe that there is a similar sequence of generations in Korea, and perhaps in other countries of Asia, but that the generations are not of the same age. In Korea, for example, Koreans pointed out that among the generation born before the end of the Korean War there was a belief in strict child rearing which emphasized very traditional Korean cultural values.

In the period immediately following the Korean War, starting in the mid-1950s, there was an extended period of great hardship, not unlike the period of the Great Depression in America, in which hard work and learning to live with little were emphasized along with very pragmatic strategies for succeeding in a harsh and difficult environment. From their point of view, this period produced a generation of people quite like the America members of the Depression/War generation.

Finally, they noted that, starting with the great boom in the Korean economy which took place during the Vietnam War, a new generation has grown up which shares some, but certainly not all, the values of the American Baby Boom generation. This younger generation has lived in a world of relatively fast economic development, becoming accustomed to the idea that they can accomplish much with relatively little effort, and that their country is an independent and strong world economic entity.

We are not presenting this analysis of Korean generations from the point of view of sociological research. These are only the general impressions of Koreans who have had relatively little time to think about these questions. Nevertheless, they did say that they recognize among themselves that there are quite clear communicative divisions and that discourse operates in different ways depending on whether one is a member of one or another of these discourse systems.

A similar informal analysis among college-age students in Hong Kong indicates that there are similar differences between members of different generations in Hong Kong as well. We believe that a study could be made of differences in generations in Japan, Hong Kong, China, Taiwan, Singapore, or any other Asian cultural group. We are certain that such differences would reflect patterns of socialization unique to those places and to different times and that historical experiences and ideological shifts would also be major factors. We are convinced that such terms as "westernization" are of little use in making this kind of analysis. The roots of generational differences are buried deeply within the cultural constructs of each cultural group. We would not expect the new forms of individualism which are developing throughout Asia to have much in common with what is called individualism in America, for example.

We would expect to find, however, that throughout Asia there are significant differences between members of different generations and that those differences would form what would amount to different generational discourse systems. We hope that future research will allow us and others to provide clearer analyses than are currently available in this area of discourse study.

Communication Between Generations

When we considered the voluntary discourse systems of corporate structures and of professional or occupational specializations, the problem we posed was for individuals who found themselves caught between the goals, ideologies, and identities of these two different systems. We might think of that as an internal problem, in that it is the individual person who needs to resolve how he or she is going to deal with this conflict in identity. Now we have described some of the differences we find between members of different generational discourse systems. The problem which arises, however, is rather different; it is an external problem of communication with those who are members of a different discourse system. The problem is not how Baby Boomers communicate with other Baby Boomers, but how members of the Depression/War generation and Baby Boomers communicate.

As a problem in interdiscourse professional communication, we would argue that communication between members of different American generations is very much the same kind of problem as communication between employees from different cultural backgrounds in a multinational corporation – each approaches situations with a different interpretive framework, and that leads to false conversational inferences and ultimately to an incapacity to develop the kind of cooperation both sides of the problem are seeking.

The differences between generations are a particularly acute problem in organizational communication. There is a fairly clear stratification along structural lines which matches generational stratification. Most of the corporations and governmental organizations of the contemporary world have a small, mostly retired now, but still very powerful group of members of the Authoritarian generation at the top. These Authoritarians, now between sixty-six and eighty years of age, were the ones who in earlier years created the organizational structures, the policies, the corporate culture, and the existing power relations with outside groups. A few of them continue to sit on boards of directors, on boards of commissioners, and in senior legislative and ministerial positions, while most exercise their power from behind the scenes.

On the whole, these members of the Authoritarian generation take it for granted that institutions will be structured hierarchically and that they will be motivated primarily out of altruistic interest in the overall good of society or the organization. They will tend to restrict or deny their own interests in these more general, overriding group interests. They will be particularly sensitive to challenges to their authority and use all their power to resist these challenges.

Just below these Olympian figures are the members of the Depression/War generation. They are now between their late forties and sixty-five years of age; that is, they are in the positions where they can most fully exercise their institutional power as the senior generation of active corporate and organizational members. This generation is much more concerned with individual power and control; this is the generation which brought stress to the attention of managers concerned with corporate health and productivity because of their own tendency to work to the point of collapsing. This is the generation with the relentless drive for scheduling, timing, and efficiency, which, in their minds, were the primary means by which one might achieve personal dominance. Their entire lives have been lived in a struggle for dominance against both the older Authoritarian generation and the younger Baby Boom generation.

This younger generation, which is now between thirty and fifty years of age, is beginning to take over the organizational structures of our business and government. While it might be said that all of the American generations are concerned with forwarding the success of the individual, the two pre-war generations found this success largely within the formal structures of corporate discourse systems. The success of a Depression/War generation member is gauged in the number of people he or she controls. This Baby Boom generation, as well as the Infochild generation to some extent, is more strongly motivated by personal freedom and enjoyment of what has come to be called "lifestyle." For them, institutional success is only useful if it provides them with the things they enjoy outside of the organizations.

Communication within organizations, then, is played out on a field of very differing pitches. While all of these corporate members might use the same words, the meanings by which they are interpreted are radically different. We will give just one example to indicate how these different generations often fail to understand each other.

In an engineering office two of the junior engineers, both members of the Baby Boom generation, came up with the idea for a project which they thought would significantly improve one of their production processes. They went to their supervisor, a member of the Depression/War generation, told him briefly about the project, and asked whether or not he would be willing to support it. His answer was, "That sounds like a great idea. Go right ahead and I'll give you my full support."

The engineers began their work and were enjoying the project, but they noticed after a while that their supervisor had never again made mention of it. He had not stopped by their office to ask into its progress, and he had not mentioned it when they had run across him at the exercise club from time to time. At the next staff meeting they waited to see if they would have a place on the agenda to bring everyone up to date, and found that, again, there was no mention. They became discouraged and ultimately abandoned the idea.

This corporation during this period of time was employing a consulting company to assist them with rethinking and developing a new corporate culture. At one of the discussion sessions with junior staff, a point was raised about supervisory staff. These two engineers argued that the biggest problem they experienced was that creativity was being smothered by the higher management. They said that they received "no support" from above when they tried to initiate new projects. They felt that the system was "too hierarchical" and that they were being forced into simply accepting and carrying out management concepts.

Ironically, in discussions with management these same consultants heard a very different story. The complaint of management was that whatever they might do to foster the corporate cultural goals of initiative and creativity among their employees, all they got was mechanical and routine following of management directives. The particular supervisor in question pointed out that two engineers had come to him with what he thought was a really creative concept and, even though he had given them complete freedom to pursue the project, they had just dropped it for no reason whatsoever.

In this communication between the two generations, the crucial word is "support." From the point of view of the members of the younger generation, "support" means to show an interest, to come around from time to time and ask how things are going, to mention to others that these people are doing something interesting. They took for granted that the organization would give them the resources to do the actual work. From the point of view of the supervisor, as a member of the older generation, "support" means to leave you entirely free and independent, to refrain from meddling, to stay away until the younger engineers can prove they did the job entirely on their own.

This is only one case of many we could cite in which the two generations sadly misinterpret each other, with results which are not satisfactory to either of them. Each is using its own discourse system to interpret the discourse exchanged between them. "Support" for the older generation is interpreted against a background of a desire for total freedom and independence, for total self-control – something which has eluded most members of this generation. For the younger generation, the word "support" is interpreted against a background of a desire for involvement, creativity, group interest, and the approval of one's seniors. Just as these Baby Boomers expected their parents to wait and watch them for signs of individual creativity, in corporations and in government they still hope for the recognition of their uniqueness.

As we will see again in our discussion below of communication between men and women, the problem of interdiscourse system communication, like that of intercultural communication, is that while the words may be understood, the meanings are interpreted within a cultural envelope created by the discourse system from which a person speaks. In the case both of different generations within the same society and even of different genders within the same family, each side believes that its interpretation is the same as that of the other side, and is simply mystified about why they are coming to different conclusions.

11

Gender Discourse

Intergender Discourse

The discourse systems of different generations cut across the central communicative systems of a culture. In a similar way, the discourse systems of
gender cut across culture and generations, corporate culture and professional specializations. As a subject of discourse research, the study of gender
discourse is relatively new. Most of what is available for analysis is based on
patterns of discourse within American society, and as a result, in what follows we will again need to restrict ourselves primarily to American discourse.

For our purposes the most useful research in this area is the work of
Deborah Tannen. From her analysis as well as that of many others, it is
clear that the discourse of men and women forms two systems which are in
many ways distinct from each other, in spite of the fact that, on the whole,
boys and girls grow up in the same families, we are educated together, we
form families together, and we work together in the same companies and
offices and are members of the same professions and occupation groups.

At first it may seem out of place in a book on intercultural professional
communication to be focusing on problems which, as Tannen has described
so well, occur across the dinner table each evening. Our own research and
consultation work has shown us, however, that not only do men and women
work within very different interpretive frames of discourse in the home, but
in professional communication these different ways of seeing the world are
a major source of miscommunication, to the frustration and loss of everyone
involved in them.

Directness or indirectness?

We will start with a common example in order to draw out the themes we
will discuss later. The conversation below is not at all unusual:

He: What would you like for your birthday?
She: I don't care, anything's OK.
He: No, really, what do you want? I'd like to get you something nice.
She: You don't have to get me anything, besides we can't afford much right
        now.
He: Well, how about if we just go out for dinner together then?
She: Sure, that's fine. I don't really want anything. You always give me
        whatever I want anyway.

Both the man and the woman in this conversation feel frustrated by this situation. He really wants to give her something nice, unusual, something she would not otherwise buy for herself because they do not usually spend much money on special things for each other or for themselves. But from this conversation he is not able to figure out what she would like, and he gives up and settles for just going out for dinner – something they have always done and which carries no special meaning for either of them. What has frustrated him is that while he has asked quite clearly and specifically what she wants, she has told him nothing. He is confirmed in his belief that this woman and perhaps all women are wishy-washy, indefinite, unable to say clearly what they want, or just passive.

The woman in this conversation is also frustrated. She would very much appreciate a special and unusual gift as a symbol of the strength of their relationship. What the gift would be is not the consideration for her at all; what is important to her is that he should know her well enough to be able to tell what would be just the right gift to symbolize this. The fact that he has asked outright indicates to her that he, like all men, is unobservant, is unable to interpret her feelings, or in the worst case does not really care for her as much as he says. She feels what he has said is just an exercise in pretending to care and that he is really quite satisfied to get out of the situation with nothing but having to go for dinner.

The result is that even though he has had the best of intentions in his mind and has sincerely wanted to express his feelings for her, what the man has communicated to this woman is quite the opposite. She feels he does not care for her very much at all.

For her part, the woman has wanted to give him a chance to demonstrate his feelings for her, and so she has been careful not to spoil this by being explicit. For her it is important not to be explicit, and so she carefully disguises any clues that she is really hoping for the nice gift he has suggested. She hopes that in spite of this conversation he will go out and buy something for her, and so is disappointed to find that he has taken her quite literally and they have only had a dinner together again.

The man and the women in this example have approached the same situation with very different interpretive frames, and so even though they have succeeded in producing a complete coherent, fluent discourse from the point of view of such matters as syntax, turn exchange, and the rest, they have not really understood each other at all. This, then, is the first issue to be considered: men and women approach communication with different interpretive frames. Where one may expect direct explicit statement, the other may be expecting indirect expression.

Before going any further, it is important to say that we do not mean that men are direct and women are indirect. No such statement can be really meaningful. What we mean to say is that when one expects directness and the other uses indirectness, wrong interpretations and miscommunication will be the result. The point is difference in expectation, not absolute differences in style or behavior.

To make this point as clearly as we can before getting into further contrastive descriptions, consider that it is a frequent complaint women make of men that they never tell them that they love them. Donal Carbaugh (1989) has described how on the American television talk show *Donahue*, which we mentioned above in discussing generational discourse, a woman complained that in some decade or more of marriage her husband had never told her that he loved her. The response many men make to this complaint is that they have worked hard at their jobs, they have been faithful husbands, they have not wasted money on themselves for years – what clearer expression of their love could they make than years of demonstrating it through their day-to-day behavior? In other words, in this case it seems that what the woman is asking for is an explicit statement in so many words, whereas what the man is doing is making an indirect statement through his actions.

To repeat our point, what is important is the difference in expectations in any particular situation. In some cases, women use indirect approaches to communication while men are expecting more direct approaches; in other cases, it is the women who are expecting direct statement and the men who are expressing themselves indirectly. The issue is not directness and indirectness; the issue is the current interpretive framework. As we will see, in many situations, men and women have different interpretive frameworks and this leads them to draw the wrong inferences from language which in another situation would be quite clear and unambiguous.

As we have discussed in chapter 4 in the section on metacommunication, the problem in discourse between men and women, and between members of any two different discourse systems, most often lies in the signaling and interpretation of metamessages. Behind everything we say is a set of standing interpretive frameworks. The boss who tells a joke forgets that people are laughing because he is the boss, not because he is very funny. Within that framework, his position of power makes his employees more responsive than they might be if he was the mailroom boy. In order to understand intergender discourse, we will have to look at the standing interpretive frameworks within which the discourses between men and women take place. All of us are the products of our histories and our socializations, and for men and women the most significant aspect of that history is the asymmetrical differentiation of the roles and statuses of men and women.

Different interpretive frames

In organizational communication, from businesses to university and public school classrooms, a clear difference between the behavior of men and women has been observed. In a business meeting of a dozen people, both men and women, it has been observed that most of the talk is dominated by the men in the group. They take the most turns at talk, and when they talk they take longer turns. From this situation one might mistakenly draw the conclusion that men talk more than women, or that women are basically taciturn. On the other hand, a similar business meeting in which the participants are all women (though in our contemporary world that is still, unfortunately, a somewhat rare occasion) finds them highly voluble with rapid exchanges of turns, much simultaneous speech, and an overall polychromatic introduction of topics.

In university classrooms in which a discussion is being led by a teacher, Tannen (1991) has observed that, again, men dominate the flow of the discussion, with women taking fewer and shorter turns. On the other hand, when the discussion takes the form of separate small groups, women who are silent in the larger setting emerge as having a good deal to say.

Both of these situations are in contrast to the common complaint of women that their men at home are sullen, silent, and withdrawn from them. This once again points up the fact that one cannot make a binary contrast between men and women, saying that women are taciturn and men are voluble. That might be said in the context of a mixed gender business meeting or a large university class discussion. On the other hand, if the context is a same-gender business meeting or a small group discussion, one would have to say that women are if anything more voluble than men. And if the context is the home, one would then want to say that men were actually taciturn.

The research literature on intergender discourse has pointed out at least nine dimensions along which men and women tend to form different interpretive frames. Many of these are quite closely related and might be considered just other ways of saying the same thing. These dimensions, which have been adapted from Tannen (1990a), are as follows:

1 intimacy–independence;
2 connection–status;
3 inclusive–exclusive;
4 relationship–information;

5 rapport–report;
6 community–contest;
7 problems–solutions;
8 novice–expert;
9 listening–lecturing.

Intimacy–independence

An example which is given by Tannen (1990a:26) concerns a couple whom she names Linda and Josh. Josh gets a call from an old friend who will be visiting town, and he immediately invites him to stay at their house. Later on, when he tells Linda, she is upset because he has not discussed it with her before making the invitation. He tells her that he does not want to be seen as asking his wife for permission in front of his old friends.

While Josh's concern is that discussing it with his wife may show weakness by suggesting that he needs her permission, Linda's concern is motivated quite differently. Her concern is that he seems to be showing a greater degree of intimacy with his old friend than with his wife. She feels he owes it to her to display his intimacy with her to this friend, not the other way around.

From this point of view, what is of concern to the man is his independence whereas for the woman it is their intimacy. In other words, he is concerned for his status as being free to make up his own mind, in contemporary western society a prerogative of higher rather than lower status, whereas she is concerned for their connection. In addition to this, there is felt to be a different distribution of the contexts in which intimacy or connection should be displayed. The intimacy within which men seem most comfortable is that of equal, semi-public status, the sports club, or the pub, or even the difficult work assignment. The difficulty men have in expressing intimacy with their wives reflects a background assumption of an asymmetrical status. For them, showing intimacy shows equality of status.

This pull between independence and intimacy, status and connection, is displayed as well in a language of inclusive and exclusive statements. A man's boss calls him into the office to discuss with him the possible transfer to an overseas assignment.

Supervisor: You've done well for us here. Do you think you could adjust to working in Frankfurt?
Employee: Well, of course, I've never been there, but I see no reason why I could not perform as well there as anywhere.

When he goes home he says to his wife, "I've been given a transfer to Frankfurt. Maybe you should start looking into schools for the kids."

Throughout these situations he has quite unconsciously used a language of exclusion. Although this transfer is a transfer for not just him but for his entire family, he has never thought to broaden out the pronoun he is using to include them. He has not said, "We've never been there," or, "We're going to go to Frankfurt and maybe we should start looking into schools." A woman in the same situation might be quite concerned in the first place with not just how she would be able to perform her work, but how the whole family might get along in such a transfer. She would most likely feel it quite natural to want to discuss it with the family before saying that she was quite sure that it would work out well.

Of course, a woman who takes such an inclusive stance in discussing the transfer with her boss might be thought to be a weak employee who could not make such crucial decisions on her own. While the man with his exclusive language communicates to his boss that he is quite independent and able to stand on his own (whether or not his family will get along), the woman communicates dependence and even suggests the possibility that if things did not go well with the family, she would not be able to perform her work up to standards.

Actual cases show that whether it is a man or a woman, work performance cannot be easily isolated from family matters, and most international corporations now recognize the need for providing support for not just the employee, but the employee's family as well. What we are concerned with here is that in such cases, the actual facts of the matter aside, the language of exclusion which a man uses will tend to emphasize his autonomy and independence and play down his intimate relationships; the language of inclusion used by a woman is more likely to play up the intimacy and relationships, recognizing them for the significant factors that they are.

Relationship–information

We have discussed differences in this dimension in several places. In chapter 5 we said that the use of deductive and inductive strategies for the introduction of topics was related to the question of whether relationship or informational functions of language predominated. In that case we were focusing largely on either situational or intercultural differences in expectations. In considering intergender discourse, the issue is the same, but with the difference that in many cases women as a group, according to the research, will tend to focus more on relationships than men, who will tend to direct their attention to information. The result, predictably, is that men will perceive women to be indirect or confused because their attention to the relationship will have led to a less deductive introduction of topics.

More generally, because women are concerned with intimacy, connection, and inclusion, they will tend to focus more attention on the use of language as a way of communicating relationships. Men, on the other hand, because of their focus on independence, status, and exclusion, will favor the informational functioning of language. Tannen (1990a) has referred to this as the distinction between rapport and report.

Even where men and women base their communications on the exchange of information, the types of information communicated are likely to be different. There is an old joke on the subject. A man says,

> My wife and I have an agreement; I make all the big decisions, but she gets to make the little ones. I decide what the United Nations should do, how to solve the world energy crisis, and who will win the next World Cup; she decides where we should live, how we should eat, how to educate the kids, and where we'll retire.

This joke, which men tend to find more amusing than women, suggests that the joke teller is henpecked and controlled by his wife. But the joke is based on observation of the fact that what men consider "information" is what we might call public affairs or news; what women consider "information" is more likely to be the close and important details of their daily lives.

One of the perennial sticking points in the debate over whether men and women in intimate relationships "talk" or not has to do with what they talk about. A man is more likely to say he had had a good talk with someone if the talk had ranged over broad subjects like the economy, politics, and sports. The more general and abstract the discussion, the more it would count as a good "talk." Women, on the other hand, are likely to consider it a good "talk" when close details of individual lives are brought out, particularly where those details show people's character, their feelings, and their reactions to the events of their ongoing lives. What women call a good talk, men might dismiss by saying it is "nothing but" gossip.

The focus of the talk of women is on the community of humans who are connected together in their daily lives. Men, on the other hand, tend to be more concerned with contest. Sports, politics, international business and economy, or, where they engage in personal details, success and advancement are the topics which interest men. Again, this reflects the ongoing concern in the discourse of women with how human beings manage to keep their communities together and functioning in spite of difficulties and conflicts. Men, being more concerned with independence and status, tend to focus on the ways in which individuals or groups manage to emerge victorious in combat, whether the combat is literal (war) or figurative (business competition).

One result of this difference in the topics men and women talk about leads to a major kind of intergender miscommunication, what we might call problems and solutions. Everyone, of course, has problems. The difference is in how we respond when others tell us theirs. Women tend to respond to hearing of someone else's problems by telling of their own problems. This indicates that they understand the situation the other person is in and that they feel sympathetic. Men, in contrast, are more likely to take it as a request for help and to offer a solution, however pointless the solution might be.

If a woman describes a problem she is having with a client, for example, to another woman, what will most likely happen is that her colleague will say, "Yes. I had one just like that last week. I felt awful, but there was nothing I could do." If she describes this same problem to a male colleague, she is more likely to hear, "Well, of course, what you should have done is *X Y Z*." He is likely either to offer a reprimand and explanation of what she did wrong, or, in a slightly more helpful case, offer some constructive suggestions about how she might deal with the problem. What he is quite unlikely to do is sympathize with her and share a similar problem.

The reason men and women take this different position goes back to the question of connection and status. A problem, for a woman, gives her an opportunity to show her sympathy and to emphasize her connections with others. A man is more likely to take the same situation as an opportunity to step into the role of the person with the status of problem solver. This dimension of novice–expert is one on which much frustration and a great deal of misinterpretation develop.

When a woman uses what Tannen (1990a) calls "troubles talk," that is, the discussion of problems, to emphasize connections, community, and sympathy for others, a man is likely to take this as a request for help and as a display of weakness or ignorance. Consequently, when a man hears problems aired, he is likely to take it as a challenge to his ability, his competence, his expertise. He is ready to rush in and show how easily he can solve this problem.

Of course, what normally happens is not a simple problem–solution sequence when men and women talk. If a woman puts forward a problem, she is looking for a symmetrical exchange of problems and sympathy. This is not what she gets; what she gets is a solution. This suggests to her either that the man has not heard her call for sympathy or that he is attempting to put her down for ignorance as a novice. Because she has not received the sympathy she is looking for, she is likely to increase the emphasis on the problem, and the man is likely to hear this as a failure to accept his solution, which directly challenges his sense of expertise. As each attempts within his or her own framework to continue the discussion, the misinterpretation gets worse until one or the other simply gives up or gets angry.

One of the regular accusations men make of women is of illogicality. This arises in part with the opposite situation, in which a man brings up a problem with a woman. He is looking for some active discussion of possible solutions, though, as we have said, he is most likely interested in quite abstract and theoretical solutions. In his mind he has brought up a topic for discussion and is probably looking forward to some active, maybe even contentious playing with the arguments for and against possible solutions. The woman, on the other hand, using her framework of connection and sympathy, brings up a problem of her own. From the man's point of view this is completely a non sequitur. Rather than one problem to solve, the woman has, in his mind, posed a second and wholly unrelated problem. If she keeps doing that, they will never get anywhere in their discussion. He sooner or later gives up, thinking that she is illogical and cannot keep her mind on the subject, his subject.

One outcome of this polarity between novice and expert is the polarity between listening and lecture. Women are quite accustomed to getting extended lectures from men on a diverse range of subjects. What often triggers these lectures is a woman's attempt to start a round of "troubles talk." As she brings up a problem for sympathy, she is taken as having presented a problem for solution. The more she elaborates on the problem, the bigger the problem needing solution seems to be to the man. The result is that he launches into a full-blown solution when all the woman was looking for was a sympathetic ear. She lapses into silence once she realizes that the more she says about her problem in an attempt to be heard, the longer the lecture is likely to last.

We have not by any means exhausted the ways of talking about differences in interpretive frames of men and women. What we hope to have done is simply to illustrate how men and women come to misinterpret each other, even when they approach communication with the best of intentions. If this were all there were to it, we could simply ask men and women to examine these and similar examples, to analyze their own speech, and then to simply say something like, "Oh, excuse me, I thought you meant . . ." Unfortunately, men and women find it difficult to make the apparently obvious corrections because, for both men and women, their sense of identity and their sense of their place in culture and society are tied up in the ideological history of relationships between men and women. These interpretive frameworks, through which we see the world in our gender-specific ways, are not just tinted glasses that one has chosen to put on and which one can simply take off. Both historically and in our earliest socialization we have been taught that these interpretive frameworks are part and parcel of being men and women.

The origin of difference: ideology and paradox

The history of the discourses of men and women and the misinterpretations which arise in communication between them is tied up in the historical development of the Utilitarian ideology. To put it in a few words, the Utilitarian ideology is based upon the concept that humans are free, equal, rational, economic entities and that all society is based upon free interactions among such individuals. Unfortunately, in practice these rights have been rather selectively distributed.

To be fair to at least one of the founding Utilitarians, J. S. Mill, it should be said that he was among the leaders in the suffrage movement – the social and political movement to grant the right to vote to women. Nevertheless, in practice the conceptual individual at the foundation of Utilitarian thinking has remained a man.

While Utilitarian ideology is strongly anti-traditional, it has, to date, done little to alter the traditional polarization between inside and outside work. In pre-industrial European society, according to the sociologist Ruth Cowan (1983), most economic activity was centered upon the household, particularly the household of the large land owners. In fact, the word "economy" was first used in discussions of the management of the resources of such large households. The relatively clear demarcation between the work of men and the work of women was based upon this distinction between outside work, which was the domain of men, and inside work, which was the domain of women.

In this, European society may not have been particularly different from many other traditional agrarian societies. With industrialization and with the rise of Utilitarian ideology, however, two major shifts produced a major asymmetry in the statuses of men and women, which play out today in the discourse between them. The first shift came about in the redefinition of economic activity. It came to be defined as just those activities of invention and technologization so idealized by Utilitarian ideology. The second shift was in placing exclusive value on those newly defined economic entities, "productive" individuals.

As creativity and invention came to be valued over tradition in the Utilitarian ideology, men came to be associated with the progressive aspects of society and women with the traditional aspects. Early in the period of industrialization, public schools were established as part of the Utilitarian agenda. By the beginning of the twentieth century, however, schools had shifted from being predominantly staffed with male teachers to having mostly women in teaching positions. Men remained in positions of authority as headmasters and principals. At the same time, the moral instruction of children had shifted away from being the father's responsibility to become an integral aspect of the mother's child-rearing practices. Even in families which earlier had given over child rearing largely to servants, the mother was encouraged to take over these tasks.

Ruth Cowan writes,

Experts repeatedly suggested that a mother was the single most important person in a child's life, and that the child raised by nursemaids was a child to be pitied. The young boy raised by servants would never learn the upright, go-getting resourcefulness of the truly American child, would never become a useful member of the egalitarian republic, and would probably fail in the business world (Cowan, 1983:179).

There are probably many reasons for this reduction in the moral authority of the father in child rearing and education. The story given at that time was that father's time was too valuable. He needed to be at work in business and industry during the days, and after work he needed to stop in the bars to make business contacts. Then, of course, in the wars so many men were lost that this shift in education and child rearing was stabilized as the normal pattern.

Even though women had come to play the major role in socialization, they were denied any role in the structures of authority and decision making. This has remained true to a considerable extent today. This attitude toward women in what had come to be considered a woman's domain, education, was even more severe in government and business, where women had virtually no direct voice in the corridors of power. The net result of these sociological changes, coupled with the growth of the Utilitarian discourse system, is that there has come to be a strong identification of the Utilitarian ideology with that of the discourse of men.

It would go beyond the scope of this book to try to decide upon the direction of cause and effect. It would be difficult to establish whether the discourse of men is what it is because of the Utilitarian ideology, or conversely the Utilitarian ideology is what it is because it was developed by men. For our purposes it is sufficient to point out that the similarity the reader will have observed between the characteristics of men's discourse we have given above and the ideology of Utilitarian discourse is not an accidental one; the two discourse systems have evolved together over the past two hundred years or so to the point that in many ways they are indistinguishable from each other.

This, then, is the background against which the misinterpretations between men and women within Utilitarian discourse take place. Men, within the Utilitarian discourse system, assume that the highest values will be placed upon independence, status, individuality, egalitarianism, the communication of information, competition, problem solving, and displaying technological and other forms of expertise. Furthermore, in many cases quite innocently, they will have come to believe in the ideological egalitarianism of Utilitarian discourse and fail to recognize the clear asymmetries of power which, in fact, exist between men and women.

On the other hand, women will be much more conscious of the actual asymmetries of power and status, and while they will hold out for the values of intimacy, connection, inclusion, relationship and rapport, problem sharing, and recognition of one's weaknesses, they will also know that these characteristics are not highly valued within the Utilitarian discourse system. They are likely to be acutely conscious of the contradictions between the equality which is expressed and the asymmetry which is practiced, especially in their discourse with men.

A simple gesture, once thought of as the minimum of civility, such as a compliment or holding open the door, has come to be interpreted within this contradictory framework as symbolic of these contradictions. A man who holds open the door for a professional woman colleague may have little awareness of the asymmetry in their status which has been experienced by the woman. She, in contrast, feels that this gesture only reasserts that he feels he is more powerful or stronger, or holds the social responsibility for protecting and guiding her through life. For her the symbolic framework in which this act is placed is a framework of conflict between professionally equal status on the one hand and asymmetrical status as woman on the other.

The maintenance of difference: socialization

A question which is often asked in discussions of miscommunications between members of different groups is this: why do people not just modify their behavior once they have realized that some aspect of it is producing difficulties or confusion? The answer we have put forward above is that, to a considerable extent, our sense of who we are as people and of our place in human society is tied up in the patterns of discourse we use in communicating with others. To change our behavior is to change who we are.

But again, the question is asked, "If who we are is producing difficulties, why do we resist undertaking these changes?" The answer to that is that, on the whole, we have been who we are from very early in life and in most cases simply cannot imagine being any different. In other words, our primary socialization is a very powerful framework around what we do for the rest of our lives. We tend to form our concept of the world as well as our own place in it very early in life, and to change that concept of the world is a threatening prospect that few of us are willing to face up to.

While there have as yet been relatively few studies of how boys and girls learn to become boys and girls, the research which has been done indicates that from very early in life we begin to rehearse the roles which we will enact throughout our lives. In a study of the play of boys and girls, Maltz and Borker (1982) observed that there were major differences in their activities which clearly parallel the differences for men and women we have described above.

For example, the play of girls tends to be organized around intimate and small groups of "best friends," who play inside with dolls and other household items. These small groups are hard to join and require constant talk to maintain the strong bonds of intimacy. Boys, on the other hand, tend to play in much larger and much more loosely organized groups. They play outside in large "packs" in competitive games, chases, and mock fights. These boys' groups are relatively easy to join, but the new members are taken in at the bottom of a rigidly hierarchical structure.

For girls, the main activity is intimate talk about problems. They use their verbal skill to produce intimacy and cooperation and generally avoid fighting and conflict. Through their "troubles talk" they produce tight bonding and feel that they have been successful when a sense of agreement and commonality is achieved.

Boys, on the other hand, organize around doing things rather than talking. The verbal activities are directed at producing and maintaining a hierarchical structure. These insults, challenges, and arguments are a ritualized fighting which produces hierarchical bonds. In contrast to the play of girls, boys seem least satisfied when everyone is in agreement, most satisfied when a struggle for position is in progress.

In another study, Tannen (1990b) studied both the verbal and non-verbal communication in conversations between females on the one hand and males on the other. She studied groups from quite young children to young adults. She found that the females oriented their bodies and gaze toward each other in what she called a direct alignment. The males, on the other hand, sat so that they did not directly face each other, but looked obliquely at some third point. The posture of the females was generally still and collected together into a small space, whereas the males spread themselves out, legs and arms wide, and were very active with much movement of their bodies as they talked.

The talk of these girls and boys paralleled this non-verbal alignment. The girls were highly voluble, but introduced relatively few topics, all of which were quite personal. They tended to focus on one person at a time and thoroughly talk out her problem before going on to the problem of the other person. The boys, on the other hand, talked relatively little and their topics were much more abstracted and diverse. They tended to talk in parallel, largely ignoring the other.

While the research on socialization to the roles of men and women is relatively new, it is clear that the differences we observe in the discourse systems of men and women have their foundations in these early behaviors of boys and girls. While the two studies we have mentioned say relatively little about what might cause these differences in behaviors, other studies have shown that in primary socialization, quite subtle cues are used by children to determine the wishes of the care givers. It would be quite wrong to think that boys always fight and girls always cry, but it is clear that differential treatment of these two behaviors tells boys and girls what is expected of them. A girl who has just fought with her brother and is crying may be told, "Don't fight. That's not nice." Her brother, on the other hand may be told, "Don't cry. Boys don't cry about a thing like that."

Messages and metamessages: forms of discourse

In describing the differences between women's and men's interpretive frameworks, we have already indicated most of the major differences in the forms of discourse used within these two systems. In a sense, because men and women operate within many of the same contexts, the forms of discourse themselves may not differ to a great extent. What has been observed to be a very important difference, however, is the attention given to message and to metamessage. This parallels, of course, the difference in attention given to relationship and to information. There is a tendency for men to focus on the information given, that is, the message, and for women to pay closer attention to the metamessage, that is, to how the information is to be interpreted.

The man we mentioned earlier who has been given a transfer to the company's Frankfurt office might say, "I've been given a transfer," focusing on the basic information that he (and, of course, the family) will be moving soon. For him the issue is the move and its consequences, not the exact wording he has used in saying this. His wife, on the other hand, has noticed his choice of the pronoun "I" and feels she is being given no choice in this issue. She feels that he is saying (once again) that he is going to do whatever he has to do and that she can choose either to go along with it or not.

So while he has brought up the subject of the move to talk about, his wife has picked up on the metamessage that he is the important one in the family, the one whose moves determine what everyone else will do, and in the following conversation she is searching for further evidence of his attitude toward them. He then follows this statement by saying, "Maybe you should start looking into schools for the kids." There it is. He has said "you," and expects her to do the work of arranging all this while still not including her in the process of making the decision.

This differential attention to message and metamessage, of course, is an expression of the Utilitarian ideological position of empiricism and positivism. As a result, the discourse of women is sometimes taken as not just emotional, but also opposing the ideological basis of this system. Women come to be thought of as willfully illogical and emotional. What for a woman is a concern for inequality, very much an expression of one aspect of the Utilitarian ideology, is taken as undermining that ideology. The result is that it is women who are taken to be contradictory, not the ideology of the discourse system which is producing this contradiction.

The struggle for equality, the struggle for power

We can return to one of the problems with which we began this section on intergender discourse. In some contexts men are said to be excessively taciturn. In other contexts it is women who are said to be the silent partners. Women complain that in their intimate relationships, their men fail to talk to them. Men see women in business meetings and in classrooms as quiet, uninfluential fixtures who have relatively little to add to the discussion. As we have said above, in chapter 3, taciturnity and volubility are not so much attributes of a person's character, though certainly individuals vary enormously in their personal style on this dimension; they are face strategies of independence and involvement, which to some extent everyone has the ability to use when they are appropriate. That is to say, whatever personal configuration someone might have, that same person will be more or less voluble, more or less taciturn, depending on the face relationships he or she is trying to express to others.

Women tend to be voluble in small and more intimate groups, taciturn in large and more formal or public situations. Men tend to be more voluble in those more public contexts and fall into taciturnity or monologues in situations of intimacy. We believe that this is a direct result of the broader framework of expectations provided by contemporary society and its background of Utilitarian discourse. As this framework grants to men the right (and, of course, obligation) to dominate in public contexts, and since public contexts are ones in which the Utilitarian discourse system expects a face system of symmetrical solidarity, men in these contexts are found to be highly voluble. That is, in these contexts men adopt the face strategies of involvement.

The question then is this: why do men become taciturn in intimate relationships? On the surface of it, it would seem that a man should assume a face system of symmetrical solidarity and feel quite comfortable expressing involvement with his wife. Of course, that would imply equality of status, and that is where the problem lies. In public contexts, at least until just recently, the dominating face systems of Utilitarian discourse were taken as the appropriate frameworks. In intimate relationships between men and women, however, there has been an ongoing struggle over the appropriate face system. Men have largely continued to assume asymmetrical status between themselves and women in all contexts. This assumption has been buttressed by claiming this status as wage earner, protector, most informed, expert, and all the other values asserted by the Utilitarian discourse system.

Women, on the other hand, have taken the Utilitarian ideology at its word and claimed equal status as human beings.

In chapter 3 we stated the problem as follows: "When two participants *differ* in their assessment of face strategies, it will tend to be perceived as difference in *power*." Men and women differ in their assessment of the face systems in which they are currently operating in western society. When men use face strategies of involvement in speaking to women, they do so within a face system of hierarchical asymmetry. Women hear these strategies of involvement as the attempt to assert dominance. To be certain that this dominance is not legitimated, women will avoid using strategies of independence in responding. In such a system, men expect women to respond to them with strategies of independence. When women speak to them with strategies of involvement, men feel they are being challenged. Men then have only one of two options. If they continue to respond with involvement strategies, they feel they will be heard as asserting their un-equal status. On the other hand, if they use strategies of independence – taciturnity is primary among them – they hope to achieve a system of neither symmetrical solidarity nor asymmetry, but a stand-off compromise of symmetrical deference. Unfortunately, this compromise solution men sometimes adopt of avoiding the asymmetry that comes with the use of involvement strategies is not perceived as the best way to foster intimacy.

In other words, there is a perennial dilemma for men and women in contemporary western society, which in most cases does not arise from ill will on the part of either men or women. It arises out of the contradictions of the domination of the Utilitarian discourse system, which advocates egalitarian relationships for members only and requires its members to display their membership through the forms of discourse of the Utilitarian system. To the extent one adopts the male/Utilitarian values of independ-ence, status, exclusion, information, contest, and problem-solving expertise, one can be perceived as a member in good standing. On the other hand, to the extent one expresses the female pole of these values, intimacy, con-nection, inclusion, relationship, rapport, community, and problem-sharing willingness to learn and to admit one's weaknesses, one is taken to be at best a marginal member of the system. The Utilitarian discourse system frames it this way for men and women: confusion will be eliminated in discourse between men and women as soon as everyone adopts a single, unambiguous system of discourse – the male/Utilitarian form of discourse.

Further Research on Gender Discourse Systems

Most of the research on gender discourse systems has been carried out in North America or in Europe, and so it is premature to speculate on how widely such discourse systems might be distributed throughout the cultures of the world. We certainly know that men's and women's speech have been seen to be markedly different in many of the languages of the world. Furthermore, it is clear that in virtually any culture, the experience of women is markedly different from the experience of men, and we expect that such experiential and social differences will be codified within markedly different systems of discourse.

What remains to be seen, of course, is not whether or not the discourse systems of men and women will be different. It would be very surprising if they were not. What remains to be studied, however, is the extent to which the women of one cultural group share a discourse system with the women of another cultural group. In other words, the question yet to be studied is whether or not women's discourse forms a discourse system which cuts across major cultural lines as well as across class, ethnic, corporate, professional, and generational lines within a particular culture.

Such questions, as interesting and important as they are, however, are not the major focus of this book. Our concern in this section has been to show that even within an otherwise very homogeneous group, such as members of the same generation within the same ethnic group within the same culture, there will be major and very significant differences between the discourse systems of men and women. Our point is that any individual must be understood to belong to multiple discourse systems, which interact with each other in any particular situation. When we are talking about the communication between Asians and westerners, for example, we must never forget that it will also be important to know whether or not there are significant ethnic, generational, gender, or other group differences between them. We believe that these other discourse systems hold the key to unlocking major difficulties in intercultural communication.

Discourse Systems and the Individual

The problem we now want to try to understand is how a person manages to cope with such a complexity of discourse systems. A person is born a male or a female in a particular region, whether rural or city, of a particular country at a particular time in history. He or she becomes educated within a certain professional sphere, cultivates certain tastes and interests, takes certain political positions, and develops a set of adult family and other interpersonal relationships. In the process of these developments a person learns a set of languages and linguistic varieties. The question is this: how does a person reach a stable identity and still navigate among all of these competing sources of identity and group membership?

Each discourse system tends to emphasize certain aspects of face relationships. These, in turn, require certain forms of discourse for their expression. To be sure members will have competence in those forms, socialization practices are instituted within the discourse system, and those socialization practices inculcate certain cultural values. Those values give rise to, support, and legitimate the face relationships expected within that discourse system. Each such discourse system forms a circle of enclosure which, on the positive side, gives identity and security to its members, but, on the negative side, tends to enclose them within its boundaries, so that it is easier for them to go on talking to each other than it is for them to establish successful communication with those who are outside this circle of the discourse system.

There are two aspects of this problem of discourse systems and the individual which we want to consider: identity and membership. Identity is, of course, a very complex concept, and we recognize that. For our purposes, what we want to emphasize is that part of every person's identity is the discourse systems within which he or she is a member. From person to person this will vary, of course, with some individuals taking great pride in their membership in a professional association while others just pay their annual dues without much further thought to the matter. Even in the case of such deeply permanent cultural identities as one's home culture, one's region, or one's family there will be considerable personal variation.

In research the authors have carried out in Alaska (Scollon and Scollon 1981), it was found that Athabaskan Indians have a tendency to resist education and literacy within the American school system even though they have clearly stated goals of succeeding within the American economic and political system. The reasons we have given for this resistance is that for Athabaskan Indians to engage in the new discourse systems of American schooling and literacy amounts to a change in identity, and it is this change in identity which is being resisted.

Recently, at the Earth Summit in Brazil, it was reported that Third World feminists had engaged in extended discussions with North American feminists on the question of cultural and gender identity. As it was reported, the problem was that Third World women felt that American feminists were asking the women of the world to take on aspects of identity which were not, in fact, those of the discourse system of women, but rather the discourse system of North Americans. They argued that American women could not set their American identity aside and claim to be simply world feminists as a means of escaping responsibility for the worldwide ecological problems which they had gone to the Earth Summit to discuss.

The point we want to make here is that one of the major functions of a discourse system is to give a sense of identity to its members. The positive side of this function is that members of a discourse system come to feel comfortable in communicating with other members of the discourse system.

It reduces the ambiguity in interpreting discourse. The negative side of this function is that it forms a boundary between ingroup and outgroup, and people who are not members of the discourse system are rejected by members and find it difficult to achieve membership. At the same time the boundary between ingroup and outgroup communication makes it less likely that members of the discourse system will be able to make themselves understood to non-members. In extreme cases this may come to seem justified: "Who wants to talk to *them* anyway?"

Identity is seen from the point of view of the person. Membership is the same thing seen from the point of view of the group. It is the group which ultimately determines who is or is not a member of the group. One might feel identity and yet be rejected by the group as a non-member. Conversely, one might be considered a member of a group, but not yet come to take it as a part of one's identity.

We wrote in chapter 7 of the study in which it was found that Japanese tended to disapprove of Japanese speaking high or complex forms of Japanese to foreigners, no matter what the foreigners' ability with the language might be. This is a case in which members of a discourse system chose to limit membership in the group, even where outgroup individuals begin to show serious competence with ingroup forms of discourse.

Discourse systems will come to have requirements for membership. These requirements may vary in their stringency depending on how closely guarded group identity comes to be. In contemporary America, for example, there is considerable discussion about whether or not men can be feminists. One position asserts that only a woman can be a feminist, because the feminist discourse system has as one of its basic requirements for membership that one can feel identity as a woman. Others take the position that it is not at all necessary to feel identity as a woman to take on and support the social and political goals and aspirations of women as one's own. In such a case, what is being debated is whether or not feminism is a gender discourse system of women or, in fact, a goal-directed discourse community.

We have used "socialization" as a general term to cover both explicit processes of training and education and implicit processes of learning which take place as part of the ongoing activities within a discourse system. A child born in Hong Kong as the child of Cantonese-speaking parents is socialized into the norms for speaking Cantonese. A person who takes a job with an international corporation such as IBM usually receives specific training which introduces him or her to the expectations of such a company. In both cases, the new member of the discourse system is given both explicit and implicit expectations of how to behave and how to communicate.

The discourse systems in which professional communicators work are a mixture of natural and goal-directed systems. A person is born into a culture, a family, a gender, a generation, and other such natural discourse systems. At the same time, a person has been educated for the position one has taken within a company. One has both corporate discourse identities and the identities that come with one's professional specialization.

It should be obvious that not all of these systems of socialization will be in agreement about what is proper behavior in every situation. A person will find himself or herself in conflict over what is the right way to speak, what are the right relationships to express or to maintain, what are the right forms of discourse to use in any particular situation. From the point of view of the analysis of discourse across discourse systems, we should see each system as trying to socialize its members into its own preferred norms and away from the norms of other systems in which he or she may be a member.

To put this all more bluntly, contemporary international business has adopted a Utilitarian discourse system. Therefore, it has as one of its goals the elimination of such other forms of discourse as might be used by participants. This discourse system, like all other discourse systems, tends to say to participants, "Leave your other ways of speaking at the door."

The result of this is that participation in such systems comes more easily to those whose other forms of identity and membership are less in competition with them. It is a greater problem for those whose other forms of identity are distinctive. For these people, it requires a temporary suspension of their personal identity and group membership to participate in transactions in these discourse systems.

Intersystem Communication

We hope that we have convinced the reader that there are many forms of discourse systems, some of which exclude others, some of which are included in others, many of which cut across other systems. All of these discourse systems are defined by features which are shared by some, but not by all, other systems. In any particular communicative situation, the participants will simultaneously be members of various discourse systems other than the system of relevance for that particular communicative situation. To summarize this situation we can say that, from the point of view of the individual, almost all forms of discourse take place at the intersections of several discourse systems.

In the conversation with which we began chapter 7, Mr Chu was described as a Chinese exporter from Hong Kong. Mr Richardson was described as an American buyer on a business trip to Hong Kong. Now we can imagine that Mr Chu is a member of quite a number of discourse systems. He is Chinese; that would place him within the broad Chinese cultural system. He is from Hong Kong; that would separate him from Chinese culture in general as most likely a speaker of Cantonese. He is probably a member of the discourse community of exporters, which would have a good competence in the laws and other regulations and procedures governing exports from Hong Kong. He is male, and that would place him within the male discourse system. In addition to that, he is likely to be employed by a company which may do importing business as well as manufacturing products. Finally, Mr Chu would most likely belong to a generation born since 1949, which in Hong Kong could mean that his family had at some point immigrated to Hong Kong from China. Possibly that would imply some form of political commitment in relation to the government of the People's Republic of China. In other words, there would be many considerations in Mr Chu's mind as he presented himself to Mr Richardson in this opening dialogue.

Mr Richardson as an American buyer is understood to be the employee of some larger corporation. As such he would have corporate identity and obligations. At the same time, he would be a member of the discourse community of the buyers of his particular products. If it happened to be clothing, he would probably belong to some clothing manufacturers' or buyers' association. In addition, Mr Richardson may perhaps be the child of Scottish immigrants to America. Perhaps he is a member of the Depression/War generation. He is also, as a male, a member of the American male discourse system.

All of these identities and memberships may well be relevant to understanding the communication between Mr Chu and Mr Richardson. We chose these two to be an example because their situation is somewhat simpler than it would be if, for example, instead of Mr Richardson it was Ms Herrera, a Latino woman, a Latina, of the Baby Boom generation.

Because of the complexity of human social organization, we believe that communication which takes place exclusively within a single discourse system is the rarest form of communication. Some form of intercultural or at least intergroup communication is probably the most normal form of communication. Certainly within the context of international professional communication this is the case.

Professional communicators are regularly faced with complex situations of communication. We began this book by saying that language is always ambiguous, whether it is at the level of the interpretation of words and sentences or at the level of making conversational inferences. This ambiguity is not the result of poor learning; it does not matter how long you study Chinese, or Japanese, or English, the things you say and hear said will never be completely and unambiguously interpretable. This is the nature of language.

Nevertheless, professional communicators depend on achieving some degree of confidence in their communications. The specialization of a professional communicator lies in his or her being able to choose the most appropriate forms of language for any particular situation so as to be as clear and effective as possible in communicating with his or her audience. One cannot lie back and simply say that language is always ambiguous, and therefore nothing we can do or study will improve the situation.

We argued at the beginning of this book that there were two basic strategies a professional communicator can use to deal with the fundamental ambiguity of language: one of these is to try to increase his or her shared knowledge with the audience, the other is to come to expect difficulties and learn how to cope with miscommunication. Much of the substance of this book is given over to detailing the many dimensions along which participants in a discourse can either come to share their understandings or fail to understand each other. We have discussed the elements of the grammar of context, face relationships, linguistic resources, conversational inferencing processes including schemata, rhetorical strategies, and focus, and cultural factors from belief systems to proxemics, kinesics, and the use of time. Finally, in these last chapters we have shown how all of these factors may combine together into multiple and cross-cutting systems and communities of discourse.

A professional communicator will be better positioned for effective communication by learning more about other participants in communicative events in any one of these areas. At the same time, there is always the insoluble problem that, at any one time, one is participating in multiple and possibly conflicting discourse systems. In some of these one will be a full member, in others one will be a novice or, perhaps, only a temporary visitor. For example, a tour guide in Hong Kong who is working with a tour group from Australia may be a full member of her own cultural group and her gender and generational discourse systems. She may be a well-established member of the travel industry discourse community as well. But she may also have just taken this position with a new travel company and, therefore, be a rather novice member of the corporate discourse system. She will have to take all of this into some consideration in planning activities for the tourists she is guiding.

For example, perhaps this group of tourists has taken a tour with this company before and they may well know this company's procedures and expectations as well as or better than the company's new employee. Or conversely, perhaps this tour guide has already worked with this group of people, who have come to this new company because they like this particular guide. In that case, she will share more with the group of tourists, her clients, than she shares with her own company. Such complexities are not so rare, and in any event, we present them here only to highlight the fact that many situations of discourse have ambiguities of this sort, which are the result of the fact that we are always simultaneously members of multiple discourse systems.

The fact that we are always members of multiple discourse systems, and the related fact that in professional communication we are also often novices in some of the relevant systems, mean that in professional communication we virtually always work under the conditions of stress which arise from such role pluralism. To put it in a nutshell, it is sometimes difficult to know just who we are and whom we represent when we speak.

The ideal solution is to share knowledge with other participants in a discourse. This is why it is easiest to communicate with other members of the same discourse system. This is why people so often gather together socially with others who are very much like them. It is easier and more comfortable to communicate when you do not have to do so much work to understand what is going on or to make your own communications clear to others.

Unfortunately, as we have said, in most cases such banding together is impossible in professional communication. We might go further to say that not only is it impossible, it is undesirable. Situations in which professional communication occur are almost always those in which one is communicating to members of a different discourse system. This is obviously true in situations of intercultural communication; but even within a cultural group, professional communication is normally outgroup communication. A maker of children's toys wants to sell toys to parents of children or others who will give them to children. It would be absurd to focus his marketing communications on other makers of children's toys just because they would be the easiest to talk to and would understand him best.

The most fundamental assumption is that professional communication is communication with members of other discourse systems, and therefore, because we have to assume that we do not share knowledge, assumptions, values, and forms of discourse with them, we must expect there to be problems of interpretation. We must look for these problems, anticipate where they will arise out of our differences, and then plan our communications to be effective as outgroup communications.

If we accept that our professional communications are outgroup communications, we then have to guard against the idea that this other group is completely different from our discourse system. No single dimension will be sufficient to compare and contrast our discourse systems. The problems of ideology arise when we accept the difference between our group and some other group and then come to assume there is a single difference between us which accounts for our differences. We must always simultaneously look for differences *and* commonalities. It is the difference in pattern, not any absolute difference, which is significant between discourse systems.

By being careful to look for both differences and commonalities, we will also avoid the fallacy of lumping. We will not fall into the error of assuming two groups are the same as each other simply because they differ from our own group on some dimension of discourse. Such an analysis will also prevent the fallacy of solidarity, in which we assume that because our group is the same as another group on the basis of a single dimension of discourse, we are the same on all dimensions. Again, it is the difference in pattern which is significant. The key is to note both differences and commonalities.

Sharing knowledge of other groups or discourse systems is not the same as becoming a member. As we have pointed out above, many discourse systems are quite resistant to taking on new members. In developing one's ability in intercultural professional communication, it is well worth remembering that it is quite unlikely that one will ever become a member of the other culture, however much one might learn about that culture or come to appreciate it. The point is to learn as much as one can about other discourse systems so that the pattern of differences and commonalities can be appreciated; the point is not to try to become a member, which may actually in some cases become offensive to members of other groups.

We conclude with what might seem a paradoxical concept, that is, that the professional communicator is one who has come to realize his or her lack of expertise. One is, of course, expert in the natural discourse systems to which one belongs, discourse systems such as one's own culture, gender and generational discourse systems, and one's professional area of expertise. Nevertheless, professional discourse in most cases produces inherent conflicts between the discourse system of one's corporate culture and the discourse community of one's professional specialization. Furthermore, intercultural professional communication requires outgroup communication in which one is never likely to take on full group membership and expertise. The dangers all lie on the side of assuming that one is an expert in such outgroup discourse systems. The American who is sure that he knows all there is to know about communication with Chinese is doomed to failure. The Japanese who is certain she is adept at communication with Koreans will have difficulties. The man who feels he really, deeply understands women is likely to know very little at all. Such outgroup certainty is virtually always a signal of binarism and stereotyping. On the other hand, a person who understands the outlines of the pattern of differences and commonalities, but fully recognizes his or her own lack of membership and state of non-expertise, is likely to be the most successful and effective communicator.

References

We have made use of references from a varied number of sources in several fields including sociolinguistics, social psychology, discourse analysis, anthropology, speech communication, philosophy of language, comparative literature, and education. The first part of this section, the research base, gives the specific references used in writing this book. The second part of this section is an extended bibliography of other sources which we have used as background in developing our thinking on this subject. They will form a useful guide to the reader who wishes to extend his or her study of any of the particular topics through further readings.

The Research Base

Chapter 1 What is a discourse approach?

The basic framework in interactive sociolinguistics has been provided by the work of Gumperz (1982). Young (1982), Scollon and Scollon (1991), and Scollon (1993b) discuss the inductive ordering of topics in discourse and their consequences for intercultural misinterpretation. Boswood (1992) is a survey of positions requiring professional communication skills for Hong Kong. Levinson (1990) presents a summary of the main conclusions of a generation of conversational analysis based on the inherent ambiguity of language. Ambiguity of communication between American men and women is treated in Tannen (1990a). Studies of both the frequency of exchanges and the duration of pauses are found in Scollon (1981, 1985), Jefferson (1989), and Feldstein and Crown (1990).

Chapter 2 How, when, and where to do things with language

Austin (1962) introduced the concept of the speech act, which was then extended by Searle (1969). Gumperz and Hymes (1972) introduced the components of speaking as an aspect of their concept of the ethnography of speaking. Saville-Troike (1989) is an excellent review of the literature in this field. Fasold (1990) gives a full discussion of address forms. Mehan (1983) discusses adjacency sequences in classrooms.

Chapter 3 Interpersonal politeness and power

R. Brown and Gilman (1960) was an early and very influential study of the connection between power and solidarity. P. Brown and Levinson (1978) introduced the theory of politeness strategies of face. Scollon and Scollon (1981, 1983, 1994) extended Brown and Levinson's theory to include the concept of global face systems. We use the symbol "W" for Brown and Levinson's "R" to indicate the weight of imposition. Brown and Levinson derived their concept of face from Goffman (1967), who, in turn, based his work on that of the anthropologist Hu (1944). Ting-Toomey (1988) has advanced that of Hu in relationship to Chinese concepts of face. Kincaid (1987) is a survey of many aspects of Asian interpersonal communication. Tannen (1984, 1989, 1990a) has used the terms "involvement" and "independence" for the two competing face wants.

Chapter 4 Conversational inference

G. Brown and Yule (1983) is a reliable and comprehensive introduction to discourse analysis. Cook (1989) is a briefer but more current account of the state of the field. McCarthy (1991) is directed to readers whose field is language education, but has much that is useful for general readers. Gee (1990) shows how the concept of discourse analysis has been extended to encompass studies of ideology. All of these sources contain excellent bibliographies of the basic research in discourse analysis.

Schegloff (1972) first showed the connection between being first speaker and being granted the right to introduce topics. Gumperz (1982) includes several papers on his seminal concept of conversational inference. Halliday and Hasan (1976) is the most comprehensive study of cohesion in English, or perhaps any language. Scollon (1993a), Tyler et al. (1988), and Field and Yip (1992) are studies of conjunction in the English of speakers of Chinese.

Schema theory is discussed in Kintsch (1977), Kintsch and Greene (1978), Carrell (1983, 1984a, 1984b, 1989), and Scollon and Scollon (1984).

Rhythm and timing are discussed in Scollon (1981), and a recent comparative study of Chinese English and Canadian English is in Feldstein and Crown (1990).

Bateson (1972) introduced the concept of metacommunication, Gumperz (1982) based his concept of contextualization cues on Bateson's idea of the metamessage, and Levinson (1990) develops the concept of interactive intelligence.

Chapter 5 Topic and face

Differences in face relationships leading to differences in rhetorical strategies are discussed in Scollon and Scollon (1991, 1994).

The *Li Ji* (or *Li Chi*) is available either in Chai and Chai (1966) or in Legge (1967).

Differences between spoken and written discourse are discussed in Ochs (1979), Tannen (1982), and Scollon and Scollon (1981), especially as these differences relate to essays. Further discussion can be found in Scollon and Scollon (1980, 1984) and in Scollon (1988).

Chapter 6 Ideologies of discourse

Scollon and Scollon (1981) introduced the concept of the discourse system, and Swales (1990) presents a comparable, though more closely defined, type of discourse system, the discourse community. Gee (1989, 1990) uses the term "Discourse" to indicate a systematic and self-legitimating set of communicative practices and identities, much like what we call a discourse system.

Lanham (1983) suggested the term "C–B–S style", and Kenner (1987) quotes Bishop Thomas Sprat. Sources on the thinking of the Enlightenment are Smith (1990), Montesquieu (1990), American State Papers (1990), Kant (1990), Locke (1990), and Bentham (1962, 1988). Kant's view on public and private is in Behler (1986); his essay regarding authorship is in Kant (1990). Mill (1990) is the foundation of Utilitarianism and includes a discussion of the ideas of Bentham.

Cook-Gumperz (1986) includes a history of the development of public schooling, Sunley (1955) analyzes the development of American patterns of child rearing, and Cowan (1983) is a sociological-historical study of what she calls the industrialization of the home.

Lakoff and Johnson (1980) discuss the anti-rhetorical nature of utilitarian discourse, though not using this terminology. Foucault (1977) brought Bentham's Panopticon to the attention of contemporary readers.

Chapter 7 What is culture?

Samovar and Porter (1988) and Carbaugh (1990) are two very useful introductory readers in intercultural communication. Hartzell (1988) has much useful information on Chinese–western intercultural communication. Hall and Hall (1987) is a rich source for communication between Japanese and Westerners.

Xu (1990) is a recent updating of the ancient *Three Character Classic* (or *San Zi Jing*). The view that children are born with evil dispositions is quoted from Sunley (1955). Confucius and Mencius may be found in convenient translations by Lau (1970, 1979). Oliver (1971) and Kincaid (1987) are good sources on comparative western and Asian rhetoric and communication. Ting-Toomey (1988) and Triandis et al. (1988) discuss the need to distinguish between individualism and collectivist social organizations.

In a long series of studies, Hsu (1953, 1983, 1985) studied the concept of the self contrastively across cultures. Scollon and Scollon (1992) raise the problem of binarism and relate it to the individualism which is emphasized in western society. Friedman and Rosenman (1974) and Friedman and Ulmer (1984) developed the idea of Type-A behavior.

Kinesics, proxemics, and the concept of time are written about in an engaging way by Hall (1959, 1969). Scollon (1987) discusses the different arrows of time. Erickson and Shultz (1982) treats the concepts of *chronos* and *kairos* time. Tannen (1990a) is a highly popular discussion of gender discourse, while Song (1985) is a comparative study which raises cautions about overgeneralization. Ross and Shortreed (1990) discuss negative reactions native speakers of a language may have toward competent foreigners.

Chapter 8 Corporate discourse

Scollon (1993b) is a study of business telephone calls. Richards and Rogers (1986) contains a history of the development of English-language teaching methodologies. Rogers and Agarwala-Rogers (1976) is a very basic analysis of communication in organizations, and Westwood (1992) is an excellent recent study of organizational behavior in a Southeast Asian cultural perspective.

Chapter 9 Professional discourse

Our discussion of the professional discourse of ESL teachers is based on the authors' own participant-observation in this discourse over more than two decades. Pennington (1992) gives an interesting discussion of various aspects of conflict which arise within this discourse system.

Chapter 10 Generational discourse

Carbaugh (1984, 1989, 1990) elaborates in considerable detail the nature of the contemporary American concept of the self and individualism. Bellah et al. (1985) followed up the observations of Tocqueville (1969) bearing upon American individualism. Postman and Paglia (1991) exemplify the generational differences in communication outlined by Scollon and Scollon (1992) and by Longfellow (1978, n.d. 1, n.d. 2, n.d. 3, n.d. 4). Goodrich (1968) is a relatively recent edition of *Infant Care*. The idea of scientific management was introduced by Taylor (1911). Cowan (1983) notes that soon after Taylor, the American home came to be industrialized. The Type-A behavior described by Friedman and Rosenman (1974) can be seen as directly an outcome of this social industrialization.
Spock (1976) is one of the most popular American books of all time.

Chapter 11 Gender discourse

Tannen (1994) includes an introduction which outlines the basic conflicts in the study of gender communication dominance, difference approaches, and "nature–

nurture" approaches. Maltz and Borker (1982) is an important introduction to the issue of socialization into gender discourse systems.

References for Further Study

The list of references which follows includes all of the bibliographic sources which are found either in the main body of the text or in the immediately preceding section on the research base. In addition to these references, we have included many which we believe the student of discourse in intercultural professional communication will find useful for further study.

Alexander, A., V. Cronen, K.-w. Kang, B. Tsou, and B. J. Banks 1986: Patterns of topic sequencing and information gain: a comparative study of relationship development in Chinese and American cultures. *Communication Quarterly*, 34, 66–78.

Allinson, Robert E. 1989: *Understanding the Chinese Mind*. Hong Kong: Oxford University Press.

American School Board Journal, January 1987.

American state papers [Declaration of Independence, Articles of Confederation, Constitution] 1990: In Mortimer J. Adler (ed.), *Great Books of the Western World*, Chicago: Encyclopaedia Britannica.

Anderson, E. N. 1988: *The Food of China*. New Haven: Yale University Press.

Austin, John 1962: *How to Do Things with Words*. Oxford: Clarendon Press.

Bateson, Gregory 1972: *Steps to an Ecology of Mind*. New York: Ballantine.

Behler, Ernst (ed.) 1986: *Immanuel Kant: philosophical writings*. New York: Continuum.

Bellah, Robert N., Richard Madsen, William M. Sullivan, Ann Swidler, and Steven M. Tipton 1985: *Habits of the Heart*. New York: Harper and Row.

Bentham, Jeremy 1962: *Introduction to the Principles of Morals and Legislation*. (Mary Warnock, ed.) Glasgow: Fontana Press.

—— 1988: *A Fragment on Government*. Cambridge: Cambridge University Press. (Originally published in 1776).

Blum-Kulka, Shoshana, Juliane House, and Gabriele Kasper (eds) 1989: *Cross-cultural Pragmatics: requests and apologies*. Norwood, NJ: Ablex.

Bolton, Kenneth and Helen Kwok 1992: *Sociolinguistics Today: eastern and western perspectives*. London: Routledge.

Bond, Michael Harris 1986: *The Psychology of the Chinese People*. New York: Oxford University Press.

—— 1988: *The Cross-cultural Challenge to Social Psychology*. Newbury Park, CA: Sage.

Boswood, Tim 1992: *English for Professional Communication: responding to Hong Kong employers' needs for English graduates*. Department of English, City Polytechnic of Hong Kong, Research Report 20, October.

Brosnahan, Irene, Richard Coe, and Ann Johns 1987: Discourse analysis of written texts in an overseas teacher training program. *English Quarterly*, 20, 16–25.

Brown, Gillian and George Yule 1983: *Discourse Analysis*. New York: Cambridge University Press.

Brown, Penelope and Stephen Levinson 1978: Universals in language usage: politeness phenomena. In Ester Goody (ed.), *Questions and Politeness: strategies in social interaction*, New York: Cambridge University Press. Republished as 1987: *Politeness*. Cambridge: Cambridge University Press.

Brown, Roger and Albert Gilman 1960: The pronouns of power and solidarity. In Thomas Sebeok (ed.), *Style in Language*, Cambridge, MA: MIT Press.

Campbell, John Angus 1987: Charles Darwin: rhetorician of science. In John S. Nelson, Allan Megill, and Donald N. McCloskey (eds), *The Rhetoric of Human Sciences*, Madison, WI: University of Wisconsin Press.

Carbaugh, Donal 1984: "Relationship" as a cultural category in some American speech. Paper presented at the annual meetings of the Speech Communication Association, Chicago.

—— 1989: *Talking American: cultural discourses on Donahue*. Norwood, NJ: Ablex.

—— 1990: *Cultural Communication and Intercultural Contact*. Hillsdale, NJ: Lawrence Erlbaum Associates.

Carrell, Patricia L. 1983: Some issues in studying the role of schemata, or background knowledge, in second language comprehension. *Reading in a Foreign Language*, 1(2), 81–92.

—— 1984a: Evidence of a formal schema in second language comprehension. *Language Learning*, 34(2), 87–112.

—— 1984b: The effects of rhetorical organization on ESL readers. *TESOL Quarterly*, 18(3), 441–69.

—— 1989: Metacognitive awareness and second language reading. *Modern Language Journal*, 73, 121–34.

Chai, Ch'u and Winberg Chai 1966: *Li Chi: Book of Rites*. Secaucus, NJ: University Books.

Chatman, Seymour 1978: *Story and Discourse*. Ithaca, NY: Cornell University Press.

Cheshire, Jenny 1991: *English Around the World*. Cambridge: Cambridge University Press.

Chinese Culture Connection 1987: Chinese values and the search for culture free dimensions of culture. *Journal of Cross-cultural Psychology*, 18, 143–64.

Chu, Godwin C. 1979: Communication and cultural change in China: a conceptual framework. In Godwin C. Chu and Francis L. K. Hsu, *Moving a Mountain: cultural change in China*. Honolulu: University Press of Hawaii.

—— 1985: The changing concept of self in contemporary China. In Anthony J. Marsella, George DeVos, and Francis L. K. Hsu (eds), *Culture and Self: Asian and western perspectives*, New York: Tavistock Publications.

Chu, Godwin C. and Francis L. K. Hsu 1979: *Moving a Mountain: cultural change in China*. Honolulu: University Press of Hawaii.

Coates, Jennifer and Deborah Cameron 1988: *Women in their Speech Communities: new perspectives on language and sex*. London: Longman.

Cook, Guy 1989: *Discourse*. Oxford: Oxford University Press.

Cook-Gumperz, Jenny 1986: *The Social Construction of Literacy*. New York: Cambridge University Press.

Cowan, Ruth Schwartz 1983: *More Work for Mother*. New York: Basic Books.

De Bary, William. Theodore 1988: *East Asian Civilizations: a dialogue in five stages*. Cambridge, MA: Harvard University Press.

De Bary, William Theodore and John W. Chaffee 1989: *Neo-Confucian Education: the formative stage*. Berkeley, CA: University of California Press.

Dredge, C. Paul 1983: What is politeness in Korean speech? *Korean Linguistics*, 3, 21–32.

Ebrey, Patricia Buckley 1984: *Family and Property in Sung China: Yuan Ts'ai's precepts for social living*. Princeton, NJ: Princeton University Press.

—— 1985: T'ang guides to verbal etiquette. *Harvard Journal of Asiatic Studies*, 45(2), 581–613.

Erikson, Erik 1950: *Childhood and Society*. New York: Norton.

Erickson, Frederick and Jeffrey Shultz 1982: *The Counselor as Gatekeeper: social interaction in interviews*. New York: Academic Press.

Fasold, Ralph 1990: *The Sociolinguistics of Language*. Oxford: Blackwell.

Feldstein, Stanley and Cynthia L. Crown 1990: Oriental and Canadian conversational interactions: chronographic structure and interpersonal perception. *Journal of Asian Pacific Communication*, 1(1), 247–65.

Field, Yvette and Yip Lee Mee Oi 1992: A comparison of internal conjunctive cohesion in the English essay writing of Cantonese speakers and native speakers of English. *Regional English Language Center Journal* 23(1), 15–28.

Foucault, Michel 1977: *Discipline and Punish*. New York: Pantheon Books.

Frank, Francine Wattman and Paula A. Treichler 1989: *Language, Gender and Professional Writing: theoretical approaches and guidelines for nonsexist usage*. New York: Modern Language Association of America.

Friedman, Meyer and Ray H. Rosenman 1974: *Type A Behavior and Your Heart*. New York: Fawcett Columbine.

Friedman, Meyer and Diane Ulmer 1984: *Treating Type A Behavior and Your Heart*. New York: Alfred A. Knopf.

Gee, James Paul 1986: Orality and literacy: from "The Savage Mind" to "Ways with Words." *TESOL Quarterly*, 20, 719–46.

—— 1989: Literacy, discourse, and linguistics: essays by James Paul Gee. *Journal of Education*, 171(1).

—— 1990: *Social Linguistics and Literacies: ideology in discourses*. Bristol, PA: Falmer Press.

Giles, H. and A. Franklyn-Stokes 1989: Communicator characteristics. In M. K. Asante and W. B. Gudykunst (eds), *The Handbook of Intercultural Communication*, Newbury Park, CA: Sage.

Giles, H., N. Coupland, and J. M. Wiemann 1992: "Talk is cheap . . . but my word is my bond": beliefs about talk. In Kenneth Bolton and Helen Kwok (eds), *Sociolinguistics Today: eastern and western perspectives*, London: Routledge.

Goffman, Erving 1967: *Interaction Ritual*. Garden City, NY: Anchor Books.

—— 1974: *Frame Analysis*. New York: Harper and Row.

—— 1981: *Forms of Talk*. Philadelphia: University of Pennsylvania Press.

Goodrich, Frederick W. Jr 1968: *Infant Care: the United States government guide*. Englewood Cliffs, NJ: Prentice Hall.

Gudykunst, W. B., Y.-C. Yoon, and T. Nishida 1987: The influence of individualism–collectivism on perception of communication in ingroup and outgroup relationships. *Communication Monographs*, 54, 295–306.

Gumperz, John 1977: Sociocultural knowledge in conversational inference. In M. Saville-Troike (ed.), *28th Annual Round Table Monograph Series on Language and Linguistics*, Washington, DC: Georgetown University Press.

——1982: *Discourse Strategies*. New York: Cambridge University Press.

——1991: Interviewing in intercultural situations. In P. Drew and J. Heritage (eds), *Talk at Work*, New York: Cambridge University Press.

——1992: Contextualization and understanding. In A. Duranti and G. Goodwin (eds), *Rethinking Context*, Cambridge: Cambridge University Press.

Gumperz, John J. and Dell Hymes 1972: *Directions in Sociolinguistics: the ethnography of communication*. New York: Holt, Rinehart and Winston.

Günthner, Susanne 1991: Chines/Innen und Deutsche im Gesprach: Aspekta der Interkulturellen Kommunikation. Universitat Konstanz: Dissertation.

——1992: The construction of gendered discourse in Chinese–German interactions. *Discourse and Society*, 3(2), 167–91.

Hall, Edward T. 1959: *The Silent Language*. Garden City, NY: Doubleday.

——1969: *The Hidden Dimension*. Garden City, NY: Doubleday.

Hall, Edward T. and Mildred Reed Hall 1987: *Hidden Differences: doing business with the Japanese*. Garden City, NY: Doubleday.

Halliday, M. A. K. 1989: *Spoken and Written Language*. Oxford: Oxford University Press.

Halliday, M. A. K. and Ruqaiya Hasan 1976: *Cohesion in English*. London: Longman.

Hartzell, Richard W. 1988: *Harmony in Conflict: active adaptation to life in present-day Chinese society*. Taipei: Caves Books.

Hayashi, Reiko 1988: Simultaneous talk: from the perspective of floor management of English and Japanese speakers. *World Englishes* 7(3), 269–88.

——1990: Rhythmicity sequence and synchrony of English and Japanese face to face conversation. *Language Sciences*, 12(2/3), 155–95.

Heritage, John 1989: Current developments in conversation analysis. In Derek Roger and Peter Bull (eds), *Conversation: an interdisciplinary perspective*, Clevedon: Multilingual Matters.

Hinds, John 1983: Contrastive rhetoric: Japanese and English. *Text* 3(2), 183–95.

Ho, David Yau-Fai 1976: On the concept of face. *The American Journal of Sociology*, 81, 867–84.

——1986: Chinese patterns of socialization. In Michael Harris Bond (ed.), *The Psychology of the Chinese People*, New York: Oxford University Press.

Hofstede, G. 1983: Dimensions of national cultures in 50 countries and three regions. In J. B. Deregowski, S. Dziurawiec, and R. C. Annis (eds), *Explications in Cross-cultural Psychology*, Lisse: Swets and Zeitlinger.

Hsu, Francis L. K. 1953: *Americans and Chinese: passage to differences*. Honolulu: University Press of Hawaii.

——1969: *The Study of Literate Civilizations*. New York: Holt, Rinehart and Winston.

——1973: *Religion, Science and Human Crises*. Westport, CT: Greenwood Press.

——1983: *Rugged Individualism Reconsidered: essays in psychological anthropology*. Knoxville: University of Tennessee Press.

—— 1985: The self in cross-cultural perspective. In Anthony J. Marsella, George DeVos, and Francis L. K. Hsu (eds), *Culture and Self: Asian and western perspectives*, New York: Tavistock Publications.

Hu, Hsien Chin 1944: The Chinese concept of "face". *American Anthropologist*, 46, 45–64.

Hwang, Kwang-Kuo 1987: Face and favor: the Chinese power game. *The American Journal of Sociology*, 92(4), 944–74.

Hymes, Dell 1966: Two types of linguistic relativity. In William Bright (ed.), *Sociolinguistics*, The Hague: Mouton.

—— 1972: Models of the interaction of language and social life. In John J. Gumperz and Dell Hymes (eds), *Directions in Sociolinguistics: the ethnography of communication*, New York: Holt, Rinehart and Winston.

Jefferson, Gail 1989: Preliminary notes on a possible metric which provides for a "standard maximum" silence of approximately one second in conversation. In Derek Roger and Peter Bull (eds), *Conversation: an interdisciplinary perspective*, Clevedon: Multilingual Matters.

Kant, Immanuel 1983: An answer to the question: What is Enlightenment? In Ted Humphrey (tr.), *Perpetual Peace and Other Essays on Politics, History, and Morals*, Indianapolis: Hackett. (Originally published in 1784).

—— 1990: *The Science of Right*. In Mortimer J. Adler (ed.), *Great Books of the Western World*, Chicago: Encyclopaedia Britannica.

Kaplan, Robert B. 1966: Cultural thought patterns in intercultural education. *Language Learning* 16(1 and 2), 1–20.

—— 1987: Cultural thought patterns revisited. In Ulla Conner and Robert B. Kaplan (eds), *Writing Across Languages: analysis of L2 text*, Reading, MA: Addison-Wesley.

Kenner, Hugh 1987: *The Mechanical Muse*. New York: Oxford University Press.

Kim, Ki-hong 1975: Cross-cultural differences between Americans and Koreans in nonverbal behavior. In Ho-Min Sohn (ed.), *The Korean Language: its structure and social projection*, Honolulu: Center for Korean Studies, University of Hawaii.

Kincaid, D. Lawrence 1987: *Communication Theory: eastern and western perspectives*. San Diego: Academic Press.

King, Ambrose Y. C. and Michael H. Bond 1985: The Confucian paradigm of man: a sociological view. In Wen-Shing Tseng and David Y. H. Wu (eds), *Chinese Culture and Mental Health*, Orlando: Academic Press.

Kintsch, Walter 1977: On comprehending stories. In Marcel Just and Patricia Carpenter (eds), *Cognitive Processes in Comprehension*, Hillsdale, NJ: Lawrence Erlbaum Associates.

Kintsch, Walter and E. Greene 1978: The role of culture-specific schemata in the comprehension and recall of stories. *Discourse Processes* 1(1), 1–13.

Lakoff, George and Mark Johnson 1980: *Metaphors We Live By*. Chicago: University of Chicago Press.

Lanham, Richard A. 1983: *Literacy and the Survival of Humanism*. New Haven: Yale University Press.

Lau, D. C. 1970: *Mencius*. New York: Penguin.

—— 1979: *Confucius: the Analects*. New York: Penguin.

Lee, Thomas H. C. 1984: The discovery of childhood: children's education in Sung

China (960–1279). In Sigrid Paul (ed.), *Kultur: Begriff und Wort in China and Japan*, Berlin: Dietrich Reimer Verlag.

Legge, James 1967: *Li Chi: Book of Rites*. New York: University Books.

Levinson, Stephen C. 1988: Putting linguistics on a proper footing: explorations in Goffman's concepts of participation. In P. Drew and A. Wootton (eds), *Erving Goffman: exploring the interaction order*, Oxford: Polity Press.

—— 1990: Interactional biases in human thinking. Working Paper No. 3, Project Group Cognitive Anthropology, Max-Planck-Gesellschaft, Berlin.

Littwin, Susan 1986: *The Postponed Generation: why America's grown-up kids are growing up later*. New York: William Morrow.

Locke, John 1990: *An Enquiry concerning Human Understanding*. In Mortimer J. Adler (ed.), *Great Books of the Western World*, Chicago: Encyclopaedia Britannica.

Longfellow, Layne A. 1978: Leadership, power, and productivity: doing well by doing good. Prescott, AZ: Lecture Theatre.

—— no date 1: Four American generations: doing well by doing good. Prescott, AZ: Lecture Theatre.

—— no date 2: Changing the rules of our lives: from high school to midlife and beyond. Prescott, AZ: Lecture Theatre.

—— no date 3: Stress: the American addiction. Prescott, AZ: Lecture Theatre.

—— no date 4: Positioning for tomorrow: the emergence of women in the workforce. Prescott, AZ: Lecture Theatre.

Lukes, Steven 1973: *Individualism*. Oxford: Blackwell.

Maltz, Daniel N. and Ruth A. Borker 1982: A cultural approach to male-female miscommunication. In John J. Gumperz (ed.), *Language and Social Identity*, Cambridge: Cambridge University Press.

Marsella, Anthony J., George DeVos, and Francis L. K. Hsu 1985: *Culture and Self: Asian and western perspectives*. New York: Tavistock Publications.

McCarthy, Michael 1991: *Discourse Analysis for Language Teachers*. Cambridge: Cambridge University Press.

McDermott, Ray 1979: Lecture. American Anthropological Association, Cincinatte.

Mehan, Hugh 1983: *Learning Lessons: social organization in the classroom*. Cambridge, MA: Harvard University Press.

Mill, John Stuart 1990: *Utilitarianism*. In Mortimer J. Adler (ed.), *Great Books of the Western World*, Chicago: Encyclopaedia Britannica. (Originally published 1690).

Montesquieu, Baron de Charles de Secondat 1990: *The Spirit of Laws*. In Mortimer J. Adler (ed.), *Great Books of the Western World*, Chicago: Encyclopaedia Britannica.

Murray, Douglas P. 1983: Face-to-face: American and Chinese interactions. In Robert A. Kapp (ed.), *Communicating with China*, Chicago: Intercultural Press.

Nakane, Chie 1972: *Japanese Society*. Berkeley, CA: University of California Press.

Nietzsche, Friedrich 1990: Beyond good and evil. In Mortimer J. Adler (ed.), *Great Books of the Western World*, Chicago: Encyclopaedia Britannica. (Originally published in 1886).

Obelkevich, James 1987: Proverbs and social history. In Peter Burke and Roy Porter (eds), *The Social History of Language*, Cambridge: Cambridge University Press.

Ochs, Elinor 1979: Planned and unplanned discourse. In Talmy Givon (ed.), *Discourse and Syntax*, New York: Academic Press.

Oliver, Robert 1971: *Communication and Culture in Ancient India and China*. Syracuse: Syracuse University Press.

Ouchi, William G. 1981: *Theory Z*. New York: Avon.

Pennington, Martha 1992: Work satisfaction in teaching English as a second language. Department of English, City Potytechnic of Hong Kong, Research Report 5.

Poole, Deborah 1992: Language socialization in the second language classroom. *Language Learning*, 42(4), 593–616.

Postman, Neil and Camille Paglia 1991: She wants her TV! He wants his book! Dinner conversation. *Harper's*, March, 44–55.

Redding, Gordon and Gilbert Y. Y. Wong 1986: The psychology of Chinese organizational behavior. In Michael Harris Bond (ed.), *The Psychology of the Chinese People*, New York: Oxford University Press.

Richards, Jack C. 1985: *The Context of Language Teaching*. Cambridge: Cambridge University Press.

——1989: Beyond teacher training: approaches to teacher education in language teaching. *Perspectives: Working Papers of the Department of English*, City Polytechnic of Hong Kong, 1(1), 1–12.

Richards, Jack C. and Theodore S. Rodgers 1986: *Approaches and Methods in Language Teaching: a description and analysis*. Cambridge: Cambridge University Press.

Richards, Jack C., John Platt, and Heidi Weber 1985: *Longman Dictionary of Applied Linguistics*. Harlow: Longman.

Rogers, Everett M. and Rehka Agarwala-Rogers 1976: *Communication in Organizations*. New York: Free Press.

Ross, Steven and Ian M. Shortreed 1990: Japanese foreigner talk: convergence or divergence? Asian Pacific language and communication: foundations, issues, and directions. *Journal of Asian Pacific Communication*, 1(1), 135–46.

Samovar, Larry A. and Richard E. Porter 1988: *Intercultural Communication: a reader*. Belmont, CA: Wadsworth.

Saville-Troike, Muriel 1989: *The Ethnography of Communication*. Oxford: Blackwell.

Sayeki, Yutaka 1983: Joint solving of physics problems by college students. In Michael Cole, Naomi Miyake, and Denis Newman (eds), *Proceedings of the Conference on Joint Problem Solving and Microcomputers*, La Jolla, CA: University of California, San Diego, Laboratory of Comparative Human Cognition.

Schegloff, Emanuel 1972: Sequencing in conversational openings. In John Gumperz and Dell Hymes (eds), *Directions in Sociolinguistics*, New York: Holt, Rinehart and Winston.

Scollon, Ron 1981: The rhythmic integration of ordinary talk. In Deborah Tannen (ed.), *Georgetown University Roundtable on Languages and linguistics 1981*, Washington, DC: Georgetown University Press.

——1985: The machine stops. In Deborah Tannen and Muriel Saville-Troike (eds), *Perspectives on Silence*, Norwood, NJ: Ablex.

——1987: *Time and the Media: notes on public discourse in the electronic age*. Haines, AK: Black Current Press.

——1988: Storytelling, reading, and the micropolitics of literacy. In John E. Readance and R. Scott Baldwin (eds), *Dialogues in Literacy Research*, Chicago: National Reading Conference.

——1993a: Cumulative ambiguity: conjunctions in Chinese–English intercultural communication. *Perspectives: Working Papers of the Department of English*, City Polytechnic of Hong Kong, 5(1), 55–73.

—— 1993b: Maxims of stance: discourse in English for professional communication. Department of English, City Polytechnic of Hong Kong, Research Report 26.

Scollon, Ron and Suzanne Wong Scollon 1980: Literacy as focused interaction. *Quarterly Newsletter of the Laboratory of Comparative Human Cognition*, 2(2), 26–9.

—— 1981: *Narrative, Literacy and Face in Interethnic Communication*. Norwood, NJ: Ablex.

—— 1983: Face in interethnic communication. In Jack Richards and Richard Schmidt (eds), *Language and Communication*, London: Longman.

—— 1984: Cooking it up and boiling it down: abstracts in Athabaskan children's story retellings. In Deborah Tannen (ed.), *Coherence in Spoken and Written Discourse*, Norwood, NJ: Ablex.

—— 1986: *Responsive Communication: patterns for making sense*. Haines, AK: Black Current Press.

—— 1990: Epilogue to "Athabaskan–English interethnic communication." In Donal Carbaugh (ed.), *Cultural Communication and Intercultural Contact*, Hillsdale, NJ: Lawrence Erlbaum Associates.

—— 1991: Topic confusion in English–Asian discourse. *World Englishes* 10(2), 113–25.

—— 1992: Individualism and binarism: a critique of American intercultural communication analysis. Department of English, City Polytechnic of Hong Kong, Research Report 22.

—— 1994: Face parameters in East–West discourse. In Stella Ting-Toomey (ed.), *The Challenge of Facework*, Albany: State University of New York Press.

Searle, John R. 1969: *Speech Acts*. New York: Cambridge University Press.

Smith, Adam 1990: *An Inquiry into the Nature and Causes of the Wealth of Nations*. In Mortimer J. Adler (ed.), *Great Books of the Western World*, Chicago: Encyclopaedia Britannica.

Smith, Larry E. 1987: *Discourse Across Cultures: strategies in world Englishes*. New York: Prentice Hall.

Sohn, Ho-Min 1983: Power and solidarity in the Korean language. *Korean Linguistics*, 3, 97–122.

Song, Weizhen 1985: A preliminary study of the character traits of the Chinese. In Wen-Shing Tseng and David Y. H. Wu (eds), *Chinese Culture and Mental Health*, Orlando: Academic Press.

Spock, Benjamin 1976: *Baby and Child Care*. New York: Hawthorne Books. (Originally published 1945).

Stevenson, Harold W., H. Azuma, and K. Hakuta 1986: *Child Development and Education in Japan*. New York: Freeman.

Stewart, E. and J. Bennett 1992: *American Cultural Patterns: a cross-cultural perspective*. Yarmouth, ME: Intercultural Press.

Stover, Leon E. 1974: *The Cultural Ecology of Chinese Civilization*. New York: Pica Press.

Sunley, Robert 1955: Early American literature on child rearing. In Margaret Mead and Martha Wolfenstein (eds), *Childhood in Contemporary Cultures*, Chicago: University of Chicago Press.

Suzuki, Takao 1986: Language and behavior in Japan: the conceptualization of personal relations. In Takie S. Lebra and W. P. Lebra (eds), *Japanese Culture and Behavior*, Honolulu: University of Hawaii Press.

Swales, John M. 1990: *Genre Analysis: English in academic and research settings*. Cambridge: Cambridge University Press.

Swann, Joan 1992: *Girls, Boys and Language*. Oxford: Blackwell.

Tannen, Deborah 1982: Oral and literate strategies in spoken and written narratives. *Language*, 58(1), 1–21.

—— 1984: *Conversational Style: analyzing talk among friends*. Norwood, NJ: Ablex.

—— 1989: *Talking Voices: repetition, dialogue and imagery in conversational discourse*. Cambridge: Cambridge University Press.

—— 1990a: *You Just Don't Understand: women and men in conversation*. New York: William Morrow.

—— 1990b: Gender differences in conversational coherence: physical alignment and topical cohesion. In Bruce Dorval (ed.), *Conversational Organization and its Development*, Norwood, NJ: Ablex.

—— 1991: Teachers' classroom strategies should recognize that men and women use language differently. *The Chronicle of Higher Education*, 37(40), B2–B3.

—— 1993: *Gender and Conversational Interaction*. Oxford: Oxford University Press.

—— 1994: *Gender and Discourse*. Oxford: Oxford University Press.

Tannen, Deborah and Muriel Saville-Troike 1985: *Perspectives on Silence*. Norwood, NJ: Ablex.

Taylor, Frederick 1911: *Scientific Management*. New York: Harper and Row.

Ting-Toomey, Stella 1988: Intercultural conflict styles: a face-negotiation theory. In Young Kim and William Gudykunst (eds), *Theories in Intercultural Communication*, Newbury Park, CA: Sage.

Tobin, Joseph J., David Y. H. Wu, and Dana H. Davidson 1989: *Preschool in Three Cultures*. New Haven: Yale University Press.

Tocqueville, Alexis de 1969: *Democracy in America*. Trans George Lawrence. Garden City, NY: Anchor Books.

Tönnies, Ferdinand 1971: *Ferdinand Tönnies on Sociology: pure, applied and empirical: selected writings*. Chicago: University of Chicago Press.

Tracy, Karen 1990: The many faces of facework. In H. Giles and W. P. Robinson (eds), *Handbook of Language and Social Psychology*, Chichester: John Wiley.

Triandis, H. C., R. Bontempo, M. J. Villarcal, M. Asai, and N. Lucca 1988: Individualism–collectivism: cross-cultural perspectives on self–group relationships. *Journal of Personality and Social Psychology*, 54, 323–38.

Tsuda, Yukio 1986: *Language Inequality and Distortion in Intercultural Communication: a critical theory approach*. Amsterdam: John Benjamins.

Tyler, Andrea E., Ann A. Jefferies, and Catherine E. Davies 1988: The effect of discourse structuring devices on listener perceptions of coherence in non-native university teacher's spoken discourse. *World Englishes*, 7(2), 101–10.

Universal Declaration of Human Rights 1948: In *Encyclopaedia Britannica*, 15th edn, vol. 12.

Waley, Arthur 1943: *Monkey*. New York: Grove Press.

West, Mrs Max 1914: *Infant Care*. Washington, DC: US Government Printing Office.

Westwood, R. I. 1992: *Organisational Behavior: Southeast Asian perspectives*. Hong Kong: Longman Group (Far East).

Wetzel, P. 1988: Are powerless communication strategies the Japanese norm? *Language in Society*, 17, 555–64.

Wheeler, L., H. T. Reis, and Michael H. Bond 1989: Collectivism–individualism in everyday social life: the Middle Kingdom and the melting pot. *Journal of Personality and Social Psychology*, 57, 79–86.

White, S. 1989: Backchannels across cultures: a study of Americans and Japanese. *Language in Society* 18, 59–76.

Whorf, Benjamin Lee 1956: *Language, Thought, and Reality*. Cambridge, MA: MIT Press.

Wolfenstein, Martha 1953: Trends in infant care. *Journal of Orthopsychiatry*, 23, 120–4.

Xu Chuiyang (ed.) 1990: *Three Character Classic*. Singapore: EPB Publishers.

Young, Linda Wai Ling 1982: Inscrutability revisited. In John Gumperz (ed.), *Language and Social Identity*, New York: Cambridge University Press.

Yu, Anthony C. 1977: *The Journey to the West*. Chicago: University of Chicago Press.

Yum, J. O. 1988: The impact of Confucianism on interpersonal relationships and communication patterns in East Asia. *Communication Monographs*, 55, 374–88.

Index